This work aims to provide the rea  hat
happened in the Ypres Salient betw ort
the visitor around sites of importar tles
of Ypres, and in so doing to bring th ing
guidebooks by providing a unique new dimension without listing memorials and cemeteries. It doesn't matter whether you are in your armchair, on foot, on a bicycle, or in a car, this book will effortlessly transport you to the Ypres Salient, where you will be able to visualise what happened. It will take you to Kruiseecke Crossroads and Gheluvelt in late October 1914, where tired remnants of the British Expeditionary Force fought desperately to prevent the Germans from breaking through to Ypres. It will lead you to the St Julien to Poelcappelle road on 22 April 1915 where Canadian soldiers near the front line formed a defensive flank after a chlorine gas attack had engulfed adjacent French colonial troops, killing many, while the survivors fled to the rear. You will visit Gravenstafel Ridge, where the Canadians were involved in bitter fighting two days later. You will go to locations throughout the Salient, which will help you to understand the four stages of the Second Battle of Ypres and the eight major phases of the Third Battle of Ypres where British, Australian, New Zealand and Canadian divisions all fought at different times. Eighteen concise chapters will focus on aspects of particular battles, explaining troop movements and strategy. Each chapter is accompanied by many maps based on those in the Official History, which have been painstakingly designed to provide clarity, while colour photographs taken by the authors in the course of many visits to the Ypres Salient will help the visitor to understand important points made in the text. After reading this book you should be able to stand at any location within Ypres Salient and be able to work out what happened there throughout the four years of the Great War. You will also be able to conjure up a picture in your mind of events which took place more than 100 years ago as though they were happening in front of you.

Thomas R. Scotland
Born in St. Andrews and brought up in
the East Neuk of Fife, Tom was educated
at Waid Academy in Anstruther. He graduated in Medicine from the University of
Edinburgh in 1971, becoming a Fellow
of the Royal College of Surgeons of Edinburgh in 1975. He developed his
interest in the Great War whilst a student, when there were still many veterans
alive. He trained in orthopaedic surgery in Aberdeen, and after spending a
year as a Fellow at the University of Toronto, returned to take up the position of Consultant Orthopaedic Surgeon with Grampian Health Board and
Honorary Senior Lecturer at the University of Aberdeen. His particular interests were knee surgery, paediatric orthopaedics and tumour surgery, and for
three years he was lead clinician for the Scottish Sarcoma Managed Clinical
Network. Over the years he has been a frequent visitor to the Western Front
and since retiring from the National Health Service in 2007 has kept in touch
with former colleagues by leading cycling expeditions to the Western Front.
He is co-author of three books with Steve, *War Surgery 1914-1918*, *Wars,
Pestilence and the Surgeon's Blade*, being an account of the evolution of
British military surgery in the 19th century, and *Understanding the Somme
1916, an illuminating battlefield guide.*

Steven D. Heys
Born in Accrington in Lancashire and educated in England, Australia and
Scotland, Steve graduated in Medicine from the University of Aberdeen in
1981 and undertook surgical training in the North-East of Scotland. He is a
Fellow of the Royal Colleges of Surgeons in England, Edinburgh and Glasgow
and underwent research training at the Rowet Research Institute in Aberdeen,
obtaining a PhD in 1992. He specialised in general and breast cancer surgery
for many years before latterly concentrating on breast cancer surgery together
with his research interests in the role of nutrition in the causation of cancer,
and has responsibilities for medical education both locally and nationally.
He has published more than 200 scientific papers and written many book
chapters on different aspects of surgery and played many national and inter-
national roles in surgery and the provision of surgical services. His interest
in the Great War was sparked by the stories of the Accrington Pals and the
Lancashire Fusiliers, by his time as a member of the RAMC (V), serving for
six years in the 51st Highland Brigade, and by Tom's famous cycling tours
around the Western Front where he has the dual role of bicycle mechanic, and
because he is a keen bagpipe player, has been appointed as Piper to the tours!
He is co-author of the three books with Tom, *War Surgery 1914-1918*, *Wars,
Pestilence and the Surgeon's Blade*, and *Understanding the Somme 1916, an
illuminating battlefield guide.*

UNDERSTANDING THE YPRES SALIENT 1914-18

AN ILLUMINATING BATTLEFIELD GUIDE

Thomas Scotland & Steven Heys

Helion & Company

Helion & Company Limited
26 Willow Road
Solihull
West Midlands
B91 1UE
England
Tel. 0121 705 3393
Fax 0121 711 4075
Email: info@helion.co.uk
Website: www.helion.co.uk
Twitter: @helionbooks
Visit our blog at http://blog.helion.co.uk/

Published by Helion & Company 2017
Designed and typeset by Mach 3 Solutions (www.mach3solutions.co.uk)
Cover designed by Paul Hewitt, Battlefield Design (www.battlefield-design.co.uk)
Printed by Henry Ling Limited, Dorchester, Dorset

ISBN 978-1-911512-50-9

British Library Cataloguing-in-Publication Data.
A catalogue record for this book is available from the British Library.

For details of other military history titles published by Helion & Company
Limited, contact the above address, or visit our website: http://www.helion.co.uk

We always welcome receiving book proposals from prospective authors.

This book is dedicated to
Daniella, Sara, Molly, Robert, Hannah and Max.

Contents

Preface

This work aims to provide you with a good understanding of what happened in the Ypres Salient between 1914 and 1918. It sets out to transport you around sites of importance for the First, Second and Third Battles of Ypres, and in so doing to bring the battlefield to life. It augments existing guide books by providing another dimension, without listing memorials and cemeteries. It doesn't matter whether you are in your armchair, on foot, on a bicycle or in a car, this book will enable you to visualise important events. It will take you to Kruiseecke Crossroads and Gheluvelt in late October 1914, where tired remnants of the British Expeditionary Force fought desperately to prevent the Germans from breaking through to Ypres. It will lead you to the St Julien to Poelcappelle road on 22 April 1915, where Canadian soldiers near the front line saved the day by forming a defensive flank after a chlorine gas attack had engulfed adjacent French colonial troops, killing many, while survivors fled to the rear. It will take you to Pilckem Ridge on 31 July 1917, when hopes of a breakout from Ypres Salient were dashed. Eighteen chapters will help you to understand what happened during the different phases of the First, Second and Third Battles of Ypres. Each chapter is accompanied by maps based on those in the Official History, which have been designed to provide clarity, while colour photographs taken by the authors in the course of many visits to the Ypres Salient augment the text. After reading this book, you should be able to stand at any location within the Ypres Salient and create a picture in your mind of events which took place more than 100 years ago as though they were happening in front of you.

Acknowledgements

The authors wish to acknowledge help given by Ruth Duncan, Curator of the Gordon Highlanders Museum, Aberdeen, and researcher Anushka Kumar, who together provided much valuable material, including the photographs of Captain James Anson Otho Brooke and Drum Major Kenny, who were awarded the Victoria Cross during the First Battle of Ypres. They also gave us information from the following sources: the War Diary of the 2nd Battalion Gordon Highlanders for events between 22–24 October 1914 and between 4–7 October 1917; a typed account of the archives of the 2nd Battalion Gordon Highlanders during the First Battle of Ypres, part of a donation of documents relating to Lieutenant Colonel James Dawson (GHPB63.59); a letter from Brigadier General A.R. Hoskins DSO to Sir Alexander Lyon, concerning the action of 25 September 1915 (GHPB146.15); and the diary of Major D.W. Pailthorpe relating to the Battle of Broodseinde on 4 October 1917 (PB375). Extracts from these documents have helped to enrich the text and bring events to life.

Chapter 1

The Ypres Salient: Introduction

British soldiers first arrived in Ypres on 13 October 1914, and over the following four years were involved in bitter fighting within a very confined area which became known as the Ypres Salient.

The definition of a salient is an outward bulge of a military line into enemy-held territory, and the salient around Ypres soon gained an infamous reputation. When visiting Ypres for the first time, it is very difficult to become orientated and to gain a good understanding of events that took place here. There are many small towns and villages, and numerous surrounding farms, which look the same in a bland landscape, so it is easy to lose one's sense of direction. Farming is a very important activity here, and the richly fertilised fields are very productive, just as they were in 1914 before the Great War.

Most local people go about their daily business, seemingly oblivious of the terrible battles which were fought here during four years of conflict, and the many cemeteries and memorials which are scattered everywhere are the only reminders of those days.

This book has been written to help the visitor to understand the Ypres Salient; to bring it to life and put events into context. It is not intended to replace the many battlefield guides that exist already. Rather, it hopes to add a new dimension to understanding the Ypres Salient.

HOW DID THE BRITISH COME TO BE IN YPRES?

When Great Britain declared war on Germany in August 1914, an expeditionary force was sent to France under the command of Sir John French. The British Expeditionary Force (BEF) consisted of four regular Army infantry divisions and a cavalry division. With appropriate support troops on lines of communication to ensure that the fighting divisions were supplied with food and munitions, approximately 90,000 men went to France. Unlike Great Britain, both France and Germany had huge armies of conscripts already in place. In August 1914, the French had 1,300,000 men and the Germans 850,000. Moreover, the Germans could mobilise a further 4,300,000 trained men within a matter of days. In the opening months of the war, the brunt of the allied fighting was borne by the French.

GERMAN STRATEGY AT THE OUTBREAK OF THE WAR

Because France and Russia had signed an alliance in 1892 which required them to support each other in the event of an attack by a foreign power, Germany knew that if she declared war on either France or her Russian ally, it would have to be fought on two fronts against both countries.

The Schlieffen Plan was devised, therefore, to ensure rapid German success against the French in the west before tackling the Russians in the east. It was assumed that the Russians would take several weeks to mobilise, and the Schlieffen Plan allowed a six-week period in which to defeat the French. Seven German armies were mobilised to attack five French armies. The three German armies to the north would sweep through Belgium; those in the centre would attack through Luxembourg and push the French back through the Ardennes; while the two German armies in the south, in Alsace and Lorraine, would soak up French pressure. The Germans knew full well that the French would be certain to attack in Alsace and Lorraine with utmost vigour after forfeiting these two provinces in the Franco-Prussian War of 1870–71. The German armies to the north would swing round behind the French, driving them towards their two armies in Alsace and Lorraine and into an encircling trap.

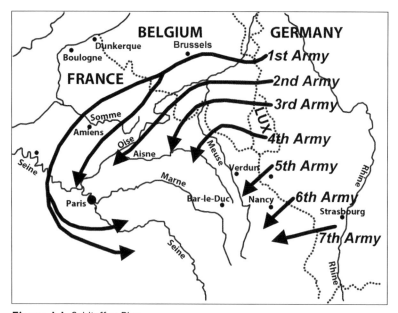

Figure 1.1 Schlieffen Plan.

FRENCH STRATEGY AT THE OUTBREAK OF THE WAR

When the Germans mounted their attack, the French implemented 'Plan 17'. Quite simply, they would attack the Germans on every front with every available resource until they were removed from French soil. French losses in the opening days of the war in these initial encounters, known as The Battle of the Frontiers, were enormous.

THE BATTLE OF MONS, 23 AUGUST 1914

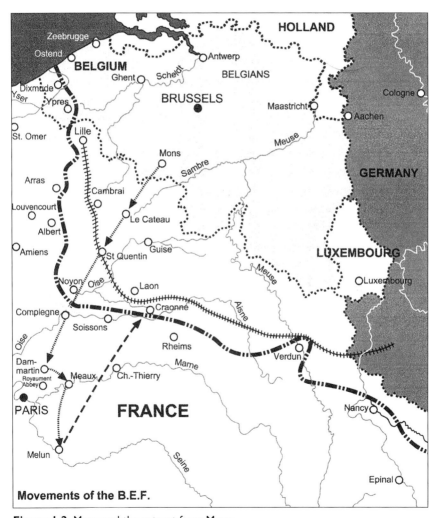

Figure 1.2 Mons and the retreat from Mons.

The British made their way to the Belgian town of Mons on the left flank of the French Fifth Army, where they fought a defensive action against a numerically superior German First Army on Sunday, 23 August 1914. They withdrew rapidly to the south that evening after the adjacent French Fifth Army had retreated, leaving the British badly exposed.

After sustaining very heavy losses, all the French armies retreated from the frontiers of Belgium, Luxembourg and Germany. The BEF kept in touch with the French Fifth Army to its left, hotly pursued by the Germans.

On 26 August 1914 at Le Cateau (Figure 1.2), the British II Corps under General Horace Smith-Dorrien turned round to deliver a counter-punch to the pursuing German First Army. This was a manoeuvre designed to slow the Germans down, as they had been so close on the heels of the retiring British that there had been no respite and the men were exhausted.

Then, with their French allies on their left flank, the British pulled back to the River Marne, less than 30 miles east of Paris. General von Kluck, commander of the German First Army, sensed that he had the British at his mercy and made a critical error of judgement. Instead of sweeping to the rear of French forces, which would have meant going to the west of Paris before herding the French into the trap in Alsace and Lorraine, he marched to the east of the city, exposing the flank of his army to a new French Sixth Army, which had been formed for the defence of Paris.

THE BATTLE OF THE MARNE

General Joffre, Commander-in-Chief of the French forces, could scarcely believe the news when he heard what the German First Army had done. He launched a major offensive between 6–9 September in what became known as the Battle of the Marne. The French Sixth Army struck hard into the flank of the German First Army, which turned towards Paris to face the threat. This resulted in a gap opening between the German First and Second Armies, which was exploited by the BEF and the French Fifth Army, while other French armies also went onto the offensive. The Germans were in disarray and withdrew to the River Aisne north of the Marne. This was a decisive victory for the Allies, because it meant the Schlieffen Plan had failed.

Soldiers of the BEF had marched for more than 150 miles since the Battle of Mons, and had been under constant German pressure. Now they had an opportunity to attack. Reinvigorated by this prospect, they assisted their French allies and harried the Germans as they retreated across the River Aisne (Figure 1.3). It was anticipated that the pursuit would continue after the crossing, but instead the Germans dug trenches on the north bank of the Aisne.

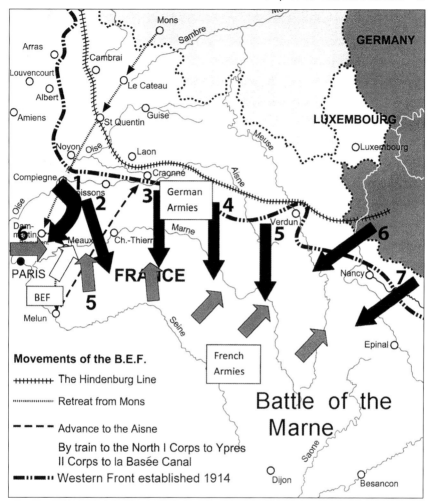

Figure 1.3 The Battle of the Marne.

Another fierce engagement, which would become known as the Battle of the Aisne, was fought between 12–15 September, when opposing entrenched forces tried unsuccessfully to break through enemy lines. Each side then attempted to outflank the other in a series of manoeuvres to the north, which became known as the 'race to the sea'. These outflanking attempts were only brought to a standstill when the sandy beaches of the Belgian coast were reached. Soon, two lines of soldiers faced each other from the Swiss border to the Channel coast, and the Western Front came into being. A war of movement was replaced by static trench warfare.

THE BEF GOES TO YPRES

During the 'race to the sea', the BEF was transported north by train to play its part in the unfolding conflict. The original BEF which had fought at Mons on 23 August 1914 comprised I Corps and II Corps, each with approximately 30,000 men. II Corps fought around La Bassée, while I Corps went further north and arrived at Ypres on 13 October. Reinforcements to meet ever-increasing demands and growing numbers of casualties were sent as quickly as possible. British III Corps arrived in time for the Battle of The Aisne, and IV Corps in time for the fighting around Ypres in October and November.

THE NATURE OF THE FIGHTING CHANGES DRAMATICALLY AROUND YPRES

The Belgian Army to the north blocked access to the coastal plain in what became known as the Battle of the (River) Yser, an engagement they only won by opening the dyke sluices and flooding the flat coastal plain from the coast as far as Dixmuide, thus securing the northern flank of the Allied line for the duration of the war. With no further outflanking option available, the Germans attempted to break directly through the Allied lines around Ypres and Messines Ridge to the south. This would be an overwhelming hammer blow. Only after first defeating the tiny British Army, and then the French, would the Germans be able to turn their full force against Russian armies on the Eastern Front. Fighting began around Ypres on 21 October 1914. Figure 1.4 shows how the Allied front line to the east of Ypres was an approximate semi-circle projecting into German-held territory, with Ypres at the hub, before swinging south through Hollebeke and Messines.

THREE MAJOR BATTLES AT YPRES

Fighting around Ypres was continuous throughout the four years of the war, and men lost their lives on a daily basis. There were, however, three distinct battles, which form the basis for the chapters of this book.

THE FIRST BATTLE OF YPRES

The First Battle of Ypres lasted from 21 October until mid-November 1914. British casualties amounted to 58,155 killed, wounded or missing.[1] Adding casualties from prior engagements in 1914, it is estimated that by the end

---

1   Neillands, R., *The Great War Generals on the Western Front* (London: Robinson Publishing Ltd, 1999), p.136.

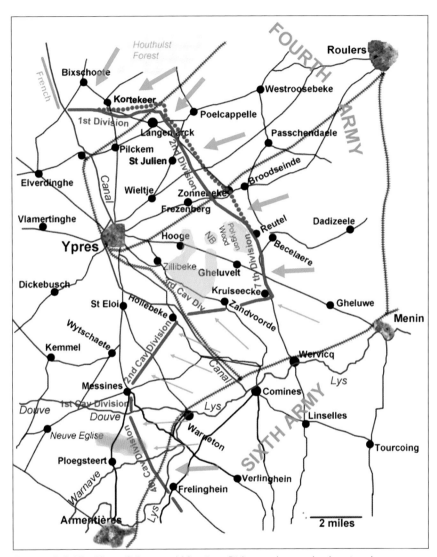

Figure 1.4 The Ypres Salient and Messines Ridge to the south, showing the disposition of British and German forces. British positions are marked with red lines, French with blue; attacking Germans are green. The dotted red line shows the front on 21 October 1914, while the solid red line shows it on 23 October after the First Battle of Ypres had begun. NB is Nonne Bosschen

Figure 1.5 This is how a German artilleryman using binoculars would have viewed Ypres from the northern end of Messines Ridge. From here he could direct shellfire onto targets within the city or onto enemy troop positions in the Ypres Salient.

of the year only one officer and 30 other ranks remained from each of the battalions of approximately 1,000 officers and men which had gone to France in August 1914.[2] The loss of these men from the Regular Army was a severe blow because they were highly trained professionals.

By the conclusion of the First Battle of Ypres, British and French forces remained in possession of most of the territory to the east of Ypres, which became known as the Ypres Salient. It was vulnerable to shellfire from the front and from the sides. The principal success of the Germans in this engagement was to force the British off Messines Ridge to the south of Ypres, pushing Allied positions to the west of Wytschaete and Messines, making the line like an inverted S-bend. Not only did the capture of Messines Ridge give the Germans the advantage of holding the high ground over their adversaries, it also provided them with the opportunity to fire on British or French soldiers in the Ypres Salient from the rear. Figure 1.5 is a German artilleryman's view of Ypres from the northern end of Messines Ridge.

---

2   Ibid., p.140.

THE SECOND BATTLE OF YPRES

The Second Battle of Ypres began on 22 April 1915, when the Germans used chlorine gas for the first time against French Colonial troops near Langemarck. This could have resulted in a breakthrough to Ypres, had the Germans been prepared to take full advantage of the surprise element of their attack. In the event they were not, and a disaster was averted. Nevertheless, much Allied territory was lost, and by the time the Second Battle of Ypres ended on 25 May 1915, the Salient had contracted to a much tighter defensive position round Ypres. Casualties in the British Expeditionary Force amounted to 59,275 killed, wounded and missing. This figure includes losses sustained by the Canadian 1st Division and the Indian Corps.[3]

THE THIRD BATTLE OF YPRES

The Third Battle of Ypres began on 31 July 1917. It was a British-led offensive aimed at breaking free from the Ypres Salient before advancing to capture the Belgian ports of Ostend and Zeebrugge, thereby denying their use to the Germans as U-boat bases. It was recognised that as the British advanced, the Salient would be pushed out further, so attacking troops would become increasingly exposed to damaging artillery fire from Messines Ridge (Figure 1.5). The Battle of Messines Ridge on 7 June 1917 was a necessary preliminary action to remove the Germans from the ridge. For nearly two weeks before the attack, 2,266 guns, 756 of which were heavy and medium pieces, pounded German positions on the ridge. Key to the attack was the detonation of 19 mines at zero hour, 0310, on 7 June, after which the infantry advanced and swept all before it.

The Battle of Messines Ridge was the most successful battle fought during the first three years of the war. Unfortunately, there was a six-week delay between it and the opening of the Third Battle of Ypres.

Hopes of a breakout from the Salient were quickly dashed when the offensive moved much more slowly than anticipated, finally becoming bogged down in the mud round the village of Passchendaele in November 1917. Here men fought and died in the most appalling conditions. The Third Battle of Ypres involved Australian, New Zealand and Canadian divisions, as well as British and South African troops, and was fought in a series of named steps. These were the Battles of Pilckem Ridge, Langemarck, Menin Road, Polygon Wood, Broodseinde, Poelcappelle, First Battle of Passchendaele and Second Battle of Passchendaele. It has been estimated that Allied losses during the Third Battle

---

3   Ibid., p.163.

of Ypres were 275,000, with 70,000 men being killed.[4] The reality is that no one knows precisely how many died and how many bodies were never recovered from the mud.

How to use this guide

The book will take you to important locations to explain the different phases of the First, Second and Third Battles of Ypres. You can read the book from beginning to end to obtain a comprehensive chronological account of events over four years of warfare. You may wish to study a specific battle, for example the Second Battle of Passchendaele, where you can follow the actions of the four Canadian divisions. Since each chapter has been constructed to be self-contained, this is easily achievable. Alternatively, you may decide to study a particular location, for example Gravenstafel Ridge, which was the scene of fighting during the First Battle of Ypres in October 1914 (British 2nd Division), the Second Battle of Ypres on 24 April 1915 (Canadian 1st Division) and the Third Battle of Ypres on 4 October 1917 (New Zealand Division). Cross referencing is provided in the relevant chapters to help you do this. It is hoped that by building up a picture of events you will be able to understand what happened in the Ypres Salient throughout the four years of the war.

We use the names of towns and villages which are employed in the *Official History of the Great War*, and avoid place names used in the present day. For example, the Third Battle of Ypres concluded with the capture of Passchendaele. We have, however, used the modern names of roads to guide you to selected locations in every chapter to help you understand what happened in these locations and why. An appendix provides a list of important place names. The maps have been carefully designed to be as clear as possible to help you to understand what happened, and are mostly based on maps in the *Official History*.

---

4   Prior R., and Wilson, T., *Passchendaele, The Untold Story* (New Haven CT: Yale University Press, 2002), p. 195.

Chapter 2

THE FIRST BATTLE OF YPRES: LANGEMARCK, 21–24 OCTOBER 1914

During October and November 1914, in what became known as the First Battle of Ypres, British and French forces fought against men of the German Fourth and Sixth Armies around the Belgian city of Ypres, where the front line held by the Allies bulged out against German positions (Figure 2.1). Langemarck is a village seven miles north-east of Ypres on the perimeter of this bulge. Fighting began on 21 October on a front extending from Armentières in the south, through Messines Ridge in the centre, to Ypres in the north. The fighting intensified around Langemarck between 22–24 October, where a major thrust was made by the German Fourth Army to smash through British positions. The Allies were equally determined to drive the Germans from Belgian soil, and the fiercely contested ground round Ypres would become known as the Ypres Salient. Langemarck was described by Edmonds in the *Official History of the Great War* as the largest of the villages near Ypres, with 1,450 houses and 7,450 inhabitants.[1] It is linked by road with Zonnebeke 4.2 miles to the south-east, Poelcappelle 2.4 miles to the north-east and Boesinghe 3.5 miles to the south-west. Figure 2.1 shows the disposition of French, British and German forces on 22–23 October.

On the evening of 19 October, the British Commander-in-Chief, Field Marshal Sir John French, issued orders to General Sir Douglas Haig, commander of I Corps (comprising the 1st and 2nd Divisions), to launch an attack on 21 October against German forces near Langemarck. Haig would be supported by French cavalry in the vicinity of Houthulst Forest. All other British forces would stand fast and hold position. The 1st and 2nd Divisions were under the command of Generals Lomax and Monro, respectively.

---

1   Edmonds, J.E., *History of the Great War Based on Official Documents by Direction of the Historical Section of the Committee of Imperial Defence. Military Operations. France and Belgium 1914 Volume 2* (London: Macmillan, 1925), p.157.

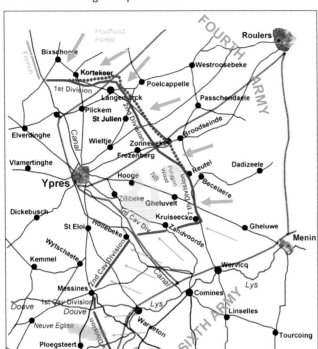

Figure 2.1 The Battles of Ypres 1914, 22 and 23 October, showing disposition of British and German forces; British positions are marked with red lines, French are in blue, while German attacks are displayed using green arrows. Dotted red line shows front on 21 October; solid red line shows front on 23 October.

Men of the 1st Division moved forward through the hamlet of Pilckem to take up position on the morning of 21 October. Unbeknown to them, at the same time, the German XXVI Reserve Corps and a division of XXIII Cavalry Corps from the German Fourth Army were planning to attack the approaches to Ypres by breaking through the Allied line between Bixschoote and Langemarck (Figure 2.1).

THE BATTLE OF LANGEMARCK, 21–22 OCTOBER 1914

Make your way from the centre of Ypres to Langemarck. The suggested route takes you through the hamlet of Pilckem, where men of the British 1st Division assembled before going to their positions in the front line. From St Martin's

Cathedral, leave by the Elverdingestraat, and after 600 yards turn right onto Haiglaan, which becomes the Veurnseweg (N8). Turn right onto N38 and cross the Yser Canal. After passing an industrial complex, the first turning to the left is the Pilkseweg, which you should take. After 1.9 miles you reach Pilckem, which is on a crossroads with the Boesinghe to Langemarck road (Figure 2.2).

Location 1: Pilckem

Figure 2.2 Approaching Pilckem from the Pilkseweg; the main road between Boesinghe and Langemarck is approximately 100 yards ahead. Boesinghe is 1.7 miles to the left; Langemarck is 1.8 miles to the right.

You are going to go straight across the main road and continue for 0.9 miles to a position called Kortekeer Cabaret, which played a very important role in the Battle of Langemarck, where men on the left flank of the 1st Division came under severe pressure. If you turn round first and look back in the direction from which you have come, soldiers from the 1st Division assembled in the fields just below you, before proceeding to their starting positions, where they replaced French Territorials (Figure 2.3).

The 1st Division should have been ready to advance from positions at Langemarck at the same time as the 2nd Division launched its attack across the Zonnebeke to Langemarck road, which you will visit shortly, but it was delayed by severe congestion of the roads on the approaches to Langemarck and still had some way to go from Pilckem.

Figure 2.3 Looking back from Pilckem in the general direction of Ypres; men of the British 1st Division would have assembled in the fields in the foreground before advancing through Pilckem and on to their positions in the front line on 21 October 1914.

Leave Pilckem by going straight across the crossroads ahead. Stop when you reach a cycle and walking track. Look to your right and you will see the church spire of Langemarck ahead (Figure 2.4). The track is the old Ypres to Staden railway line, where you may consider events as they unfolded when forward positions were reached.

Location 2: Pilkseweg – Where it crosses Ypres to Staden Railway

When men from the 1st Division arrived, they were informed that German forces were attacking Allied positions at Langemarck and between Langemarck and Bixschoote. The French Cavalry on the left of the 1st Division (Figure 2.1) had surprisingly withdrawn behind the Yser Canal, leaving the British left flank exposed. General Sir Douglas Haig wrote in his diary:

> Wednesday October 21. Without any warning whatsoever, the French Cavalry on our left received orders to retire west of the canal. The reason for this withdrawal was stated to be that the enemy was advancing in strength of about a division. The GOC of the French Cavalry Division on the immediate left of our 1st Division fully realised the effect of his withdrawal and declined absolutely to obey this order until it was repeated.[2]

---

2   Blake, R., *The Private Papers of Douglas Haig 1914–1919* (London: Eyre and Spottiswoode, 1952), pp.74–75.

Figure 2.4 Langemarck Church seen from Ypres to Staden railway line where Pilkseweg crosses it; many of the men of the 1st Division would have made their way to Langemarck, while others would have followed the route you are taking along the Pilkseweg.

As a result of the French withdrawal, the British front line at Kortekeer Cabaret came under attack. Kortekeer Cabaret was an inn at an otherwise unremarkable crossroads on the Bixschoote to Langemarck road. In itself, it was of little significance, but it played a very important role as German forces tried to smash through the British line around the crossroads.

Go along the Pilkseweg for approximately 0.9 miles. You will see the church spire at Bixschoote ahead and over to your left (Figure 2.5). Kortekeer Cabaret (Figure 2.6) is 500 yards ahead of the position from which Figure 2.5 was taken. Bixschoote was lost to the Germans on 22 October when French Territorial forces were driven out.[3]

Location 3: Kortekeer Cabaret

On 22 October, while German efforts at Langemarck were repulsed with relative ease, the situation at Kortekeer Cabaret was critical, as they tried to break through to Pilckem. Attacks began at 1530, advancing soldiers singing '*Die Wacht am Rhein*' and waving their rifles over their heads with complete disregard for their personal safety. Kortekeer Cabaret was defended

3   Edmonds, J.E., *History of the Great War Based on Official Documents by Direction of the Historical Section of the Committee of Imperial Defence. Military Operations. France and Belgium 1914 Volume 2* (London: Macmillan, 1925), p.180.

Figure 2.5 From the Pilkseweg approaching Kortekeer Cabaret, the church spire at Bixschoote is visible.

Figure 2.6 Crossroads at Kortekeer; Bixschoote is half a mile along the main road to the left. Langemarck is 1.9 miles to the right.

by the 1st Cameron Highlanders. Through sheer weight of enemy numbers, the Camerons were forced to withdraw, but not before they had killed 1,500 Germans. Two companies of the Black Watch to their right held firm, but the Germans now held part of the British line.

The 1st Battalion Northampton Regiment attempted unsuccessfully to retake the trenches, and the Cabaret itself remained heavily defended by the Germans. Haig ordered all the troops he could muster to retake the position. The 2nd KRRC, 1st Queen's, 1st Loyal North Lancashire and 2nd South Staffordshires assembled at Pilckem under Brigadier General Bulfin at 0245 on 23 October. This force advanced from Pilckem on the road you have just travelled along and launched a successful counter-attack with the help of the 1st Northampton Battalion and 1st Cameron Highlanders. The 1st Battalion Scots Guards, positioned to the left of Bulfin's force, came under attack, but successfully repulsed it.[4] The Germans launched several unsuccessful counter-attacks to retake Kortekeer Cabaret. In spite of successfully forcing them back, Bulfin concluded that the Kortekeer position was too difficult to hold and withdrew to a line just south of the Langemarck to Bixschoote road.

The British 1st Division sustained 1,344 casualties in carrying out the counter-attack on 23 October, while it was thought that losses sustained by the German XXIII Reserve Corps must have been considerably higher. The German effort to break through between Bixschoote and Langemarck on 22 and 23 October had failed.

Turn right at the Kortekeer Crossroads and go through Langemarck on the road to Poelcappelle to appreciate what happened on the right flank of the British 1st Division during the Battle of Langemarck. Stop when you get a good view of Poelcappelle village ahead and to your left (Figure 2.7).

Location 3: Near Poelcappelle Village

When the British arrived in Langemarck, they were informed that Germans were advancing from Poelcappelle railway station, some 2,000 yards from Langemarck. On 21 October, the 1st South Wales Borderers and 1st Queen's were ordered to attack Poelcappelle village and railway station, respectively. The Germans fell back to their original positions in Poelcappelle, by which time German reinforcements were arriving and the British could make no further progress. Soon the entire British advanced guard was deployed thinly, covering a front line between Poelcappelle and Bixschoote (Figure 2.1).

There were no trench systems at this stage in the war, and the British fought in small groups in short sections of hastily dug trenches, many only 3ft deep,

---

4   Ibid., p.179.

Figure 2.7 Germans advanced from positions in Poelcappelle railway station and Poelcappelle village; the British 1st Division advanced from the direction of Langemarck towards Poelcappelle. Isolated groups of British soldiers would have formed a front line by digging in close to the position from which this photograph was taken, with Poelcappelle church in the background.

and separated by gaps of between 200–400 yards, with at best only a small amount of barbed wire to protect them.[5] These could be defended easily enough in daytime using enfilade rifle and machine-gun fire, but holding them at night-time was a different matter. However, apart from difficulties experienced at Kortekeer Cabaret on 21 and 22 October, the British 1st Division coped well with the German onslaught. Repeated German attacks on Langemarck were thrown back. Despite heavy German shelling of Langemarck, there were few British casualties as the front line was well outside the village.

Advancing Germans were easy targets for trained British infantrymen, who kept firing until their rifles were too hot to handle. The Germans sustained heavy casualties due to the high standard of British marksmanship and stout defending. Edmonds states:

> Struck by gun and machine gun fire as soon as they came well into sight, the German masses staggered, and as one British diary states, their dead and wounded were literally piled up in heaps, almost before a rifle shot had been fired. Led by their officers, some still struggled on, only to meet their fate at the hands of a reserve company.[6]

5 Ibid., pp.173–75.
6 Ibid., p.178.

THE ATTACK OF THE BRITISH 2ND DIVISION

On 21 October, the 2nd Division to the right of the 1st Division was ready and in position to cross the Langemarck to Zonnebeke road at 0700.[7] Travel into Poelcappelle, where you will reach a roundabout with the statue of a stork in the middle which commemorates French aviator Georges Guynemer (Chapter 16). Turn right in the direction of St Julien for approximately 1.2 miles, where you will see a Canadian memorial commemorating men from the Canadian 1st Division who died during the opening days of the Second Battle of Ypres (Chapters 6 and 7). Turn left on the road to Zonnebeke. Go along it for approximately 1.2 miles until you reach a crossroads (Figure 2.8). The road to the left is the sGraventafelstraat, which leads to the hamlet of Gravenstafel approximately three-quarters of a mile away. The crossroads where you stand subsequently became a German strongpoint known as Kansas Cross (Chapter 14).

Location 4: Kansas Cross

Figure 2.8 Approaching a crossroads on the Langemarck to Zonnebeke road; Zonnebeke is approximately 1.2 miles ahead and Langemarck 2.5 miles behind. The village of Gravenstafel is three-quarters of a mile along the road to the left. The crossroads here would subsequently become a German strongpoint known as Kansas Cross. Men of the British 2nd Division crossed the road from shallow trenches in the fields to your right, attacking Germans over to your left.

7 Ibid., p.158.

The British 2nd Division assembled at 0630, with leading troops stretched in a broad front to the right of the Langemarck to Zonnebeke road. At first everything went well, but as soon as the road was crossed, enemy fire from advantageous positions on higher ground over to the left became heavy. Two companies of the 3rd Coldstreams reached the hamlet of Gravenstafel. Continue along the Zonnebeke road to Dochy Farm Cemetery, where a clear view may be obtained of this high ground (Figure 2.9).

Location 5: Dochy Farm Cemetery

Figure 2.9 Men of the British 2nd Division advanced towards the higher ground straight ahead, where their progress was halted by Germans firing from advantageous positions. Three years later, the New Zealand Division would advance across these same fields (Chapter 15).

Figure 2.9 was taken from Dochy Farm Cemetery, looking across the Langemarck to Zonnebeke road. You can see the high ground from which the Germans were firing as men of the 2nd Division advanced. On the left of the photograph, there are four poplar trees enclosing a New Zealand Memorial (Chapter 15). The memorial marks Gravenstafel Crossroads, and was close to where the two companies of Coldstream Guards reached on 21 October. By 1400 that day, the division had advanced between 1,000–2,000 yards. No further progress could be made. German counter-attacks were easily held off.

The Coldstream Guards had fought their way forward into an isolated position and were withdrawn at dusk on 21 October.

Continue towards Zonnebeke, and after entering the village look out on your left for a cycle track, which takes you past a modern building where the railway station at Zonnebeke once stood. The cycle track becomes continuous with the old Ypres to Roulers railway line. Stop when you get a good view of Zonnebeke Church (Figure 2.10).

Location 5: Old Ypres to Roulers Railway Line

Figure 2.10 Zonnebeke Church from the Ypres to Roulers railway line close to where Zonnebeke Station once stood; Zonnebeke was lost by the British 7th Division on 21 October 1914, and regained by the French 17th Division on 24 October.

The railway line was the divisional boundary between the 2nd and 7th Divisions (Figure 2.1). As a result of German pressure on 21 October, the British 7th Division (of IV Corps) withdrew from Zonnebeke. Next day, 22 October, the 2nd Division between Zonnebeke and Langemarck had no difficulty holding their line, though heavily bombarded. The reserves of the 2nd Division, the 1st Royal Berkshires, were sent to the Ypres to Roulers railway position close to where you stand to support the left flank of the 7th Division. By the evening of 22 October, Zonnebeke was still in enemy hands, as was the high ground beyond Zonnebeke at Broodseinde, from where the Germans had an excellent view over Allied positions.

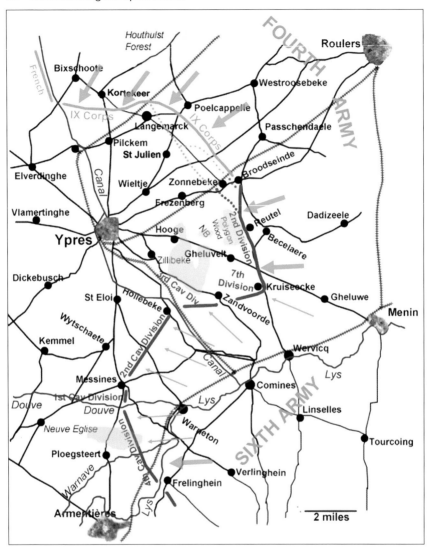

Figure 2.11 Map showing troop disposition on 24-25 October 1914. Blue lines show French positions after taking over line from British 1st and 2nd Divisions. Red lines show British front-line positions. Closer dotted lines are front-line positions on 23 October; looser dotted line the front-line positions on 24 October; solid line the front-line positions on 25 October.

On the evening of 23 October, after holding off further German assaults, the 2nd Division was relieved by the French 17th Division, under the command of General Dubois. The 2nd Division returned to the line between Broodseinde and Becelaere, adjacent to the 7th Division. On learning that Zonnebeke was in German hands, Dubois ordered the French 17th Division to recapture the village. An attack was launched between Langemarck and Zonnebeke, which began at 0700 on 24 October. While 1,000 yards of ground was gained near Langemarck, little progress was made in Zonnebeke, where there was close engagement with street fighting. By the evening, however, Zonnebeke was in French hands (Figure 2.11). On the left of the French 17th Division, the British 1st Division had a quiet day until dusk on 24 October, when it came under heavy shellfire as it was about to be relieved before redeploying to join the 2nd Division in the south near Kruiseecke (Chapter 3).[8] On 25 October, the high ground around Broodseinde fell to the French (Figure 2.11).

8   Ibid., p.194.

Chapter 3

THE FIRST BATTLE OF YPRES: KRUISEECKE AND THE KRUISEECKE RIDGE, 25–30 OCTOBER 1914

After failing to break through Allied lines at the Battle of Langemarck between 21–24 October 1914, the Germans focussed attacks on British positions in the south, beginning at the village of Kruiseecke. As previously discussed, the First Battle of Ypres was an encounter between opposing forces, each intent on attack, and neither fully aware of the strength of the other. Sir John French, Commander-in-Chief of the BEF, planned to advance against the Germans, and with the help of his French allies evict them from Belgian soil and push them back to Germany. At the same time, the Germans under the command of General von Falkenhayn made preparations to break through the British and French lines and capture Ypres, forcing the British back to the channel ports and to England. They would then destroy the French before turning their might against the Russian armies on the Eastern Front.

On 19 October, men of the British 7th Division were pushing eastwards towards the German-held town of Menin, intending to capture it. They encountered heavy German artillery fire and were forced to stop just beyond the village of Gheluvelt. The village of Kruiseecke and nearby Kruiseecke Crossroads came under intense pressure.

Location 1: Kruiseecke Crossroads

Take the N8, the Menin Road, going eastwards out of Ypres and you will come to a large roundabout. This was the approximate site of a junction between the Menin Road, the road from St Jean to Zillebeke and the Ypres to Roulers railway line. As both roads were key for transportation of supplies to the front line, German artillery frequently shelled this position, making it one of the most dangerous places to be. To conceal troops, canvas screens were positioned to shield the area from view. It fully deserved the name 'Hell Fire Corner', and all who passed through did so at speed (Figures 3.1 and 3.2).

Figure 3.1 and Figure 3.2 These photographs show 'Hell Fire Corner' as it was in 1917 and how it looks today.

If you look carefully at the side of the roundabout, you will see a British demarcation stone which marks the closest the Germans ever got to Ypres. This was in April 1918 during the Battle of the Lys, when the Ypres Salient was evacuated (Chapter 17).

Continue along the Menin Road and through the villages of Hooge and Gheluvelt. You will see a roundabout at the junction with the N303 ahead. In 1914, this was a crossroads called the Kruiseecke Crossroads, and it was here, as you face the roundabout, that the British front line ran to your left and right. The village of Kruiseecke is to your right.

The 1st Coldstream Guards held the line to your left. They had been considerably weakened by earlier fighting and were reinforced by the 1st Black Watch. To your right, the line was held by the 1st Grenadier Guards. Turn right at the Kruiseecke Crossroads (Figure 3.3), and approximately 800 yards along this road (N303) you will come to the village of Kruiseecke (Figure 3.4). You will return to Kruiseecke Crossroads soon, but fighting in Kruiseecke itself will be considered first.

Location 2: Kruiseecke

Kruiseecke was in an extremely vulnerable position on the British front line. Heroic fighting here just managed to stop the Germans from breaking through.

Figure 3.3 This is the Kruiseecke Crossroads as it is today. The approximate position of the British front line is shown by the road leading into Kruiseecke.

Figure 3.4 Looking along the main street to the village of Kruiseecke.

Since few people visit this area, its significance is not well understood. In 1914, the village comprised a road 300 yards long running in a north-south direction with a few houses.

The road to Kruiseecke marks the approximate position of the British front line in October 1914 before the German assault on Kruiseecke on the 25th. You may be able to find some shell fragments in the fields to your left. The line continued past the village before turning sharply west towards Zandvoorde (Figure 3.5).

A glance at Figure 3.5 shows how the British front line at Kruiseecke projected towards German positions, making it vulnerable to attack from the front and the sides. Holding the front line between Kruiseecke Crossroads and the village were two companies of the 1st Grenadier Guards. As you look towards Kruiseecke, a company of 2nd Scots Guards were at the apex of this projecting salient, and next to them were the 2nd Borders and 2nd Gordon Highlanders.[1]

On 20 October, the German Fourth and Sixth Armies attacked over the entire front in preparation for their major thrust at Langemarck (Chapter 2). They made small gains around the Menin Road, where the 7th Division

---

1   Edmonds, J.E., *History of the Great War Based on Official Documents by Direction of the Historical Section of the Committee of Imperial Defence. Military Operations. France and Belgium, 1914* Volume 2 (London: Macmillan, 1925) pp.239–40, 245–47.

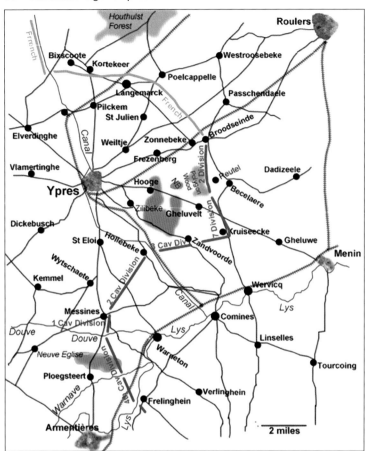

Figure 3.5 This shows the position of the front line as of 25 October 1914.

fought without respite. Over the following days, almost 40 percent of the 7th Division became casualties holding the line between the Menin Road and Zandvoorde. Drummer Kenny of the 2nd Gordon Highlanders won a Victoria Cross rescuing some wounded (Figure 3.6). A contemporary account of the action includes the following:

> On 22 and 23 October the 2nd Gordons on the south side of the Kruiseecke salient were called on to face minor attacks, repulsed by straight shooting. They were also subjected to occasional bursts of artillery fire, and vicious and accurate sniping. On 23 October Drummer William Kenny rescued five wounded men in succession in the most fearless manner under heavy fire. He was awarded the

Figure 3.6 Drum Major
Kenny VC. (Courtesy of
the Gordon Highlanders
Museum, Aberdeen)

Victoria Cross for this and previous heroic conduct in saving machine
guns and conveying urgent messages over fire swept ground.[2]

At 2000 on 25 October, Kruiseecke came under a sustained German artillery bombardment which preceded an infantry attack made by some 500
Germans. As they advanced in pouring rain under cover of darkness, they
encountered Scots Guards at the apex of the salient. The Scots Guards tried to
push them backwards, but the Germans broke through behind two companies
over a distance of 400 yards, which put the Scots Guards at great risk of being
cut off. Reinforcements were sent to stem the German advance. Although
initially unsuccessful, a further counter-attack pushed the Germans back and
restored the British front line. The 1st South Staffordshires were deployed to
strengthen the Scots and Grenadier Guards.

---

2   GHPB63.59: Copy of description of events from 10.10.1914–29.10.1914 at the 1st Battle
    of Ypres; from a typed account of the archives of the 2nd Battalion Gordon Highlanders
    from part of a donation of documents relating to Lieutenant Colonel James Dawson;
    courtesy Gordon Highlanders Museum.

On 26 October, the Germans attacked again. An artillery bombardment in the morning targeted the Scots Guards' trenches, destroying them and burying many of the occupants, not all of whom could be dug out and saved. Artillery fire was next directed onto the Grenadiers' trenches. One hour after this heavy bombardment, 15 German infantry battalions attacked. Some Germans penetrated the British front line, and shouted in English 'retire'. Many of the South Stafford Battalion thought that this was a genuine command and complied, much to the Germans' advantage, who by midday had broken into the salient around Kruiseecke and were behind the Scots and Grenadier Guards. The situation in Kruiseecke was hopeless, and 309 Scots and Grenadier Guards, who were completely cut off, surrendered. Kruiseecke was in German hands. A few Grenadiers evaded capture and fought their way back to the new British line.[3]

FIGHTING BEHIND KRUISEECKE AND ON THE KRUISEECKE RIDGE

You will now go through Kruiseecke to the west of the village. You will see Kruiseecke Ridge, where fighting continued after the capture of the village, and will have a vantage point providing you with a panoramic view of the southern half of the defensive semicircle around Ypres where several important engagements took place as the First Battle of Ypres progressed and the Ypres Salient became established. After entering Kruiseecke, turn right into a small street, the Bootstrap. Look for the first right turn labelled Tabakstraat and then first right again, which takes you onto Nieuwe Zoetendaalstraat. Go along this road until you pass a farm house on your right, from where you will have an excellent vantage point.

Location 3: Farmhouse on Nieuwe Zoetendaalstraat

You will see the church spires at Gheluvelt to your right and of Zandvoorde on a hillside ahead. Hollebeke is to the left of Zandvoorde and Wytschaete is on Messines Ridge to the far left. Messines church is in the distance beyond Wytschaete. You can identify them using the maps and photographs shown in Figures 3.7, 3.8 and 3.9. The church spires have distinctive shapes, and by imagining a line between them you can visualise British positions to the south of Ypres. A set of binoculars will help. As you look towards Gheluvelt, you can appreciate the higher ground that you occupy on the Kruiseecke Ridge.

---

3   Edmonds, J.E., *History of the Great War Based on Official Documents by Direction of the Historical Section of the Committee of Imperial Defence. Military Operations. France and Belgium 1914* Volume 2 (London: Macmillan, 1925) pp.239–40, 245–47.

Figure 3.7 This shows the view to the left from your position.

Figure 3.8 The view with church spires labelled, and with views towards the front from your position.

Figure 3.9 The view with Gheluvelt church to the right from your position. Further to your right and out of the photograph is Kruiseecke Crossroads.

Why was fighting here so important to the Germans?

The engagement here was part of a German attack to break through the Allied line. Although they had captured Kruiseecke on 26 October, their Fourth and Sixth Armies had failed to make significant progress. The German commander, General von Falkenhayn, brought other units together to form a new battle formation, Army Group Fabeck, under the command of General von Fabeck. It comprised six regular and one volunteer divisions, with an artillery power of 262 howitzers and 484 smaller guns, and was positioned between the Fourth and Sixth Armies (Figure 3.10). It would carry out a major attack on 30 October, with the objective of breaking the British line between Zandvoorde and Messines before pushing on to Mount Kemmel. The Germans would then have control of the high ground of Messines Ridge and would be well placed to advance north to the Channel coast and gain control of its vital ports.

The coming German attack

Sweep your gaze round from Gheluvelt on your right, to Zandvoorde and Hollebeke in the centre, to Wytschaete and Messines on the far left. You can see exactly where this attack would take place. Von Falkenhayn was determined this attack would succeed and his order stated:

The break-through will be of decisive importance. We must and will therefore conquer, settle for ever with the centuries' long struggle, end the war, and strike the decisive blow against our most detested enemy. We will finish with the British, Indians, Canadians and Moroccans, and other trash, feeble adversaries, who surrender in great numbers if they are attacked with vigour.[4]

Facing the might of Army Group Fabeck was the British 7th Division, which had lost almost half its strength, and British Cavalry units, which were small. In some places the Germans were six times as strong as the Allies. Figure 3.10 shows the disposition of German forces around where you are standing now.

A diversion first before the main German attack

To disguise his intentions, von Falkenhayn ordered that Gheluvelt should be captured the day before (29 October). As part of this deception, the British defenders here on Kruiseecke Ridge would also come under attack. After this had succeeded, there would be a massive assault by Army Group Fabeck, with the Fourth and Sixth Armies (Figure 3.10) in support to prevent reinforcements being sent from elsewhere by the Allies to counter Army Group Fabeck's progress.

FIGHTING ON THE KRUISEECKE RIDGE

On 29 October, men from the 2nd Battalion Royal Scots Fusiliers were involved in fighting close to where you now stand. At 0700, the Germans attacked them as part of the assault around Gheluvelt to your right. The assault extended along a line as far as Becelaere, and although you can't see this village, you can position it from Figure 3.10. The Royal Scots Fusiliers held off strong German infantry attacks throughout the day and night of 29 October and into the following morning, despite sustaining heavy casualties.[5] On the morning of 30 October, the Germans launched another attack, strengthened by their reserves. The Royal Scots Fusiliers still held the Kruiseecke Ridge, but to your right the German attack on either side of the Menin Road (towards Gheluvelt) pushed the British back along the road, leaving the Scots very exposed. Germans also overcame the British in Zandvoorde, who were forced to withdraw and the Germans captured the village. The Royal Scots Fusiliers were now under attack from the front and the sides by Germans who had moved into Zandvoorde and towards Gheluvelt. They were in fact becoming

---

4   Ibid., p.282.
5   Brice, B., *The battle book of Ypres: a reference to military operations in the Ypres Salient 1914–1918* (Stevenage: Spa Books Ltd., 1987).

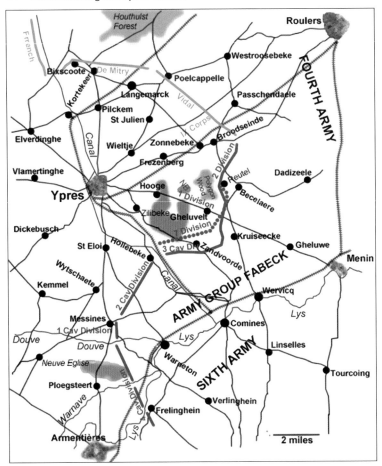

Figure 3.10 This shows the disposition of the German forces for the attack on 30 October 1914, and in particular Army Group Fabeck. The solid red line shows the British line before the attack; the dotted red line shows its position after the loss of Zandvoorde on the morning of 30 October.

surrounded by the Germans. Nevertheless, they held their position until the night of 30 October, although the situation was hopeless. They tried to withdraw towards the British lines, taking as many of their wounded as possible. German advances meant that they were almost completely cut off, and most were captured. Only a few made it back to the British line. Leave your position here and return to Kruiseecke Crossroads.

Chapter 4

THE FIRST BATTLE OF YPRES: KRUISEECKE CROSSROADS, 29 OCTOBER 1914

Leave Kruiseecke and retrace your steps to the position of the Kruiseecke Crossroads. It was here, and on either side of the Menin Road, that the Germans mounted their attack on 29 October (Chapter3). If you stand with your back towards Ypres, you are close to the British front line facing the Germans, who were a few hundred yards in front of you (Figure 4.1).

Location 1: Kruiseecke Crossroads

Turn and face towards Ypres and look at the view in Figure 4.2, which looks back along the Menin Road and shows Gheluvelt and the Gheluvelt Plateau.

Figure 4.1 Facing Kruiseecke roundabout with the German line a short distance in front, and with the village of Kruiseecke to the right and just out of the photograph, but which can be seen when you look to the right a short distance away.

Figure 4.2 With your back facing the Kruiseecke roundabout, the view is shown towards Gheluvelt along the Menin Road and in the direction of Ypres.

To your left is the village of Kruiseecke, captured by the Germans on 26 October (Figure 4.3). The British line then cut back to Zandvoorde, and from there to Hollebeke before swinging south to Wytschaete and Messines on the higher ground of Messines Ridge. To your right, the Allied line passed to Becelaere, before turning north towards Broodseinde, Poelcappelle, Langemarck and Bixschoote in an approximate semicircle with Ypres at the centre. These locations were contested vigorously during the First Battle of Ypres, by the end of which the Ypres Salient became established.

FIGHTING AT THE KRUISEECKE CROSSROADS AND ALONG THE MENIN ROAD TOWARDS GHELUVELT ON 29 OCTOBER 1914

Sir John French knew that the Germans planned to attack Gheluvelt at 0530 on 29 October because a radio message sent by the German Fourth Army to the XXVII Reserve Corps had been intercepted. The British anticipated that the attack would come along the Menin Road, and from the direction of Kruiseecke. While some preparations were made to co-ordinate artillery of

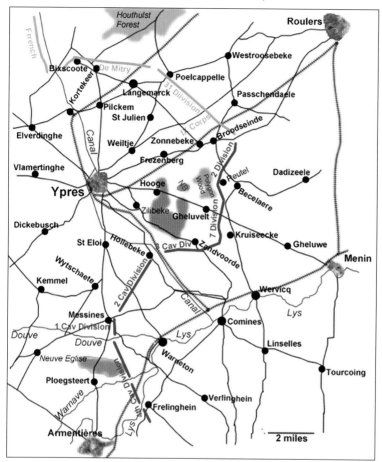

Figure 4.3 Map showing the Germans in possession of Kruiseecke.

the 1st, 2nd and 7th Divisions to deal with this potential German threat, Sir John French wanted the 2nd Division under, Major General Monro, to make its own attack.

The start of the German attack

At 0530 on 29 October, the expected German offensive was launched towards your position at Kruiseecke Crossroads and to the south of the Menin Road. It began with a fierce artillery bombardment before German infantry advanced along the Menin Road under cover of dense fog, reaching close to the British line without being seen. This was the opening of what would become known as the Battle of Gheluvelt.

Face towards the German line and look to your left (north). The 7th Division was here, and closest to you was the 1st Battalion Coldstream Guards, with about a third of its initial strength remaining. Major General FitzClarence sent two companies of 1st Black Watch and the 1st Gloucesters to support them. One company of the Black Watch was positioned immediately adjacent to the crossroads to the north of the Menin Road, and another to the left of the Coldstream Guards. Despite these reinforcements, the front line had gaps.

Now look towards the right (south) side of the Menin Road. Men of the 1st Battalion Grenadier Guards from the 7th Division were here, and next to them the 2nd Gordon Highlanders. In support were remnants of the 2nd Scots Guards and the 2nd Battalion, Border Regiment, which had sustained major losses in the fighting around Kruiseecke (Chapter 3). Figure 4.4 shows part of the line to the south of the Menin Road.

British defences consisted of hastily dug shallow trenches which did not communicate with each other, and which had significant gaps between them. Sometimes a single strand of barbed wire was all that provided protection. Trenches to the south of the Menin Road were so poor that General Henry Rawlinson, commander of the 7th Division, considered building a better defensive line behind them, but there was no time.

Figure 4.4 This photograph illustrates the view from Kruiseecke back towards the crossroads (now the roundabout) and along the approximate position of the British line.

The British were very short of artillery and shells to repel German attacks, and on 24 October Sir John French sent a telegram to Lord Kitchener, the Secretary of State for War, informing him about this shortage. He told him that the BEF would soon be fighting without artillery support. Kitchener replied that the BEF should be "economical" with its use of shells. Each gun would have a limited number of shells (nine per gun per day), and these would only be used against German artillery and not to repel attacking infantry.

FIGHTING TO THE NORTH OF THE MENIN ROAD

The key events on the north side of the road are as follows:[1]

- The inadequate trenches were difficult to defend. Many rifles and two machine guns near the crossroads jammed, partly because of lack of maintenance and partly because some ammunition cartridges were too large to fit into the rifles.
- The attacking Germans were the 16th Bavarian Reserves from the 54th Reserve Division of the XXVII Reserve Corps.
- The Black Watch and the adjacent Coldstreams were the first to be attacked.
- Within an hour, Germans entered the trenches near the crossroads and got behind the Black Watch and Coldstreams, and fired on them from a wooded area a short distance behind their trench.
- The survivors of the Black Watch and about half of the Coldstreams were taken prisoner. The remaining Coldstreams fought on. The Germans then moved further north behind the Scots Guards and tried to take them from the rear as well, but despite sustaining many casualties the Scots Guards held their part of the line.
- To try to restore the situation, especially just to the north of the Menin Road, three companies of the 1st Gloucesters were sent forwards to support the Coldstreams, and initially were successful. However, the might of the German attack resulted in heavy losses, and over the next few hours, the British line was forced back 300 yards. A fourth company of the Gloucesters was sent to help south of the Menin Road.

The War Diary of the 1st Battalion Coldstreams stated:

An attack by the Germans of which notice was given was beaten off at 0530 in dense mist but was successful further S. At the crossroads E.S.E. of Gheluvelt: the result being that the battalion trenches were almost immediately attacked from the rear.

---

1   Neillands R., *The Old Contemptibles* (London: John Murray, 2004).

OTHER FIGHTING FURTHER NORTH

The Germans also attacked the British front line at Becelaere without any prior artillery bombardment, surprising the 1st Battalion Scots Guards.

FIGHTING TO THE SOUTH OF THE MENIN ROAD

To the south of the road, men of the 1st Battalion of the Grenadiers (7th Division) were very nearly caught out.

- The Grenadiers were not aware of what was happening on the north side of the Menin Road due to the fog and because adjacent houses obstructed their view.
- They decided that the Germans were not actually going to attack and so sent back the 2nd Scots Guards and the 2nd Borders at 0645.
- They were taken by surprise when German artillery bombarded them suddenly and followed up very quickly with an infantry attack, with men just emerging from the fog onto their positions.
- Not only did Germans attack from the front, they also attacked from the rear, because some of the Germans who had broken through the trenches to the north of the Menin Road were able to cross the road and attack them from behind.
- The Grenadiers were forced back, despite their best efforts.
- They made counter-attacks, supported by the 2nd Gordons, and did retake some trenches temporarily, but again the Germans forced them backwards.
- They regrouped to the east of Gheluvelt just south of the Menin Road, and were joined by the fourth company of the Gloucesters and the 2nd Borders (who had been sent to the rear just before this attack).
- The 2nd Gordons also came under repeated attacks from their front but held their position through the day, although like the Grenadiers suffered heavy losses.

It was during this action that Captain James Anson Otho Brooke of the 2nd Gordons led two counter-attacks, one of which resulted in the recapture of a Grenadier trench. Brooke was clearly a leader, having been the outstanding cadet at the Royal Military Academy, Sandhurst, in 1905, where he won the Sword of Honour. Brooke was killed in the counter-attack, and for his bravery and leadership was awarded the Victoria Cross (Figure 4.5).

His citation reads:

> For conspicuous bravery and great ability near Gheluvelt on the 29th October, in leading two attacks on the German trenches under heavy

rifle and machine gun fire, regaining a lost trench at a very critical moment. He was killed on that day. By his marked coolness and promptitude on this occasion Lieutenant Brooke prevented the enemy from breaking through our line, at a time when a general counter-attack could not have been organised.

London Gazette (supplement) No. 29074, 16 February 1916

The following contemporary account of the fighting on 29 October conveys vividly what things were like around where you stand:

The morning of October 29th was foggy. The heavy German bombardment was not at first followed by an infantry attack, and Major General Capper drew back the two supporting battalions, 2nd Scots Guard and 2nd Border Regiment, because they had no cover and would, when the light improved and the fog cleared, be at the mercy of the German artillery. Then, at 7.30am the German artillery began to pound the 1st Grenadiers. Almost immediately a swarm of Germans swept down on their left flank, broke through, and attacked them in rear, while simultaneously the enemy assaulted frontally. The Grenadiers were almost cut to pieces and the remnants, with the left flank company of the Gordons pushed back toward Gheluvelt. But the Gordons sent aid in

Figure 4.5 Captain James Anson Otho Brooke VC.
(Courtesy of the Gordon Highlanders Museum, Aberdeen)

the shape of the reserve company; the Borders and the Scots Guards hurried back into action; and a counter-attack north of the Menin road somewhat eased the situation. At the worst moment, when a counter-attack had failed and the defence had seemed to be on the edge of disaster, the heroism of Captain J A O Brooke had done much to restore it. Brooke was killed, and received the posthumous award of the Victoria Cross.[2]

As explained in Chapter 3, the advancing Germans had taken the Kruiseecke Ridge. Around the Menin Road, the British were pushed backwards to a new line approximately 800 yards from the crossroads. The Germans were in control of the Kruiseecke Crossroads and the Kruiseecke Ridge.[3] By the end of the day on 29 October, the British had sustained major losses, which amounted to three battalions. The *Official History of the Coldstream Guards* states there were no officers left and only 80 men.

2   GHPB63: Copy of description of events from 10.10.1914–29.10.1914 at the 1st Battle of Ypres; from a typed account of the archives of the 2nd Battalion Gordon Highlanders from part of a donation of documents relating to Lieutenant Colonel James Dawson; courtesy Gordon Highlanders Museum.
3   Neillands, R., *The Old Contemptibles* (London: John Murray, 2004).

Chapter 5

THE FIRST BATTLE OF YPRES:
THE BATTLE OF GHELUVELT,
30–31 OCTOBER 1914
THE BATTLE OF NONNE BOSSCHEN,
11 NOVEMBER 1914

Following fighting on 29 October, the British lost front-line trenches around the Menin Road and were pushed back approximately 800 yards towards Gheluvelt. The Germans were in control of Kruiseecke Crossroads and Kruiseecke Ridge. On 30 October, Sir John French still planned to attack, despite the setbacks of the previous day's fighting. Sir Douglas Haig urged caution and a re-evaluation of the situation before committing to an offensive. He wanted the three British divisions to secure their positions by strengthening defences. Men of the 2nd Division were fortunate to have acquired some barbed wire which they could use to protect their trenches, but soldiers of other divisions could only deepen their trenches as much as possible.

That day also happened to be the day for Army Group Fabeck's offensive (Chapter 3). During the night of 29–30 October, five fresh German infantry divisions were brought forward to attack. The Germans planned to break through the British front line between Gheluvelt and Messines and capture Messines Ridge, then cut off defenders at Ypres to the north, forcing a retreat to the coast. The British 7th Division and three cavalry divisions would bear the brunt of the German attack (Figure 5.1). In the north, the Germans had a numerical superiority ratio of three to two, while towards the south they had three times as many men. Army Group Fabeck had five divisions and a reserve supported by artillery, whilst the British 7th Division had lost almost half its strength and the three British Cavalry units defending Messines Ridge were so small that the Germans were six times as strong there.

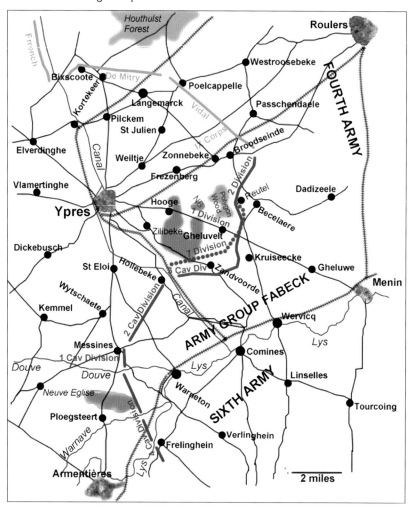

Figure 5.1 British (red line) and French (blue line) front lines as on the start of 30 October 1914 are the solid line. By 10 a.m., the British line has been pushed back west of Zandvoorde and is shown by the dotted red line. NB stands for Nonne Bosschen.

To explain events as they unfolded, you will begin by going a few hundred yards from Kruiseecke Crossroads along the Menin Road towards Gheluvelt, to where the British line had pulled back after the loss of the crossroads. Gheluvelt is on an upward incline leading onto Gheluvelt Plateau beyond, which was valuable to the British because it allowed them to look down on German positions (Figure 5.2).

Location 1: Near Foot of Gheluvelt Plateau

Figure 5.2 This photograph is taken moving up towards the Gheluvelt Plateau, with Ypres in the distance but not seen. The plateau gives a prominent position for whoever occupies it to look over the enemy lines.

Look in the direction of Ypres. You can visualise Zandvoorde, Hollebeke, Wytschaete and Messines over to your left, where a furious German assault took place on 30 October. You will have the opportunity to visit these places, and it might help to refer to Figure 5.1 and Figures 3.7–3.9. To your right, directly north of Gheluvelt at a distance of 2.8 miles as the crow flies, is the village of Zonnebeke (Figure 5.1), the scene of a diversionary German attack on 30 October. An artillery barrage at 0600 was followed 30 minutes later by an infantry attack. The Germans hoped that the British and French would divert reserves to Zonnebeke. This diversion did not work, and by 0900 it was over. Two further attacks at 1100 and midday were also successfully repelled without any need to send additional troops to the area.

Attack on Gheluvelt on 30 October 1914

- At 0800 the German 54th Reserve and 30th Divisions attacked Gheluvelt and the front line to the south of the village.
- Men of the British 1st Division and adjacent 7th Division who were attacked withstood the fierce German assault.

- The Germans did not make any progress and entrenched about 300 yards in front of the British line.

Location 2: Zandvoorde

You may simply wish to read the following section while you continue your journey along the Menin Road, but making a detour to visit the places described will give you a better idea of the extent of the German attack. Whilst the Germans failed to break through at Gheluvelt, the situation at Zandvoorde was very different. To reach this village, go into Gheluvelt and turn left on the Zandvoordestraat. Figure 5.3 shows the view as you make your way to Zandvoorde.

Figure 5.3 View taken heading from Gheluvelt towards Zandvoorde; Gheluvelt is directly behind where the photograph was taken.

Zandvoorde came under a bombardment which started at 0645 and lasted for 75 minutes.

- The men of 7 Cavalry Brigade (1st and 2nd Life Guards) were in trenches in front of Zandvoorde, which were shallow and on the slope facing the Germans. They were easily seen by the enemy and their trenches were quickly destroyed by shellfire. Some soldiers in them were buried alive.

- By 0800, survivors faced an infantry attack by the German 39th Division. In the face of this German onslaught, those who could retreat did so. By 1000, Zandvoorde had fallen to the Germans, and a new British line was established west of the village.
- Attempts made by the British, supported by French and British Cavalry reserves, to retake Zandvoorde failed (Figure 5.1).

Look towards Gheluvelt. The fall of Zandvoorde caused a problem for units fighting between Zandvoorde and the Menin Road (1st Royal Welch, 2nd Royal Scots Fusiliers and 2nd Green Howards). When the Germans captured Zandvoorde, they attacked the flank of the Royal Welch Fusiliers, who were also being attacked from the direction of Kruiseecke Crossroads. The battalion suffered heavy casualties, with only 86 survivors from a force that a few weeks earlier had consisted of 1,100 officers and men.

Go through Zandvoorde onto the Houtemstraat, and after half a mile take the Hollebekestraat. Keep going till you reach Hollebeke, where you will see the church ahead. Stop just before you reach the village.

Location 3: Hollebeke

Attack on Hollebeke on 30 October 1914

- The Germans made little progress against the defenders at Hollebeke in the morning. By midday they were raining shellfire against the trenches in front of the village (Figure 5.1 and Figure 3.8).
- The bombardment forced the defenders to withdraw. These included 3 Cavalry Brigade, the 2nd Cavalry Division and some Indian battalions.
- A new front line was established west of Hollebeke, closer to Ypres, now three miles away.

Leave Hollebeke and continue on the Hollebekestraat towards Wytschaete. Stop when you reach the junction of the Hollebekestraat and the N365. Look towards the church at Wytschaete on the ridge ahead, while you consider what happened here on 30 October 1914.

Location 4: Foot of Wytschaete Ridge

Attack on Wytschaete and Messines, 30 October 1914

- The British line was heavily bombarded, and the artillery attack was particularly strong against the 1st Cavalry Division and the right of the 2nd Cavalry

Division.

- The 1st and 2nd Cavalry Divisions withdrew to their second-line positions on the crest of Messines Ridge.
- Despite attempts made throughout the day. the Germans failed to break the British line.

THE MAIN IMPACT OF THE FIGHTING ON 30 OCTOBER 1914

The Germans attacked in an arc between Gheluvelt and Wytschaete, forcing the central part of the Allied line back by about one-and-a-half miles towards Ypres as a result of the losses of Zandvoorde and Hollebeke (Figure 5.4).

Figure 5.4 The relative positions of the villages, so you can visualise how the attack would have pushed back the British front line.

On the evening of 30 October, Haig discussed his plans with Sir John French at his HQ at White Château near 'Hell Fire Corner'. He planned an attack at 0630 on 31 October to recapture Zandvoorde and Hollebeke, using the 1st and 2nd Cavalry Divisions and three French divisions stationed at Zillebeke. Sir John French met General Foch in the early hours of 31 October to ask for additional French support. Foch promised another five French infantry battalions and three artillery batteries. Uncertain about what the Germans might be planning at Messines Ridge, Haig sent the 1st London Scottish (a Territorial battalion) to reinforce the ridge. Meanwhile, German reserves were brought

Figure 5.5 The view from the road from Wytschaete, looking towards Messines church. The Germans were attacking the British on the ridge and in the town, and would have been coming up from the left of the photograph towards the road and the village ahead.

forwards and positioned opposite Wytschaete where you stand to reinforce an attack on the ridge.

Make your way up to Wytschaete and turn in the direction of Messines. Figure 5.5 shows cyclists on Messines Ridge, with the village of Messines ahead. They have stopped at a London Scottish Memorial.

Location 5: London Scottish Memorial (Figure 5.6)

Messines and the surrounding area were heavily bombarded throughout the early hours of 31 October. The line was held by 1 Cavalry Brigade, part of 2 Cavalry Brigade, some of the 57th Rifles and by men of the 4th Division who were at Ploegsteert. They faced a German infantry attack at 0430 which centred on the village of Messines, and on the line north and south. The Germans were at first beaten back by rifle fire and close-quarter fighting. At 0800, the Germans broke the British line at Messines and the defenders fell back to the second line on the western outskirts of the village. The Germans entered Messines and blew most of it up, while the British held their second line.

Figure 5.6 The London Scottish Memorial on Messines Ridge.

Between Wytschaete and Messines, the front line was held by the 2nd Cavalry Division, three batteries of horse artillery, six batteries of French artillery (from 32nd Division), Hussars from 3 Cavalry Brigade and the 14th London Battalion(London Scottish). This was the first Territorial battalion to be brought into action. As the men made their way to the front line, they were hit by artillery fire. One non-commissioned officer, in an unfinished letter, encapsulates the fear and confusion of the ordinary soldier:

> We go on, shells coming over us, and pass behind our own guns. Then we go into a field and up to a wood. All of a sudden we're in it, and bolt like rabbits along a wet ditch beside a road. God knows what's happening. I'm nestling against the bank with my feet in water, sweating with terror, and shells shrieking over me and busting close behind. Mostly they burst four at a time then a lull. Presently we get

wise to this and when the lulls come we mount our trenching tools and dig feverishly into the bank. I look at my watch. Three hours till dark. Damn it, they must get me before then.[1]

Despite losing more than 300 men, the London Scottish supported the cavalry and succeeded in holding the line against further German attacks. Fighting continued through the night, and by the morning of 1 November the Germans had captured Wytschaete and Messines Ridge.

THE ATTACK ON GHELUVELT ON 31 OCTOBER 1914

Location 6: Close to Gheluvelt Church

Return to Gheluvelt to continue your journey along the Menin Road. Stop 300 yards from the church. You are close to where the British front line crossed the road. The battalions defending the main route into Ypres are shown in Figure 5.7. The artillery support for this part of the line was provided by 34 Brigade RFA positioned some 500 yards behind the front line, with the 1st Gloucesters close by.

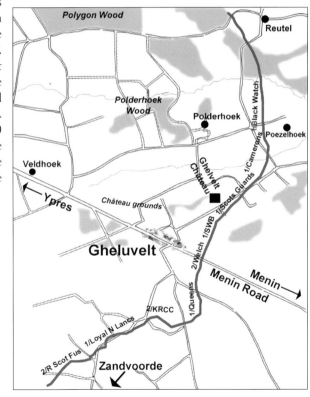

Figure 5.7 British defence of Gheluvelt.

1   Lloyd, M., *The London Scottish in the Great War* (Barnsley: Pen and Sword Limited, 2001), p.39.

To the south of the Menin Road, an orchard projected from the British front line and was occupied by men of the 2nd Kings Royal Rifle Corps and the 1st Queens. This would prove to be a weak point.

Location 7: Approximate Site of Orchard

You can visit the approximate sight of the orchard by going along a road called Oude Komenstraat on your left just before the turn-off to Zandvoorde (Zandvoordestraat). After approximately 200 yards take the second turn on your right, the Blokstraat. After 400 yards there is a farm on your right and a road to the right just after the farm. This road marks the approximate position of the front line, and the orchard was a short distance in front of this road (Figure 5.8).

Figure 5.8 Photograph taken from Oude Zandvoordestraat, looking towards Zandvoorde; the approximate site of the orchard is marked. The positions of the battalions located here can be seen by comparing with Figure 5.7.

At 0600, the Germans (16th Bavarian and 246th Infantry regiments) advanced in miserable wet conditions, and although held initially by rapid rifle fire, captured the orchard and held it despite several counter-attacks by the British. The German attack intensified with a heavy artillery bombardment. At the same time, enfilade fire was poured from the orchard onto the 1st Queens and the 2nd Royal Welch Fusiliers, inflicting many casualties. These men were between the orchard and the Menin Road.

By 0930, the right flank of the 2nd Royal Welch was blown out of its trenches and withdrew. The 1st Queens remained in position, unaware of what was happening on its immediate left (Figures 5.7 and 5.8). A gap appeared in the front line, and although a company of Gloucesters was sent forward to fill it, heavy casualties were sustained and the gap could not be plugged. To the right of the Queens, in the direction of Zandvoorde, the 1st Loyal North Lancs and 2nd Royal Scots Fusiliers were surrounded and most were killed, wounded or captured. The breach in the British line grew even wider.

Retrace your steps to Gheluvelt and cross the Menin Road. Turn towards Ypres for a few yards and turn right into the Kasteelstraat, then left into Gheluveldplaats (a small square). At the end of the square, turn to your right and you will see the entrance to the grounds of Gheluvelt Château. Look towards the château (Figure 5.9).

Location 8: Gheluvelt Château Grounds

Figure 5.9 Gheluvelt Château and grounds can be seen. The Worcesters would have come in, most likely, from the left of the photograph.

To the north of the Menin Road, the line was held by part of the 2nd Royal Welch, 1st South Wales Borders and 1st Scots Guards. They were forced back into the château grounds, sustaining many casualties. They pushed the

Germans back a short distance, but only to the eastern edge of the grounds. Brigadier General FitzClarence VC (awarded in 1899 in the Boer War) was in command of the Guards, and he sent up men he had left from the Black Watch and one company of 2nd Worcestershires to reinforce survivors in the château grounds. Drastic action was needed to prevent an overwhelming breakthrough. FitzClarence returned to his headquarters at nearby Glencorse Wood, and from there went to Major General Lomax's Battle HQ at 'Clapham Junction'. The 2nd Worcesters were reserves of the 2nd Division, and were employed to deliver a counter-attack on the German flank. Their attack was made from the direction of Polygon Wood with utmost vigour. At 1300, FitzClarence gave the order to Major Hankey commanding the 2nd Worcestershires to advance to Gheluvelt and restore the British line. The path followed by these men is shown on the map in Figure 5.10.

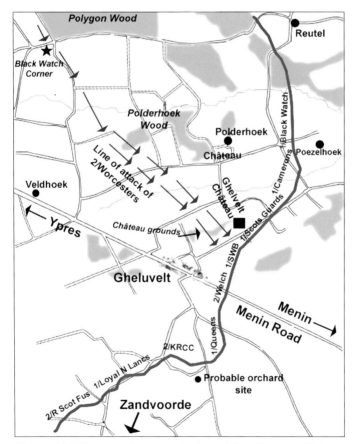

Figure 5.10 This map illustrates the line of the advance made by men of the 2nd Worcesters as they moved forward.

To understand this attack, go along the Polderweg at the far end of the square and skirt round the right of the church. You will soon reach a cemetery, which you should walk through and find a track at the far end. Walk along this track for a short distance until you come to a road, where you will see a plaque marking the approximate position of Polderhoek Château. Look ahead with the cemetery behind you, where you will see the view shown in Figure 5.11. The 2nd Worcesters would have been coming towards you.

Figure 5.11 The view with your back to Gheluvelt Château, from the approximate site of Polderhoek Château. If you look in the distance you can see Polygon Wood, and whilst Black Watch Corner is hidden by trees, its approximate position is indicated.

Turn to face Gheluvelt Château (Figure 5.12). The Worcesters would have been coming past you, moving down the slope towards the wall of the château gardens. If you retrace your steps towards the cemetery, then you will pass the boundary of the gardens where the wall was.

As the 2nd Worcesters advanced, the Germans pounded them with shell-fire. Approximately 100 were killed or wounded before they even reached the château. They attacked 1,200 Germans in the château grounds, with hand-to-hand fighting, and such was the ferocity of the Worcesters' attack that around 100 Germans lay dead, many killed by the bayonet, while those who could, fled. The Worcesters kept going until they reached the survivors of the South Wales Borderers and Scots Guards in the south-west part of the grounds, who

Figure 5.12 Facing Gheluvelt Château, you can see the village and the trees marking the château grounds. The 2nd Worcesters would have been coming past you as they moved forwards.

Figure 5.13 The memorial to the Worcesters and the remnants of the old mill; the latter was destroyed by German artillery fire.

Figure 5.14 Clapham Junction.

were fighting for their lives. Major Hankey deployed his men in a sunken lane which ran from the château to the village. Fighting continued, but Gheluvelt had been made secure and was back in British hands by late afternoon. The Worcesters lost three officers and 189 men in this action.

Leave the château and make your way out of Gheluvelt by returning to the Menin Road. If you turn left, you will find a small lane which takes you to the Worcesters' Memorial and the site of an old mill (Figure 5.13). This mill had been used as an observation post and had been shelled by the Germans before the battle. Remnants of the mill are adjacent to the memorial.

Return to the Menin Road and turn right towards Ypres. Keep going to 'Clapham Junction', where General Lomax, Commanding Officer of the 1st Division, had his battle headquarters. Two memorials mark the position of 'Clapham Junction'. One on the left commemorates the 18th Division, while that on the right is the Gloucesters' Memorial (Figure 5.14).

Location 9: Clapham Junction

Having heard about the crisis at Gheluvelt Château, Lomax left his HQ and rode along the Menin Road to the 2nd Division HQ at Hooge Château. Here he met with General Monro, Commanding Officer of the 2nd Division. Whilst there, Hooge Château was hit by shellfire. Lomax sustained severe wounds, which resulted in his death several months later. Monro was knocked unconscious but recovered, while several senior staff officers were killed or wounded. Major General Bulfin took command of the 1st Division. Haig, who was at his HQ at White Château near 'Hellfire Corner', set off up the Menin Road to see for himself what had happened and to try to rally the men.

Leave 'Clapham Junction' and go a short distance down the Menin Road. Turn right onto Oude Kortrijkstraat. Keep going past a wooded area to your left. This is Glencorse Wood, where FitzClarence had his HQ. Just beyond Glencorse Wood is Nonne Bosschen. There is a turning to the right called Wulvestraat, where there is an explanatory plaque about FitzClarence.

Location 10: Fitzclarence Plaque, Wulvestraat

Turn into the Wulvestraat and stop. Gheluvelt is about 800 yards straight ahead. You can see Gheluvelt church (Figure 5.15).

Now turn to your left. You can see Nonne Bosschen to the left, while Polygon Wood is straight ahead beyond the buildings (Figure 5.16).

It was near where you stand that FitzClarence spoke to the Commanding Officer of the 2nd Worcesters, who were in reserve near Polygon Wood. The Worcesters assembled to launch their vital counter-attack and advanced across the fields towards Gheluvelt Château, and a German breakthrough was prevented. Despite their heroic action, Haig decided that the British line should be moved back to the Ypres side of Gheluvelt, since this would be an easier position to defend.

OUTCOME OF 31 OCTOBER 1914

Of the original BEF, it was estimated that between a half and two-thirds of its original strength had been lost. The Germans had gained little by the end of the day, except for a part of Messines and Gheluvelt, which was occupied when the British withdrew. The Battle of Gheluvelt ended on 31 October. The Germans captured Messines Ridge on 1 November, and Wytschaete fell to them on 2 November. The high ground at Kemmel remained in British hands.

A PERIOD OF RELATIVE CALM BEFORE THE STORM-NONNE BOSSCHEN

The Germans too had sustained major losses, and although fighting continued over the following days, it was not as severe. The British and French believed mistakenly that the Germans were preparing to send divisions to the Eastern Front to fight the Russians. In fact, Army Group Fabeck was being reinforced by more men and artillery in preparation for a further major attack. The Germans were determined to break through, and six more divisions, together

Figure 5.15 The view from close to the site of FitzClarence's headquarters. Gheluvelt church can be seen, with the approximate position of Gheluvelt Château and its gardens indicated.

Figure 5.16 Nonne Bosschen is to the left. Polygon Wood is beyond the buildings ahead.

with a Prussian Guard Division, strengthened Army Group Fabeck. In addition, the Germans formed another smaller army group commanded by von Linsingen, which was strategically placed along the Menin Road.

On the morning of 11 November, the Germans launched a massive and prolonged artillery bombardment, which started at 0630 and was directed against the British 1st and 2nd Divisions. It was of greater ferocity than anything before. Gunner C.W. Burrows of the Royal Field Artillery recorded:

> By nine o'clock the bombardment had built up to a crescendo the like of which no living soldier had heard before. There was nothing to be done but crouch in trenches, in ditches, in hollows, in any hole or nook and cranny in the quaking earth that could offer the slightest shelter from the inferno of tumbling shells; to stomach it, to stick it out, to wait and to hope but without much hope that when the shelling stopped and the enemy came on, they would be fit and ready to fight.[2]

An infantry attack started at 0900 using 12½ German divisions over a front of nine miles, from Messines in the south to Polygon Wood in the north. While the assault was launched on a broad front, the main thrust was between the Menin Road and Polygon Wood. When the artillery barrage lifted, soldiers of the Prussian Guard moved forward on either side of the Menin Road. The British line was breached between Polygon Wood, close to where you stand, and the Menin Road. The 1st Royal Scots Fusiliers and 2nd Royal Sussex were brought forward to plug the gap before the Prussians could dig in. It was becoming very hard indeed to break the momentum of the Prussian Guard.

Continue along Oude Kortrijkstraat towards Polygon Wood. You will soon come to a bridge over the motorway. You can see Polygon Wood and Black Watch Corner on the far side (Figure 5.17).

Location 11: Black Watch Corner (Figure 5.18)

First look back in the direction of the motorway and Nonne Bosschen beyond. Then turn left to consider what happened here on 11 November. Men of the 1st Black Watch were swept from their advance trenches. They withdrew to Polygon Wood, where they stopped in improvised positions close to where you stand and forced back several attacks by the Prussian Guard. Frustrated by this stubborn resistance, the Prussians sought an alternative way forward through Nonne Bosschen, where they were confronted by the 2nd Oxford and Buckinghamshire Light Infantry and the 2nd Highland Light Infantry, who

---

2   MacDonald, L., *1914: The Days of Hope* (London: Penguin Books Ltd, 1989), p.410.

Figure 5.17 Location of the Black Watch Memorial, looking across the motorway to Black Watch Corner.

Figure 5.18 The Black Watch Memorial.

attacked with great vigour before the Germans had the opportunity to dig in and prepare their defences. Some of the Prussian Guard turned and ran, while others were taken prisoner. Very few of the Oxford and Buckinghamshires were killed and wounded, while the German casualty figure ran into several hundred, such was the impetus of the attack.[3]

Brigadier General FitzClarence, who had masterminded the 2nd Worcesters' counter-attack on 31 October, was keen to launch an attack by the 2nd Oxford and Buckinghamshires and 2nd Highland Light Infantry to recover lost ground. However, because of very poor weather conditions, the attack was put on hold for a few hours. On the night of 11/12 November, FitzClarence personally joined a forward reconnaissance party. His silhouetted figure was spotted against the trees by a German sniper, and he was shot and killed. His body was never found. He is commemorated on the Menin Gate, where his is the highest-ranking officer's name inscribed there on Panel Number 3.

The Prussian Guard had failed to break through, and no further serious attack was made. The First Battle of Ypres was over. British losses for the period 14 October–30 November total 58,155 men killed, wounded or missing. The killed and missing totalled 25,833, and while this figure included a relatively small number taken prisoner, most were men whose bodies were never found. With winter coming, and as 1914 drew to a close, men on both sides dug in and the Ypres Salient became established.

Table 5.1 German armies facing the British front line in the Ypres area

	Army Commander	Corps	Divisions
Fourth Army	Albrecht, Duke of Württemberg	III Reserve	5th Reserve, 6th Reserve and Ersatz
		XXII Reserve	43rd and 44th Reserve
		XXIII Reserve	45th and 46th Reserve
		XXVI Reserve	51st and 52nd Reserve
		XXVII	53rd and 54th Reserve
Sixth Army	Rupprecht, Crown Prince of Bavaria	II	3rd and 4th Regular
		VII	13th and 14th
		XIII	25th Reserve, 5th Bavarian Reserve and 26th
		XIX	24th and 40th
		XIV	28th and 29th

---

3   Palmer, A., *The Salient: Ypres 1914–18* (London: Constable, 2007), p.88.

Chapter 6

THE SECOND BATTLE OF YPRES: BATTLE OF GRAVENSTAFEL RIDGE, 22–23 APRIL 1915

HISTORICAL OVERVIEW

The First Battle of Ypres ended in mid-November 1914, by which time the Ypres Salient had become established. On Christmas Day 1914, two British armies were formed. The First Army, under General Sir Douglas Haig, consisted of I Corps, IV Corps and the Indian Corps, and was involved in fighting in northern France between March and September 1915. The Second Army, under General Sir Horace Smith-Dorrien, comprised II Corps, III Corps and the 27th Division, until more divisions arrived in France to form V Corps under General Sir Herbert Plumer. The Second Army was responsible for the defence of the Ypres Salient.

In 1915, the British First Army fought at Neuve Chapelle (10–12 March), Aubers Ridge (9 May), Festubert (15–27 May), Givenchy (15–16 June) and Loos (25 September–13 October) (Figure 6.1). These battles were fought at the request of General Joffre, Commander-in-Chief of French forces, who wanted British support while the French attacked the Germans further south at Vimy Ridge and Champagne. The Battle of Loos in particular had an impact on events at the Ypres Salient (Chapter 9).

Allied and German lines round Ypres had remained practically unaltered over the winter months of 1914–15, but that changed dramatically on 22 April 1915 when the German Fourth Army began the Second Battle of Ypres with a chlorine gas attack around Langemarck and broke through French positions. The French 45th (Algerian) and 87th (Territorial) Divisions held the line in the northern part of the Salient between the St Julien to Poelcappelle

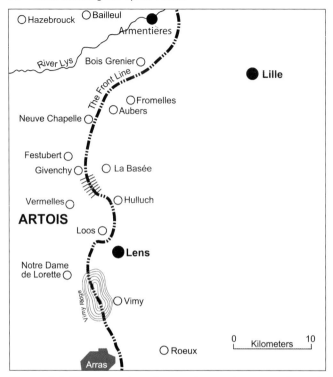

Figure 6.1 Map of northern France showing locations where the British First Army fought between March and October 1915.

Road and the Yser Canal.[1] Figures 6.2 and 6.3 show the position of the line before and after the gas attack.

At 1700 on 22 April 1915, a furious artillery bombardment was directed against Ypres, and soon afterwards greenish-yellow clouds of chlorine gas were seen near Langemarck drifting over French positions. One cloud was between Langemarck and Poelcappelle and the other between Langemarck and Boesinghe. The Second Battle of Ypres lasted until 25 May 1915, and was divided into four phases:

- Battle of Gravenstafel Ridge, 22–23 April 1915.
- Battle of St Julien, 24 April–5 May 1915.
- Battle of Frezenberg, 8–13 May 1915.
- Battle of Bellewaarde Ridge, 24–25 May 1915.

1   Christie, N.M., *For King and Empire; The Canadians in the Second Battle of Ypres* (Ottawa, Ontario: CEF Books, 1999).

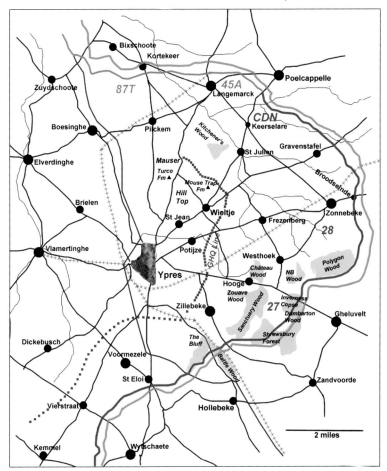

Figure 6.2 Allied line before the Second Battle of Ypres. French Colonial troops held the northern part of the line from Steenstraat to the Ypres to Poelcappelle road. The British held the Salient to the south of that road.

THE BATTLE OF GRAVENSTAFEL RIDGE, 22–23 APRIL 1915

Although called the Battle of Gravenstafel Ridge, most of the fighting took place close to the road between Ypres and Poelcappelle. From the centre of Ypres, follow the N8 (Meenseweg) to the roundabout at 'Hell Fire Corner'. Take the fifth exit, and go straight on at the next roundabout through Potijze. When you reach a T-junction at St Jean, turn right onto the N313 (Brugseweg) and past the village of Wieltje. The road joins the N38 towards Poelcappelle. Note the names of the villages, because they all played important roles in the

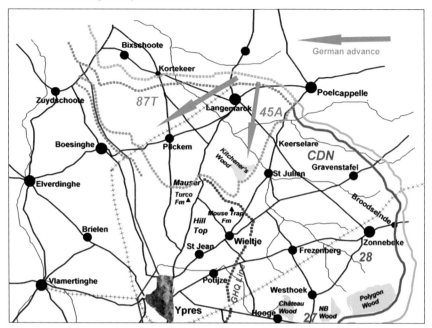

Figure 6.3 The front line after the release of the poison gas; the entire northern part of the Ypres Salient caved in. Keerselare and St Julien, which had been deep within British-held territory, became front-line positions on the Ypres to Poelcappelle road.

days after 22 April 1915. Pass through St Julien. After a mile you will reach the hamlet of Keerselare, where a Canadian Memorial called 'The Brooding Soldier' stands adjacent to a staggered crossroads with the road between Zonnebeke and Langemarck (Figure 6.4). Designed by Frederick Clemesha, the memorial commemorates soldiers of the Canadian 1st Division who fought nearby at the start of the Second Battle of Ypres.

Location 1: The Canadian Front Line on the road between Brooding Soldier and Poelcappelle

Go past the memorial and proceed to Poelcappelle, where there is a round-about with a stork statue (Chapter 16). Return in the direction of 'The Brooding Soldier' for approximately 550 yards and turn round to face Poelcappelle. You are on the approximate position of the Allied front line on 22 April.[2] Men of the Canadian 1st Division held the line here. Their position began in the field

---

2   Ibid.

Figure 6.4 The Brooding Soldier.

50 yards to your left, from where French forces held the line in the northern part of the Salient. The Canadian line extended to your right as far as the Gravenstafel to Passchendaele road (Figure 6.2).

Make your way back towards 'The Brooding Soldier', being sure to obtain a clear view of Langemarck Church steeple to your right as you proceed (Figure 6.5). If you face in the direction of the church steeple, the Allied line passed to the east (right) of the village, and was held by French Colonial soldiers of the 45th Division.

You should also look out for a windmill on top of a gentle slope to your left, which is Gravenstafel Ridge (Figure 6.6). The Canadians held a strong position here which had a commanding view of the surrounding countryside (Chapter 7).

Location 2: The Brooding Soldier

At the Canadian Memorial, face the St Julien to Poelcappelle road. This road ran through the heart of British-held territory before the German attack on 22 April; the villages of Wieltje and St Julien and the hamlet of Keerselare, where you now stand, were well behind the Canadian front line. Canadian reserves, support troops and Brigade headquarters were located in these apparently relatively secure villages you passed through to reach the Canadian front line. If you had been standing near here on 22 April at 1700, you would have seen

Figure 6.5 Facing Langemarck Church from the Poelcappelle to St Julien road close to the position of the Allied front line; the French part of the line passed to the right (east) of Langemarck.

Figure 6.6 The windmill marks the position of Gravenstafel Ridge, held by the Canadians.

Figure 6.7 Photograph taken from the approximate position of the French front line on 22 April 1915 before 5 p.m.; Poelcappelle Church spire is visible.

a green cloud of chlorine gas drifting past Langemarck Church ahead and to your right and across the fields on the far side of Keerselare from right to left, engulfing the defending Algerians of the French 45th Division. Many were asphyxiated, and those who survived fled, abandoning Langemarck and leaving the trenches of the northern part of the Salient empty.

You may wish to follow the retreat of the French Colonial soldiers on 22 April. Alternatively, you may simply want to read the next section to appreciate what happened. If you decide to proceed, go into Poelcappelle until you reach the stork roundabout. Take the exit marked Langemarck. Figure 6.7 was taken from a field 900 yards from the stork roundabout, and gives an idea of the approximate position of the French front line. Soldiers who survived the gas attack would have fled to the rear from near here. It is not recommended that you walk around farmers' fields, however.

Figure 6.8 was taken from number 57 Poelkapellestraat, on the Poelcappelle to Langemarck road close to Langemarck. The outskirts of the village are visible on the left beyond the long, low building to the right. The gas cloud would have engulfed French troops in fields to the left of the road.

In a single stroke, Langemarck was lost to the Germans and would not be recovered until 16 August 1917 during the Third Battle of Ypres (Chapter 11). The northern portion of the Ypres Salient had caved in. This could have been catastrophic, but was not, because the Germans were slow to exploit the huge

Figure 6.8 The Poelcappelle to Langemarck road; the cyclists have nearly reached the outskirts of Langemarck, which is at the end of this straight stretch of road. The chlorine gas cloud, moving right to left, would have engulfed French soldiers in the fields to the left.

gap which had suddenly appeared. Their forces around Langemarck were the 51st and 52nd Reserve Divisions from XXVI Reserve Corps. By 1730, the 52nd had reached Pilckem (Figure 6.3), but for the time being went no further. The 51st moved more slowly, because the gas cloud had not dissipated and German infantry were reluctant to advance through it.[3]

Go through Langemarck, taking the road to Boesinghe. Stop at Cement House Cemetery. Many retreating French soldiers would have crossed the Langemarck to Boesinghe road here as they escaped from the chlorine gas cloud (Figure 6.9).

The French did not stop until they reached the security of the west bank of the Yser Canal. The entire northern segment of the Ypres Salient had been abandoned. Proceed towards Boesinghe and turn left onto the Oostkaal, approximately 250 yards before you reach the Yser Canal. Stop when you can see across the canal to Boesinghe and look towards the church (Figure 6.10).

3   Neillands, R., *The Great War Generals on the Western Front 1914–1918* (London: Robinson Publishing Ltd, 1999), p.150.

Figure 6.9 Looking towards Langemarck Church from the Langemarck to Boesinghe road at Cement House Cemetery. Chlorine gas cloud would have been seen coming past the church towards the position from which the photograph was taken.

Figure 6.10 The Yser Canal at Boesinghe. The church spire is towards the left of the photograph on the west bank of the canal. French Colonial soldiers who had survived their ordeal did not stop until they reached the west bank.

The *Official History of the Great War* states:
French coloured troops without officers began drifting down the roads through the back area. Soon afterwards, French Territorial troops were seen hurriedly crossing the bridges over the canal north of Ypres. It was impossible to understand what the Africans said, but from the way they coughed and pointed to their throats, it was evident that if they were not suffering from the effects of gas they were thoroughly scared.[4]

CANADIAN IMPROVISATION, 22 APRIL 1915

Return to 'The Brooding Soldier' to understand what the Canadians did to deal with the crisis. Two Canadian medical officers, Colonel Naismith and Captain Scrimger, were riding behind divisional lines when they saw the green cloud in the distance. They detected the pungent smell of the gas carried on the wind from the front line. Naismith was a chemist and recognised this to be chlorine. They worked out a temporary solution. Urine contains uric acid, which reacts with chlorine to form dichlorourea, which crystallises, neutralising the gas. Instructions were sent to Canadian soldiers in the front line to urinate on their hankies and hold them against their noses.[5]

As indicated, the Germans moved hesitantly and did not exploit their success as vigorously as they might have done. This prevented a deeper penetration into Allied territory and gave Canadian soldiers along the Ypres to Poelcappelle road time to improvise. They were presented with the problem of defending their positions after French Colonial troops to the north had fled. They would have seen survivors running across the fields from right to left behind Keerselare as they made their way towards the safety of the Yser Canal.

Brigadier General Turner of 3 Canadian Infantry Brigade instructed Canadians of the 13th Battalion (Black Watch of Montreal), who were positioned on the left flank of the British line, to set up a refusing flank on the northern side of the Ypres to Poelcappelle road from their front line, extending past the far side of Keerselare where you now stand and St Julien to prevent German soldiers getting through. Although the Canadians managed to set up defensive positions, these were by no means complete, but they held on.

4   Edmonds, J.E., *History of the Great War Based on Official Documents by Direction of the Historical Section of the Committee of Imperial Defence. Military Operations. France and Belgium 1915* Volume I (London: Macmillan, 1927), p.177.
5   Neillands, R., *The Death of Glory: The Western Front 1915.* (London: John Murray, 2006), p.92.

Lance-Corporal F. Fisher, from Montreal, won Canada's first Victoria Cross of the Great War defending the line. His citation reads:

> On 23rd April, 1915, in the neighbourhood of St Julien, he went forward with the machine-gun, of which he was in charge, under heavy fire, and most gallantly assisted in covering the retreat of a battery, losing four men of his gun team. Later, after obtaining four more men, he went forward again to the firing line and was himself killed while bringing his machine-gun into action under very heavy fire, in order to cover the advance of supports.[6]
>
> *London Gazette*, No. 29, 202, 23 June 1915.

Sir Arthur Currie, who was in command of 2 Canadian Infantry Brigade, sent reinforcements to help shore up the new line, as did the British 28th and 27th Divisions which held the remainder of the British part of the Salient (Figure 6.3). This activity extended from the Canadian front line near Poelcappelle, past your present position and all along the road past St Julien and Wieltje.

ACTION ON NIGHT OF 22 APRIL 1915 AT KITCHENER'S WOOD

Having survived a catastrophe, perhaps it would have been wise if the Canadians had consolidated their improvised line along the Wieltje to Poelcappelle road, but instead they launched a counter-attack. The French 45th Division, which had pulled back to the Yser Canal, requested British support to regain lost ground. In the event, the French were incapable of mounting an attack and never showed up. One of the features which would come to characterise the fighting over the next few days was lack of French support to regain lost territory. The French regarded holding their new line on the west bank of the Yser Canal to be of over-riding importance, and this took priority over any counter-attack. They must have had one eye on forthcoming offensives in Artois and Champagne, where they were launching major attacks with many thousands of soldiers, and were reluctant to commit reinforcements to help resolve the crisis round Ypres. Responsibility for the counter-attack fell to Canadians of the 10th (Alberta) and 16th (Canadian Scottish) Battalions of 3 Canadian Infantry Brigade. Their aim was to attack and capture a copse of trees known as Kitchener's Wood.

To reach the approximate location of Kitchener's Wood, you must retrace your steps through St Julien towards Ypres. After leaving St Julien, look out

---

6 Fisher's body was never found. He is commemorated on the Menin Gate (Panel 24–26–28–30).

Figure 6.11 Cheddar Villa.

for Seaforth Cemetery on the right side of the road, which is adjacent to a German blockhouse called Cheddar Villa (Figure 6.11).

Turn right a few yards after the cemetery and go along a minor road for about half a mile, where you will find a small Canadian Memorial commemorating fighting at Kitchener's Wood, which is no longer present but was near the spot. Look back in the direction of St Julien.

Location 3: Canadian Memorial on Road beyond Seaforth Cemetery

On 22 April, the Germans captured Kitchener's Wood from the French. It was an ideal location from which to launch an attack on improvised Canadian defences along the road between Wieltje and Poelcappelle and cut though the British line. Figure 6.12 shows the view the Germans would have had of St Julien. The Canadians received an order to attack Kitchener's Wood, and by the time the Canadian 10th and 16th Battalions were in position, it was midnight. In pitch darkness, and not knowing the terrain, inexperienced Canadian soldiers stumbled towards Kitchener's Wood from the direction of St Julien over unfamiliar ground, against enemy forces of unknown strength and location. Despite sustaining heavy casualties (over 1,000 men killed and wounded) in fierce hand-to-hand combat, they succeeded in driving the Germans out of the wood.

Figure 6.12 View from the approximate location of Kitchener's Wood, looking towards St Julien. Canadian soldiers attacked across the field towards your position on the night of 22/23 April 1915 as they tried to recapture lost ground.

The 2nd Canadian (Eastern Ontario) and 3rd (Toronto) Battalions arrived as reinforcements in the early hours of 23 April. The 2nd Battalion was ordered to attack Kitchener's Wood as quickly as possible, but because of unfamiliarity with the terrain, the attack was delayed until daylight, when once again very heavy casualties were sustained. With the arrival of daylight, the survivors of the 10th and 16th Battalions could not hold on in the wood and were forced to withdraw to a position approximately 250 yards from where you now stand in the direction of St Julien.

CANADIAN ATTACK ON MAUSER RIDGE, 23 APRIL 1915

Leave your position, retrace your steps and continue in the direction of Ypres. There is a minor road on your right with a signpost to Buff's Cemetery. Take this road. You will soon pass a large farm on your right which was called Mouse Trap Farm in 1915. More will be said of it later. After 500 yards you will pass Buff's Road Cemetery. There is a turning to the right a short distance afterwards. Take this turning, which leads you to Track X Cemetery. Face the entrance of the cemetery and then look to your left, where you will see higher ground which was called Mauser Ridge (Figure 6.13).

Location 4: Track X Cemetery

Figure 6.13 The ridge ahead running in a west-to-east direction is Mauser Ridge, which the Germans captured from the French on 22 April 1915.

The night of 22/23 April saw intense activity to close the gap in the line between the Canadian left and the Yser Canal, which is one and a half miles to your left as you face Mauser Ridge. Even then, the line was incomplete and tenuous. During the night, the Germans launched unsuccessful attacks against positions held by the British 27th and 28th Divisions on other parts of the Salient (Figure 6.3). Ypres was bombarded heavily, as was the road between Ypres and Boesinghe along the west bank of the Yser Canal. In the early hours of 23 April, General Smith-Dorrien, commander of the British Second Army, asked for French help to launch a counter-attack to recapture Mauser Ridge, an elevated position running east to west where German soldiers were digging in and establishing advantageous positions. Kitchener's Wood was in close proximity to the eastern end of Mauser Ridge. The French announced that their 45th Division would be ready to launch a counter-attack at 0500 on 23 April.

Once again, Canadians were given the task of helping the French. On this occasion, the 1st (Western Ontario) and 4th (Central Ontario) Battalions of Brigadier General Mercer's 1 Canadian Infantry Brigade were given the responsibility. The starting time for the attack at 0500 came and went with no sign of the French. The Canadians elected to attack Mauser Ridge without

Figure 6.14 Geddes Detachment assembled in Wieltje, visible on the skyline, before passing by on its way to Mauser Ridge to the north of your position. Mouse Trap Farm is on the left.

them. They advanced over the open in broad daylight, exposed to enemy fire from key machine-gun positions and had no chance of success. As you stand looking towards Mauser Ridge, the Canadians would have come past your position and onwards towards the ridge.

Now turn round and look in the direction of Wieltje (Figure 6.14). Early in the morning of 23 April, four battalions comprising the 2nd Buffs, the 3rd Middlesex, the 5th King's Own and the 1st Yorks and Lancs formed the Geddes Detachment, under Lieutenant Colonel A.D. Geddes, which was tasked with helping the Canadian 1st and 4th Battalions. The men congregated at Wieltje on the far side of where the main road runs today and advanced to attack Mauser Ridge. As you face towards Wieltje, Geddes' force would have been coming towards you.

Very heavy casualties were sustained. British and Canadian losses totalled more than 2,000 officers and men. The commanding officers of the 4th Canadian Battalion, the 3rd Middlesex and the 1st Yorks and Lancs were killed in the attack on Mauser Ridge. On the afternoon of 23 April, another attack was made on the ridge, this time by British 13 Brigade, with the same result. Figure 6.15 shows British positions on the evening of 23 April.

By the conclusion of what became officially known as the Battle of Gravenstafel Ridge, the Allied left flank had been bent back as far as the Yser

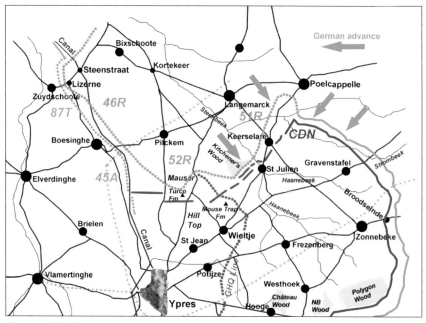

Figure 6.15 Showing British positions on the evening of 23 April 1915. The Germans are massing for an attack the following day.

Canal, and the line was thinly held. Heavy casualties had been sustained in failed attacks against Kitchener's Wood and Mauser Ridge. Instead of simply holding on and reinforcing their positions, costly counter-attacks had been made, even in broad daylight, with heavy loss of life. The *Official History of the Great War* states that if preparations had been made for a methodical advance with artillery support, men could have crept forward under cover of darkness and dug in closer to German positions without sustaining such heavy casualties in useless attacks. This seems a rather fanciful suggestion, since British artillery support was woefully inadequate due to a severe shortage of guns and shells.

One further attack was made in this vicinity on 25 April after the Battle of Gravenstafel had officially ended. It was launched against well-established machine-gun positions on Mauser Ridge by a force commanded by Brigadier General Hull, who was given 10 Brigade of the 4th Division. This attack was a disaster for several reasons. Hull and his staff had just arrived in the Salient and were unfamiliar with the ground. He had no opportunity to brief his commanders about any plan of attack and there was poor artillery support. The attack should have gone in at 0330, but was delayed for two hours until 0530. Unfortunately, nobody bothered to tell the artillery, which fired all its ammunition before the attack began![7] Casualties amounted to 73 officers and 2,236 men for absolutely no gain.[8] The attack on 25 April was the same day British and ANZAC forces landed on the Gallipoli Peninsula.

POSTSCRIPT: THE GAS ATTACK, 22 APRIL 1915

The gas attack had taken the Allies by complete surprise, although it should not have done. There was mounting evidence that something like this was going to happen. The *Official History of the Great War* states:

> A reliable agent of the Detachement of the French Army in Belgium reports that an attack on the Ypres Salient has been arranged for the night of 15th/16th April. A prisoner of the 24th Regiment, XXVI Corps, taken on 14th April near Langemarck, reports that an attack has been prepared for noon on the 15th.[9] The Germans intend making use of tubes with asphyxiating gas, placed in batteries of 20 tubes for every 40 metres along the front of XXVI Corps, then, as far as was known, in the line on either side of Langemarck, wholly opposite the French. The prisoner had in his possession a kind of gauze or cotton waste which would be dipped in some solution to counteract the effect of this gas.[10]

It was decided, however, that the captured soldier had known and volunteered too much. He must have been sent over with the intention to deceive. General Plumer, in command of British forces to the right of the French, passed the information to his divisional commanders "for what it was worth". It was duly ignored.

Chlorine gas and Fritz Haber

Chlorine gas in high concentration causes pulmonary oedema and kills by asphyxiation. German chemist Fritz Haber (1868–1934) (Figure 6.16), who would be awarded the Nobel Prize for Chemistry in 1918 for discovering a method to synthesise ammonia from nitrogen and hydrogen (Haber Process), successfully manufactured chlorine gas on an industrial scale during the war. He was present on 22 April 1915 behind the German front line to oversee its

---

7   Neillands, R., *The Death of Glory: The Western Front 1915* (London: John Murray, 2006), p.108.

8   Ibid.

9   Originally planned for 15 April, the attack was postponed because the direction of the prevailing wind was unfavourable.

10 Edmonds, J.E., *History of the Great War Based on Official Documents by Direction of the Historical Section of the Committee of Imperial Defence. Military Operations. France and Belgium 1915* Volume I(London: Macmillan, 1927), p.163.

Figure 6.16 Fritz Haber (Wikimedia Commons)

release on unsuspecting French Colonial soldiers. The use of the gas was so successful that he was presented to the Kaiser upon his return to Germany and was given a Prussian officer service revolver. Haber's wife, Clara, suffered from severe depression, aggravated by his work with poison gas, which she strongly opposed. Following an argument with her husband, she committed suicide on 2 May 1915 by shooting herself in her chest with his revolver. Haber left Germany within days of her death to supervise release of chlorine against the Russians on the Eastern Front.

Haber's work after the war included research on pesticides, from which Zyclon B was developed. This was used by the Nazis to gas Jews during Hitler's Final Solution. Haber went into exile in 1933, staying at various times in Paris, Spain, England and Switzerland before his death in 1934. He had to leave because he was born a Jew. It is a bitter irony that the scientist 'credited' with being the inventor of poison gas was indirectly responsible for the deaths of millions of fellow Jews in the Second World War. Several members of Haber's own family died in Nazi concentration camps, gassed using Zyclon B, developed in the laboratory of one of the most controversial scientists of the twentieth century.

Chapter 7

THE SECOND BATTLE OF YPRES:
BATTLE OF ST JULIEN, 24 APRIL–5 MAY 1915

BATTLE OF ST JULIEN, 24 APRIL–5 MAY 1915

The Battle of St Julien was the second of four phases of the Second Battle of Ypres. It began on 24 April and lasted until 5 May 1915. If you are continuing from Chapter 6, which deals with the Battle of Gravenstafel Ridge, then leave Track X Cemetery and retrace your steps on the minor road, passing Buff's Road Cemetery on the way. Look out for a large farm on your left, just before you rejoin the main road. This is where Mouse Trap Farm was in 1915, an important Canadian position during the Battle of St Julien. Further reference will be made to it throughout this chapter. Mouse Trap Farm also played an important role in the Battle of Frezenberg between 8–13 May 1915 (Chapter 8) and the Battle of Bellewaarde on 24–25 May 1915 (Chapter 9).

If you are studying this chapter in isolation, then make your way from Ypres to Mouse Trap Farm. Proceed from Ypres to 'Hell Fire Corner' roundabout and take the exit to Potijze and St Jean (N345). Go straight across the next roundabout, then turn right onto the Brugseweg (N313) at the next road junction. You will reach a junction with the N38, where you need to take the left exit lane to go across to a minor road nearly opposite called the Hogeziekenweg. After a short distance you will see Mouse Trap Farm on your right.

Location 1: Mouse Trap Farm

Mouse Trap Farm (Figure 7.1) was the headquarters of 3 Canadian Infantry Brigade. After the gas attack at 1700 on 22 April, it was very close to the new front line (Figure 6.15). The Germans were a short distance beyond the farm as you look towards it. Reference has been made in Chapter 6 to Captain Scrimger, one of the two medical officers who devised a way to mitigate the effects of chlorine gas released by the Germans near Langemarck. Scrimger was subsequently responsible for looking after Canadian wounded at Mouse Trap Farm, which had been converted into a makeshift dressing station. Given its close proximity

Figure 7.1 Mouse Trap Farm.

to the new Canadian front line, it was subjected to heavy shellfire, which became intense on 25 April. Scrimger displayed great bravery as he looked after the wounded and was awarded a Victoria Cross. His citation reads:

> On the afternoon of 25th April 1915 in the neighbourhood of Ypres, when in charge of an advanced dressing station in some farm buildings, which were being heavily shelled by the enemy, he directed under heavy fire the removal of the wounded, and he himself carried a severely wounded officer out of a stable in search of a place of greater safety. When he was unable alone to carry this officer further, he remained with him under fire till help could be obtained. During the very heavy fighting between 22nd and 25th April, Captain Scrimger displayed continuously day and night the greatest devotion to his duty among the wounded at the front.
>
> *London Gazette*, No. 29, 202, 23 June 1915

Leave Mouse Trap Farm and make your way to the Canadian front line near Poelcappelle, which came under attack on 24 April, marking the beginning of the Battle of St Julien. As you go, the improvised Canadian front line was a short distance to your left (Figure 6.15). To reach the front line near Poelcappelle, you should go to the roundabout in Poelcappelle and retrace your steps by approximately 600 yards.

Location 2: Canadian Front Line, 24 April 1915

Face towards Poelcappelle village and turn to your left. Following the German attack on 22 April, the Canadian front line where you stand on the St Julien to Poelcappelle road cut back almost parallel to the road along which you have just come from Mouse Trap Farm, passing through the fields very close to Keerselare and St Julien. Now turn to your right. The Canadian front line extended across the road fields in front of you in a south-easterly direction for a distance of approximately1.9 miles, where it intersected with the Gravenstafel to Passchendaele road. For reference, you will see the windmill shown in Figure 7.2. It is on Gravenstafel Ridge to the south of your position, and was behind the Canadian front line.

Windmill on
Gravenstafel Ridge

Figure 7.2 The Canadian front line ran through the fields ahead. It passed to the left of the windmill on Gravenstafel Ridge in the centre of the photograph and went towards the Gravenstafel to Passchendaele road approximately 1.9 miles away.

GERMANS LAUNCH ATTACK USING GAS AGAINST CANADIANS, 24 APRIL 1915

The front line where you stand was held by men of the Canadian 13th Battalion. Adjacent to them, in order and away from you, were the 15th, 8th and 5th Battalions, the latter occupying the right of the Canadian line on the Gravenstafel to Passchendaele road, which you will visit in due course. At

0400 on 24 April, the Germans released chlorine gas opposite the Canadian front line near the St Julien to Poelcappelle road, and followed it with an infantry attack. The 13th Canadian Battalion at the apex of the line, where you stand, and which had been deployed on 22 April to form a refusing flank along the Poelcappelle-St Julien road, held firm. The adjacent 15th Canadian Battalion (48th Highlanders of Toronto) across the fields in front of you (Figure 7.2) gave way. You can visualise the gas cloud crossing these fields from left to right, and men of the 15th Battalion pulling back.

A contributory factor to their withdrawal was that the Ross rifles, with which they had been equipped, jammed and were useless. Ross rifles were inferior to the Short Magazine Lee Enfield (SMLE) rifle, and would soon be replaced by them. The 8th Canadian Battalion beyond the 15th Battalion held firm, but there was now a sizeable gap in the Canadian front line which the Germans exploited. Some Germans advanced parallel to the road you are on towards St Julien, to attack Canadians defending the village from the rear, while others moved towards the windmill on Gravenstafel Ridge.

Make your way to the Canadian Memorial at Vancouver Corner, and turn left in the direction of Zonnebeke 2.5 miles away. After 200 yards, take the first turning to the left, which goes onto Gravenstafel Ridge. You pass the afore-mentioned windmill on the left as you go (Figure 7.3). The windmill which stood here in 1915 was the command position of the 15th Canadian Battalion.

Figure 7.3 The gentle incline up Gravenstafel Ridge. The windmill here in 1915 was the command position of the 15th Canadian Battalion.

Location 3: Summit of Gravenstafel Ridge near Locality C (Canadian Strongpoint)

Keep going past the windmill. The incline is very gentle as the road takes you in a west to east direction across the Gravenstafel Ridge. The distance from one end of the ridge to the other is approximately 1.8 miles. Stop near the top. There was a Canadian strongpoint nearby called Locality C, which held a commanding view, just as you have now. If you look to the north, you can see Poelcappelle village with its recognisable church (Figure 7.4). Poelcappelle was behind the German front line.

Turn slowly to your left and you will see Langemarck Church steeple to the north-west (Figure 7.5). Langemarck was behind the Allied front line until 22 April, when it fell into German hands. The straight line of trees in the middle distance marks the position of the road between Poelcappelle and St Julien, along which men of the 13th Battalion formed the refusing flank on 22 April (Chapter 6). When the Germans attacked Canadian positions on 24 April, the chlorine gas cloud would have moved across the fields in the foreground of Figure 7.5 from right to left. The 13th Battalion held firm, but men of the 15th Battalion withdrew, leaving a large gap. Some Germans would have attacked towards your position here on Gravenstafel Ridge. Others would have advanced parallel to the Poelcappelle to St Julien road, getting behind Canadian soldiers who were defending the refusing flank as well as those in St

Figure 7.4 Taken from close to the Canadian position at Locality C on the summit of Gravenstafel Ridge looking north; Poelcappelle church steeple is visible to the right of the trees in the middle. Poelcappelle was behind the German front line.

Figure 7.5 Langemarck church; the Poelcappelle to St Julien road is marked by the line of trees in the middle distance.

Figure 7.6 The view towards St Julien from Gravenstafel Ridge. Some Germans who broke through the Canadian line held by the 15th Battalion close to the Ypres to Poelcappelle road infiltrated behind the Canadian positions in St Julien, moving from right to left as you look towards the village.

Julien less than a mile-and-a-half away. Keep turning round to your left and you will see St Julien to the west (Figure 7.6).

You may now consider events here as they unfolded. Look towards Poelcappelle Church once more. Many Germans advanced towards Canadian positions up here on the Gravenstafel Ridge, where they encountered men of the 7th Canadian Battalion, who were in support defending the ridge. These Canadians would have been in trenches in front of you, facing in the general direction of Poelcappelle and Langemarck. Chlorine gas would have been drifting across the ridge, but the men of the 7th Battalion held firm, taking a heavy toll of Germans advancing towards their position, as exemplified by the following account of Captain E.D. Bellew of the 7th Battalion, who was awarded a Victoria Cross near to where you stand, and whose citation reads:

> For most conspicuous bravery and devotion to duty near Keerselare on 24th April, 1915, during the German attack on the Ypres salient. Capt. (then Lieut.) Bellew, as Battalion Machine Gun Officer, had two guns in action on the high ground overlooking Keerselare. The enemy's attack broke in full force on the morning of the 24th against the front and right flank of the Battalion – the latter being exposed owing to a gap in the line. The right Company was soon put out of action, but the advance was temporarily stayed by Capt. Bellew, who had sited his guns on the left of the right Company. Reinforcements were sent forward but they in turn were surrounded and destroyed. With the enemy in strength less than 100 yards from him, with no further assistance in sight, and with his rear threatened, Capt. Bellew and Serjt. Peerless, each operating a gun, decided to stay where they were and fight it out. Serjt. Peerless was killed and Capt. Bellew was wounded and fell. Nevertheless, he got up and maintained his fire till ammunition failed and the enemy rushed the position. Capt. Bellew then seized a rifle, smashed his machine gun and fighting to the last, was taken prisoner.
>
> *London Gazette*, No. 31, 340, 15 May 1919

Bellew remained a prisoner of war until the end of the conflict, returning to British Columbia in Canada and dying aged 78 in 1961.

Despite a vigorous defence, the Germans captured Locality C, close to where you stand, late in the day of 24 April, but were unable to take Boetleer's Farm. This was the headquarters of Lieutenant Colonel Lipsett of the 8th Battalion, which you will visit as you continue your journey over the ridge. Continue for a few hundred yards. Stop when you see a farm on a corner of the road as you descend from the ridge. This was the approximate position of Boetleer's Farm (Figure 7.7).

Figure 7.7 The cyclist is approaching the position of Boetleer's Farm on Gravenstafel Ridge, which was the headquarters of Lieutenant Colonel Lipsett of 8th Battalion. Passchendaele church is visible to the left (north-east).

Location 4: Boetleer's Farm

When cycling across Gravenstafel Ridge on a tranquil spring day, it is hard to imagine the events which took place in the fields round about you. Company Sergeant Major Frederick Hall of the 8th Battalion won a Victoria Cross near here. His citation reads:

> On 24th April, 1915, in the neighbourhood of Ypres, when a wounded man who was lying some 15 yards from the trench called for help, Company Sergeant-Major Hall endeavoured to reach him in the face of a very heavy enfilade fire which was being poured in by the enemy. The first attempt failed, and a Non-commissioned Officer and private soldier who were attempting to give assistance were both wounded. Company Sergeant-Major Hall then made a second most gallant attempt, and was in the act of lifting up the wounded man to bring him in when he fell mortally wounded in the head.
>
> *London Gazette*, No. 29, 202, 23 June 1915

Hall's body was never found. He is commemorated on the Menin Gate (Panel 24–26–28–30). The 8th Canadian Battalion fought around Boetleer

Farm for the entire day on 24 April, alongside the 5th Canadian Battalion on the Canadian right flank, defending the road leading from Gravenstafel to Passchendaele. They held out against German attacks, while to their left and behind them much of Gravenstafel Ridge was taken by the Germans.

Continue until you leave Gravenstafel Ridge and reach a New Zealand Memorial (Chapter 15). Turn left and continue for approximately 50 yards. The right flank of the Canadian 5th Battalion held the front line here.[1]

Location 5: Canadian Front Line on Gravelstafel Road

Figure 7.8 A photograph taken from the approximate position of the Canadian front line, looking back in the direction of Gravenstafel Ridge. The New Zealand Memorial is just round the bend in the road.

Turn around and face in the direction of the New Zealand Memorial. As you stand on the approximate position of the Canadian front line on 24 April, you can sense how exposed and isolated this position was (Figure 7.8). Locality C, which you have just visited, was taken by the Germans on 24 April, and they now occupied most of Gravenstafel Ridge, making the position here very vulnerable. Germans had infiltrated behind the Canadian line at St Julien,

---

1   Christie, N.M., *For King and Empire; The Canadians in the Second Battle of Ypres* (Ottawa, Ontario: CEF Books, 1999), p.44.

Figure 7.9 Kansas Cross at the junction of sGravenstafelstraat with Zonnebekestraat. Zonnebeke is approximately 1.2 miles to the left and Langemarck 2.5 miles to the right. The road straight ahead leads to Wieltje.

making matters even more precarious. Canadians here came under a direct frontal attack on 25 April, forcing them to withdraw to positions near to where the New Zealand Memorial stands today (Figure 7.11).

It has already been stated that some of the Germans who broke through the Canadian line attacked St Julien from the rear. You will now go to a position which gives you an impression of what happened around St Julien. Leave the Canadian front line on the Gravenstafel to Passchendaele road and turn around. Go along the sGravenstafelstraat until you reach the position of Kansas Cross at the crossroads with the Zonnebekestraat (Figure 7.9).

Go straight across and continue for approximately a third of a mile towards Wieltje. Stop when you reach a road to the right with a stream adjacent to it. Look to your right. St Julien is a short distance straight ahead of you (Figure 7.10).

Location 5: Looking towards St Julien from Tributary of Steenbeek

Germans who broke through Canadian defences on 24 April and infiltrated behind Canadian positions in St Julien would have been visible from your present position moving from right to left close to the village. By 1530 on 24 April, 1 Canadian Infantry Brigade around St Julien had retired and 3 Brigade

Figure 7.10 St Julien, taken from a position east of the village. The tributary of Steenbeek is visible in the foreground. After capturing St Julien, the Germans would have attacked across these fields towards British positions.

was in the process of doing so. Only 2 Brigade was left defending the village, and its commander, Brigadier General Sir Arthur Currie, urgently needed reinforcements if St Julien was to be held. There is a story of Currie leaving his headquarters and making for the rear to find reinforcements and bring them forward, an action much frowned upon by his superiors, since Currie's place was perceived to be in his headquarters, where he was contactable. Perhaps a previous urgent request for reinforcements had gone unheeded, or it had never been received. Despite his appeals in person, Brigadier General Bush, in command of the reserves of 150 Brigade, refused to send reinforcements without the direct order of his superior, Major General Snow, commanding officer of the 27th Division. Undeterred, Currie then went off to find Snow, and was told by Snow in no uncertain terms that he should never have left his headquarters and that had it been in his power, he would have had Currie shot for abandoning his position. Currie's efforts were in vain and St Julien fell to the Germans on 24 April. British units forming a new defensive line would have been digging in round about you, facing Germans coming from the direction of St Julien (Figure 7.11).

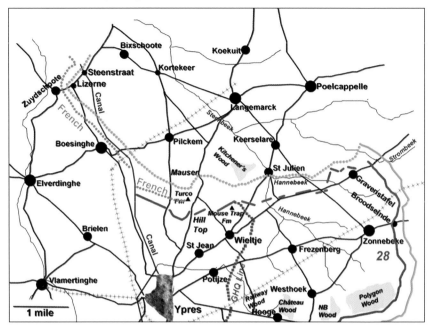

Figure 7.11 The British line on 25 April 1915, after St Julien had fallen to the Germans.

CRITICAL TIME IN BRITISH HIGH COMMAND, 27 APRIL 1915

Despite efforts made by British and Canadian soldiers to at times regain lost ground and at other times to hold what territory they had, the French helped very little, even although it was they who had lost the northern part of the Ypres Salient in the first place. Lack of French cooperation was a contributory factor to the downfall of General Smith-Dorrien, who was an infantryman, unlike Field Marshal Sir John French, who was a cavalryman through and through. Smith-Dorrien had once had the audacity to suggest to his superior that cavalry would be of more use if they functioned as mounted infantry, an observation which earned him the everlasting hatred of Sir John French. As far as the Field Marshal was concerned, Smith-Dorrien had to "quieten down" the Salient to allow General Sir Douglas Haig's First Army to make an attack on Auber's Ridge in northern France without having the distraction of a crisis in the Ypres Salient at the same time.

On 27 April, Smith-Dorrien wrote a letter to Lieutenant General Sir William Robertson, the BEF Chief of Staff, expressing the opinion that unless the French made a significant contribution to help recapture the ground lost on 22 April, a partial withdrawal from the Ypres Salient was inevitable. He

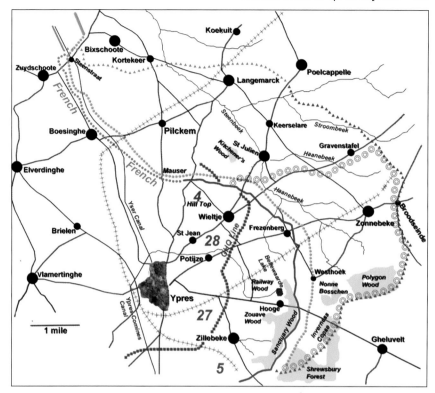

Figure 7.12 Map showing the line to which the British withdrew between 1–3 May 1915.

suggested the British Second Army should pull back and occupy the GHQ Line (Figure 7.11), a defensive position closer to Ypres made previously by French forces. The GHQ Line was well constructed, with many dugouts and strongpoints and was a good fallback position. It passed just east of Wieltje, not far from where you stand. Smith-Dorrien suggested curving an extension going through the high ground on the Bellewaarde Ridge, in the vicinity of Hooge, before swinging round through Sanctuary Wood, Hill 62 and Hill 60.[2]

Later the same day, Sir John French contacted Smith-Dorrien by telephone, telling him that matters were not as bleak as he seemed to think and that he was being defeatist. A letter soon followed, not from Field Marshal French, but from a staff officer, stripping Smith-Dorrien of his command and instructing

2 Neillands, R., *The Death of Glory* (London: John Murray, 2006), p.113.

him to hand over all necessary staff to General Plumer, commander of V Corps, who would assume command of the Second Army and communicate directly with Sir John French's headquarters to receive his instructions.

Later the same day, French soldiers launched a half-hearted attack, which failed like all others before it. Sir John French immediately told Plumer to make preparations to withdraw to a position east of Ypres, linking with the line held north and south of the city. In other words, he told him to do exactly what the sacked Smith-Dorrien had suggested earlier that same day. When two further French attacks failed, one on 29 April and the other on 30 April, Sir John French issued the instruction to withdraw from the rim of the Ypres Salient to the newly prepared positions. The withdrawal took place between 1–3 May.

The new line ran from close to Mouse Trap Farm, to the east of Wieltje, through Frezenberg and round the higher ground of Bellewaarde Ridge behind Hooge and Bellewaarde Lake, before curving round to cross the Menin Road near Clapham Junction and joining up with the line at Hill 62 and Hill 60 (Figure 7.12). In places, the withdrawal went unnoticed and German artillery bombarded empty trenches for a while. The scene was now set for the third phase of the Second Battle of Ypres, the Battle of Frezenberg Ridge.

Chapter 8

THE SECOND BATTLE OF YPRES: BATTLE OF FREZENBERG RIDGE, 8–13 MAY 1915

As a result of German successes at the Battles of Gravenstafel Ridge (Chapter 6) and St Julien (Chapter 7), the British were forced to withdraw from the southern perimeter of the Ypres Salient between 1–3 May 1915. The high ground of Broodseinde Ridge to the east of Zonnebeke, and Zonnebeke itself, were evacuated, as was Polygon Wood, while the British around the Menin Road withdrew towards Sanctuary Wood. The new line ran from near Mouse Trap Farm in the north, through Frezenberg and Bellewaarde Ridge in the centre, before crossing the Menin Road near Sanctuary Wood to Hill 62 and Hill 60 in the south (Figure 7.12).

The Germans now held Broodseinde Ridge, with excellent views over the new improvised British trenches which lay beneath them. The Ypres Salient was defended from north to south by the 4th, 28th and 27th Divisions (Figure 7.12). The Germans spent four days moving heavy artillery forward to positions on Broodseinde Ridge, whilst Duke Albrecht von Wurttemberg massed three corps of the German Fourth Army to attack. His plan was to break through British lines in the centre and capture Ypres. Newly dug British trenches were narrow, only 3ft deep, and lacked sandbags and barbed wire. There was a shortage of artillery and shells, and the British were constantly outgunned by the Germans.[1] The scene was set for the Battle of Frezenberg Ridge, fought between 8–13 May.

---

1 Edmonds, J.E., *History of the Great War Based on Official Documents by Direction of the Historical Section of the Committee of Imperial Defence. Military Operations. France and Belgium 1915* Volume I (London: Macmillan, 1927), p.312.

BATTLE OF FREZENBERG RIDGE, 8–13 MAY 1915

You may now visit a location where you can see Frezenberg Ridge and understand the battle. From the centre of Ypres, go to 'Hell Fire Corner' and take the Menin Road (Meenseweg or N8) towards Hooge. After approximately half a mile, turn left towards the signposted Royal Engineers Grave. You will reach a wood straight ahead called Railway Wood. Turn right onto the Oude Kortijkstraat, which curves round Railway Wood adjacent to the Royal Engineers Grave. You will soon pass a farm on your right called Bellewaarde Farm. Take the next turning to your left (Oude Bellewaardestraat) and stop after 150 yards. If you look ahead you will see Zonnebeke Church steeple and two roads from Zonnebeke to Ypres crossing the motorway. A very tall communications mast stands near the first (Figure 8.1).

Location 1: Viewpoint from Oude Bellewardestraat

The N37 (Briekestraat) is the closer (Figure 8.1). It goes to the roundabout at 'Hell Fire Corner'. The more distant N322 (Zonnebekeseweg) goes to Potijze. Both roads cross the motorway at the northern end of Frezenberg Ridge. You

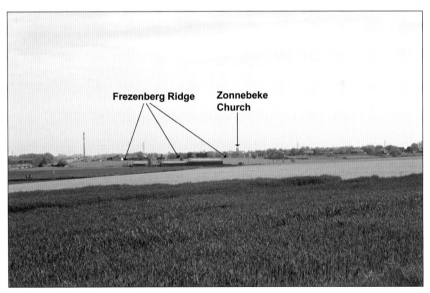

Figure 8.1 The row of houses amongst the trees ahead marks the position of the Frezenberg Ridge. Zonnebeke Church is beyond them in the centre of the photograph. The road from Zonnebeke to Ypres visible on the left of the photograph is the N37. A communications mast is a useful guide to the position of this road just after it has crossed the motorway which cuts through the northern part of Frezenberg Ridge.

Figure 8.2 Houses on Frezenberg Ridge; Zonnebeke Church is beyond. Men of the British 28th Division were on the far side (forward slope) of the ridge in full view of Germans in Zonnebeke. After the German onslaught on 8 May, their front line moved to the near side of the slope.

are referred to Figure 14.2, which is a relief map of the Ypres Salient. It shows Frezenberg Ridge running north to south where it becomes continuous with Westhoek Ridge. Look from the telecommunication mast to the right, where you can see houses on Frezenberg Ridge (Figure 8.2). The ridges played an important role in the forthcoming battle. Men of the 28th Division were in an exposed position on the far side of Frezenberg Ridge before the battle began, while men of the 27th Division were relatively sheltered behind the near side of the Westhoek Ridge.

Look back towards the telecommunications mast. You should be able to make out the village of Frezenberg beyond and to the left of the N37 where it crosses the motorway (Figure 8.3). Unfortunately, the motorway has completely distorted the topography of the battlefield here by transecting the ridge.

Look from the mast further to the left, to the N322 (Zonnebekeseweg) crossing the motorway (Figure 8.4). If you look beyond the N322 it is possible on a clear day to see the church spire of Poelcappelle in the distance.

As already noted, the British front line in the centre was on the gentle forward slope of the Frezenberg Ridge, in full view of German artillery along Broodseinde Ridge to the east of Zonnebeke. It would have been safer to

Figure 8.3 Taken from the same position as Figure 8.1, using a zoom lens and thus foreshortened, the communications mast is clearly visible. Houses in Frezenberg village can be seen beyond and to the left of the bridge over the motorway.

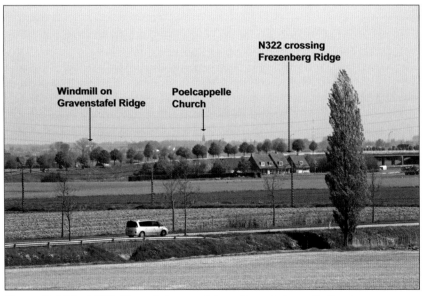

Figure 8.4 The N322 (Zonnebekeseweg) from Zonnebeke to Potijze; it too crosses the motorway and the Frezenberg Ridge. The church spire at Poelcappelle can be seen in the distance near the centre of the photograph.

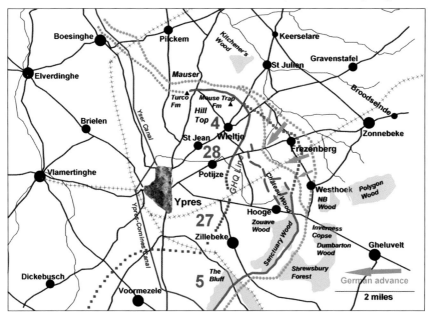

Figure 8.5 Map showing disruption of the centre of British line. There was a two-mile gap between the intact line of the 2nd Northumberland Fusiliers of the 28th Division in the north and the PPCLI of the 27th Division in the south (see text).

position the front line on the reverse slope of the ridge, where some protection would have been provided against incoming shellfire, but that would have meant abandoning more ground than was considered desirable. At 0530 on 8 May, men of the 28th Division in and around Frezenberg came under heavy German artillery fire. Between 0710 and 0910, the bombardment intensified, and soon the British trenches were destroyed. German infantry attacked at 0830. The 3rd Monmouthshire and 2nd King's Own of the 28th Division bore the brunt of the attack.

It was impossible to send reinforcements down the exposed forward slope of the Frezenberg Ridge because of the intense bombardment. At 1000, after three German attacks, these forward slopes were abandoned and makeshift new positions taken up on the reverse slope approximately 400 yards to the rear (Figure 8.2). This action would have been visible from your vantage point. The 2nd East Yorkshire Battalion was in reserve at Potijze, and was ordered forward to reinforce positions on the Frezenberg Ridge.[2] Germans who had occupied abandoned British positions continued to advance and soon

2 Ibid., pp.314–15.

infiltrated sections of the new British line. Figure 8.5 shows the disruption in the central two miles of the British line caused by the German attack.

This two-mile gap centred on Frezenberg is what you are looking at from your vantage point. To the north, the 2nd Northumberland Fusiliers on the left flank of the 28th Division held firm, while to the south, the Princess Patricia's Canadian Light Infantry (PPCLI) on the left flank of the 27th Division were steadfast in the defence of their line. Here is a summary of events:

- The 28th Division held the line as far as Mouse Trap Farm, which you have visited in Chapter 7 and is shown in Figure 8.5.
- The 1st Suffolk, 2nd Cheshire, 1st Monmouthshire and 2nd Northumberland Fusilier Battalions of the 28th Division suffered appalling casualties as the Germans smashed through the centre and began to roll up their line.
- The 1st Suffolks lost 12 officers and 432 other ranks, and only one officer and 29 men answered roll call next day.
- The 2nd Cheshire Battalion was overwhelmed at 1300 on 8 May, with nearly all the battalion killed, wounded or taken prisoner.
- The 1st Monmouthshire Battalion was almost annihilated.
- Only the 2nd Northumberland Fusiliers held on grimly near Mouse Trap Farm, and by doing so prevented matters from becoming considerably worse than they were already.
- A British counter-attack was launched in an attempt to recapture lost trenches. The 3rd Middlesex and 1st York and Lancaster were directed to attack. The 9th East Surreys soon joined in, but these reinforcements were unable to engage the Germans to drive them back, such was German artillery supremacy.

As you look across the fields towards Frezenberg Ridge, you can imagine the gap in the line, with clusters of defending British soldiers fighting for their lives with Germans who had infiltrated their lines. At least there was a fall-back position in case things became even worse, and this was the GHQ line, a well-designed defensive position closer to Ypres (Figure 8.5). It had been constructed previously by the French and consisted of a trench with a series of connected dugouts and strongpoints 500 yards apart, each designed for a garrison of around 30 men, with good fields of fire and a strong barbed-wire hedge 2m wide on its eastern side facing the Germans. It ran for nearly two miles from Zillebeke towards Mauser Ridge.[3]

You will now visit the place where men of the PPCLI, on the left flank of the 27th Division, defended their front line on 8 May. Return to the Oude Kortrijkstraat. Turn left and keep going until you reach a PPCLI Memorial,

---

3   Neillands, R., *The Death of Glory: The Western Front 1915* (London: John Murray, 2006), p.87.

which stands at a junction of two roads, the Princess Patriciastraat and the Grote Molenstraat (Figure 8.6).

Location 2: PPCLI Memorial

Figure 8.6 Memorial to Princess Patricia's Canadian Light Infantry. The front line of the PPCLI passed close to here. The wooded area immediately behind the cyclist is Lake Wood, surrounding Bellewaarde Lake and continuous with Hooge Château Wood, while Bellewaarde Farm is just visible in front of the trees to the right.

The PPCLI Memorial is close to where men of the PPCLI stood and fought on 8 May at the Battle of Frezenberg. They were defending Bellewaarde Ridge behind them, the last area of elevated ground in British possession before reaching the flat basin around Ypres. Since the German attack on 22 April, the British had lost all other advantageous ground. The PPCLI were facing towards the Germans coming from the direction of Westhoek on Westhoek Ridge. If you look straight along the line of the Princess Patriciastraat (Figure 8.7), you will see the Westhoek Ridge and the village of Westhoek. You will be able to follow the Westhoek Ridge round to the left as it becomes continuous with the Frezenberg Ridge and follow it as far as the communications mast where the motorway transects the ridge.

Now look along the Grote Molenstraat; you will see Château Wood ahead to the right and Glencorse Wood to the left (Figure 8.8). The PPCLI held the

Figure 8.7 Looking towards Westhoek Ridge from close to the PPCLI Memorial. German soldiers would have attacked the PPCLI from this direction on 8 May.

front line across the field in the foreground as far as Château Wood, before the 4th King's Royal Rifle Corps (KRRC) took it over as it passed round the far side of Château Wood to the Menin Road (Figure 8.5).

The PPCLI were exposed to a German artillery bombardment described as a "perfect inferno".[4] Their front line near where you stand was almost obliterated by shellfire. German infantry swarmed down Westhoek Ridge to attack them. The PPCLI desperately tried to maintain contact with B Company of the 3rd Monmouthshire Battalion and 1st Battalion, King's Own Yorkshire Light Infantry (KOYLI) (28th Division) on their left. Here is an extract from the memoirs of Private J.W. Vaughan, PPCLI, which gives you some idea what was happening where you stand. Part of it concerns a Lieutenant Papineau, whose name is mentioned in Chapter 17, which deals with the Canadian capture of Passchendaele in October/November 1917.

> We were hit dead centre with heavy guns and machine-guns and then we were enfiladed from the right and enfiladed from the left along the trench both ways and it seems that they were using tear-gas too because your eyes were smarting and watering and you had quite a time fighting that off. All the officers practically were gone and of course these trenches weren't much good even to begin with.

4   Ibid., p.317.

Figure 8.8 From the vicinity of the PPCLI Memorial, the British front line ran between Château Wood to the right and in the foreground and Glencorse Wood, which is ahead and to the left and further away. The PPCLI would have held the first part of this front line, while 4th KRRC held positions round Château Wood.

You didn't have much chance. I was hit with a shell splinter and I was just lying in the trench, what there was of it, and Lieutenant Papineau came along. He was a wonderful man from Quebec. He came from one of the oldest French-Canadian families, so he came along, and he had his automatic in his hand ready for Germans to come on, but he stopped and knelt beside me. One of my buddies had already ripped my puttees off and slit my pants down because I was hit in the leg and my leg had started to swell. Lieutenant Papineau looked at it and he shoved a cigarette in my mouth and lit it, and he said. Don't worry Vaughan, we'll get you out just as fast as we can.

One fellow had just been leaning over talking to me and he stood up and the next minute he got it, and he fell down dead nearly on top of me. That really upset me because he was one of the married men. In fact, that's when I began to get scared. It was all hell let loose, and laying there at the foot of that trench you didn't know what was going on-except that it was bad.[5]

---

5   MacDonald, L., *1915: The Death of Innocence* (London: Penguin Books, 1997), p.287.

Figure 8.9 The upward incline of the Westhoek Ridge to the village of Westhoek; there is a road at the top called the Frezenbergstraat. If you turn left, it takes you to Frezenberg, which is less than one mile as the crow flies, but is a rather tortuous route now, thanks to the disruption caused by the motorway.

Leave the PPCLI Memorial and take the left fork (Princess Patriciastraat). Keep going for approximately 450 yards towards the village of Westhoek ahead. You will soon start going up the incline of the Westhoek Ridge to join the Frezenbergestraat at the top (Figure 8.9).

Before you reach the top of the ridge, and while you have a good view, turn around and look back in the direction from, which you have come (Figure 8.10).

Location 3: Westhoek Ridge

German infantry attacked from Westhoek Ridge towards the line of the PPCLI across the ground in front of you. As you look towards the PPCLI Memorial, you can use it as a guide to the position of the front line. Over to your right was the right flank of the 28th Division. There was a danger that a gap might open between the left flank of the PPCLI (27th Division) and the right flank of the adjacent 3rd Monmouthshire Battalion (28th Division). Had they lost touch, the Germans would have been able to penetrate the British front line and gain access to Château Wood behind. Orders were given for the Patricias' line to be extended towards the Ypres to Roulers railway line, which was beyond Railway Wood. While the PPCLI and 3rd Monmouthshires

Figure 8.10 View from Westhoek Ridge. This is what the Germans would have seen as they attacked on 8 May. Bellewaarde Farm is visible. Château Wood is behind and to the left of the farm.

were fighting to hold their front lines and stay in contact with each other, reserves formed a defensive position behind the PPCLI, which extended across to Railway Wood to your far right, thereby closing off any possible gap should the Germans penetrate British forward positions. The 2nd Battalion, King's Shropshire Light Infantry, 9th Argyll and Sutherland Highlanders and 3rd Battalion, KRRC carried out this task. While all this was happening behind them, the 1st Battalion, KOYLI and B Company of 3rd Monmouthshire Battalion of the 28th Division fought for their lives. By the evening, only one officer and 29 men of the two companies of 3rd Monmouthshire Battalion answered roll call.

Turn around now, continue to the Frezenbergstraat and go straight over a crossroads, from where you will get a good view of Zonnebeke with Broodseinde Ridge beyond. As you look, you will be able to appreciate the amount of ground lost when the British evacuated their trenches on Broodseinde Ridge (Figure 8.11).

There are two further locations to visit to appreciate the full impact of the Battle of Frezenberg. The first is the Menin Road. Return to the Frezenbergstraat and turn left. Keep going until you reach a junction with the Oude Kortrijkstraat, where you should turn right. After 50 yards you will

Figure 8.11 Looking towards Zonnebeke from Westhoek Ridge; Zonnebeke Church is behind the central pole. German artillery on the high ground of Broodseinde Ridge beyond Zonnebeke pounded positions held by the British 27th Division behind Westhoek Ridge and the 28th Division on the exposed forward slope of Frezenberg Ridge to the left.

reach the Menin Road near Clapham Junction. You will see an 18th Division Memorial on the far side of the road (Chapter 12). Look beyond the memorial in the direction of Gheluvelt (Figure 8.12).

Location 4: Clapham Junction

When the perimeter of the Ypres Salient was evacuated between 1–3 May, the British front line moved past your position at Clapham Junction to the eastern margin of Sanctuary Wood behind you, a total distance of approximately one mile (Figure 7.12). Between 9–12 May, the Germans tried to push men from the British 27th Division astride the Menin Road from their remaining hold on the Gheluvelt Plateau to the flat basin around Ypres. Now look to your right from the 18th Division Memorial. There was a strongpoint within the wooded area adjacent to the memorial called Stirling Castle, which was occupied by the Germans after the British withdrawal (Figure 8.13).

Men from the 2nd Gloucestershire Battalion dug an advanced flanking trench shaped in the form of an arrow head which extended from the new British line in the margin of Sanctuary Wood towards Stirling Castle. Many were killed when the Germans attacked them, and many more from the

Figure 8.12 Clapham Junction, looking along the Menin Road in the direction of Gheluvelt. Before the Second Battle of Ypres began, the British line crossed the Menin Road approximately half a mile away in the direction of Gheluvelt.

Figure 8.13 Stirling Castle was in the wooded area to the right.

battalion died when attempts were made to retake this trench. The British line in Sanctuary Wood came under a fierce artillery bombardment, and German forces successfully occupied part of the wood.

The final important location to visit when considering the Battle of Frezenberg is Mouse Trap Farm in the northern part of the Salient. You may have visited this location already if you have read Chapter 7, where a cross-reference to this chapter was made to avoid a long trip to Mouse Trap Farm now.

If you wish to visit Mouse Trap Farm from Clapham Junction, proceed to 'Hell Fire Corner' and take the exit to Potijze and St Jean (N345), where you should turn right onto the Brugseweg (N313). You will reach a junction with the N38, where you need to take the left exit lane to go straight across to a minor road opposite called Hogeziekenweg. Go along this minor road and you will soon pass a road to the right with a large farm ahead. This is the location of Mouse Trap Farm (Figure 8.14).

Location 5: Mouse Trap Farm

To the right of Mouse Trap Farm as you look towards it, the line was held by the 28th Division on 8 May, where the 2nd Battalion Northumberland Fusiliers stood firm. To the right of the Northumberland Fusiliers as you look,

Figure 8.14 Mouse Trap Farm.

the line of the 28th Division had been broken as far round as the PPCLI of the 27th Division on Bellewaarde Ridge, as you have seen. To the left of Mouse Trap Farm, the 4th Division held the front line towards the Yser Canal one and a half miles away.

Location 6: Track X Cemetery

Leave Mouse Trap Farm and continue past Buff's Road Cemetery on your right. Follow a signpost for Track X Cemetery to your right after a short distance. Stop outside the cemetery and look towards Ypres to appreciate how close the British front line was to the city. The 4th Division front line ran across the field in front of you towards the Yser Canal (Figure 8.15).

Now look in the direction of Mouse Trap Farm. The situation here was critical, and a counter-attack was launched by men of the 4th Division from its vicinity.

The houses of Wieltje can be seen to the right of the farm. There is a gap between Mouse Trap Farm and Wieltje, through which the 4th Division

Figure 8.15 German's eye view of part of the line held by British 4th Division taken from Track X Cemetery close to Mouse Trap Farm (see text below); the spire of the church at St Jean is visible behind the trees to the left. Ypres Cathedral is to the far right. The Cloth Hall is almost completely concealed by the modern building in the middle distance. The 4th Division front line passed across these fields towards the Yser Canal.

Figure 8.16 Mouse Trap Farm (left) and Wieltje (ahead) from Track X Cemetery. The arrow shows the direction of the 4th Division counter-attack in the evening of 8 May 1915.

counter-attack went in a direction away from your position (Figure 8.16). The 5th South Lancashires, 1st Royal Irish Fusiliers, 1st Royal Warwicks and 2nd Royal Dublin Fusiliers were given the task, which started at 1900. Its aim was to strike the enemy in the flank, which it did. While fading light brought the attack to a stop before it had done very much, it nevertheless dislodged the Germans from positions east (left) of Wieltje, and may have had the effect of putting the entire Fourth German Army on the defensive.

In terms of territory lost, the day was far from being as disastrous as at first appeared. The 28th Division lost 1,000 yards of ground which was too exposed to enemy fire in any case to be held permanently. Loss of life, however, was very heavy. No fewer than 11 battalion commanders were killed or wounded, and a high proportion of officers and senior NCOs were killed or wounded. Since the start of the Second Battle of Ypres, the 28th Division had lost more than 15,000 men. The depleted 28th Division was withdrawn from the line and replaced by the Cavalry Corps. A further German attack on 13 May achieved very little.

EVENTS AT MOUSE TRAP FARM, 25 MAY 1915

Mouse Trap Farm had been subjected to, and had withstood, repeated attacks during the Battles of St Julien and Frezenberg Ridge. It finally fell to the Germans on 24 May during the Battle of Bellewaarde Ridge.

Look towards Mouse Trap Farm from your position at Track X Cemetery. It was held on 24 May by two platoons of Royal Dublin Fusiliers. After artillery, gas and infantry attacks, Germans closed in on the farm, overwhelmed the defenders and captured the position. By then it had been reduced to a pile of rubble. This created a breech in the front line which the Germans exploited by bombing along British trenches adjacent to the ruins of the farm, and soon a gap in the British front line extended beyond both sides of the farm, and the Germans would have been in possession of British trenches in front of you (Figure 8.15). The situation was untenable. At 2000 on 24 May, the 4th Division pulled back to a line between Turco Farm and a position west of Wieltje (Figure 9.4). As you look towards Mouse Trap Farm and Wieltje, all the ground you see in Figure 8.16 was evacuated. St Jean became the nearest village that was behind the British front line (Figure 8.15).

Chapter 9

THE SECOND BATTLE OF YPRES: BATTLE OF BELLEWAARDE RIDGE, 24–25 MAY 1915

EVENTS AT BELLEWARDE AND HOOGE JUNE–SEPTEMBER 1915

The Battle of Bellewaarde Ridge on 24–25 May 1915 was the final phase of the Second Battle of Ypres. The Battles of Gravenstafel Ridge, St Julien and Frezenberg Ridge resulted in loss of territory to the Germans, as the Allied line was forced closer to Ypres. By the conclusion of the Battle of Frezenberg Ridge, Bellewaarde Ridge was the only high ground which remained in British hands before reaching the flat basin around Ypres.

To reach Bellewaarde Ridge, take the Menin Road (N8, Meenseweg) from 'Hell Fire Corner' and then the second turning to the left, the Begijnenbosstraat, where a signpost directs you to the Royal Engineers Grave. Stop a short way from the bottom of this road, called Cambridge Road during the war.

Location 1: Cambridge Road

Look straight ahead and use Figures 9.1 to identify important landmarks in front of you. Turn right and look in the direction from which Figure 9.2 was taken to see other key locations for the Battle of Bellewaarde Ridge. By the conclusion of the Battle of Frezenberg, the British had lost Château Wood to the Germans but still held Hooge. Using Figures 9.1 and 9.2, you can picture the front line passing through Sanctuary Wood on the far right, round Hooge, across the fields in your direction and then along the side of Railway Wood closest to the Royal Engineers Memorial.

Location 2: R.E. GRAVE

Continue to the Royal Engineers Grave. Look back in the direction from which you have come to get a good view of Ypres (Figure 9.3). You are standing on

Figure 9.1 Looking up Cambridge Road to the crest of Bellewaarde Ridge. The farm on the left was called Witte Poort, and the wood behind it on the crest of the ridge is Railway Wood. The Ypres to Roulers railway once ran beyond the ridge on the far side of Railway Wood. The Royal Engineers Grave is in front of the trees to the right.

Figure 9.2 Looking towards Hooge from Cambridge Road, the trees beyond the ploughed fields are in Château Wood. Hooge is just to the right of Château Wood. Sanctuary Wood is low on the skyline on the far right of the photograph.

Figure 9.3 View from Royal Engineers Grave. Witte Poort Farm is to the left and Railway Wood to the right. Ypres can be seen between the two.

Bellewaarde Ridge, where there was fierce fighting on 24 and 25 May. You should remember that the Battle of Bellewaarde Ridge was fought over the whole length of the Ypres Salient, and Mouse Trap Farm in the north once again featured prominently (see also Chapters 7 and 8).

Figure 9.4 shows the disposition of British forces. The northern part of the Salient was defended by the 4th Division, which linked with the French on the British left at Turco Farm near the foot of Mauser Ridge. The central part of the line, including Bellewaarde Ridge, was held by the 28th Division, while the line adjacent to the Menin Road was held by the 1st Cavalry Division, fighting as infantry.

As you stand at the RE Grave, you can visualise what happened on 24 May 1915. At 0245, German artillery opened fire and the largest cloud of chlorine gas yet seen spread across most Allied positions over a 4.5 mile front. German trenches were so close in some places that the hiss of escaping gas could be heard emerging from cylinders. While the British had anticipated the gas attack, which no longer carried any element of surprise, the close proximity of German trenches meant that there was little time to put on gas masks and there were many casualties. As you look towards Witte Poort Farm and Railway Wood from the RE Grave, the gas cloud would have come from behind you and would have drifted across towards Railway Wood and Witte Poort Farm. It would have reached a height of

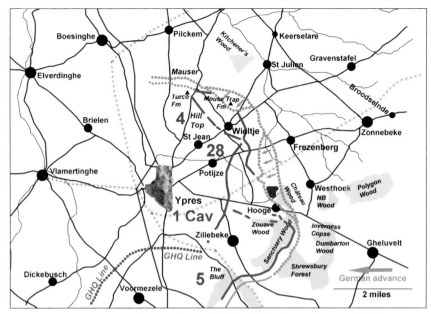

Figure 9.4 Disposition of British forces, 24 May 1915, for the Battle of Bellewaarde Ridge.

40ft, blotting out what remained of Witte Poort Farm and trees as it slowly moved along.[1]

The first onslaught of German infantry here was driven back, as it was in most locations except at Mouse Trap Farm two miles away in the northern part of the Salient, held by the 4th Division. You are referred to Chapter 8 for a description of events at Mouse Trap Farm on 24 May. The Germans subsequently broke through the British front line between the Ypres to Roulers railway and the Menin Road, both north and south of Hooge, as shown in Figure 9.4. They smashed through your position, reaching the eastern margin of Railway Wood and driving the British to the far side of Cambridge Road. Witte Poort Farm fell briefly into German hands. A counter-attack was launched at 1700 by men of the 28th Division, which successfully evicted the Germans from Witte Poort Farm and from the trenches east of Cambridge Road. Looking towards Witte Poort Farm, these trenches would have been a short distance within the field on your side of Cambridge Road and roughly parallel to it. A night attack was launched by men of the 27th and 28th

---

1   Edmonds, J.E., *History of the Great War Based on Official Documents by Direction of the Historical Section of the Committee of Imperial Defence. Military Operations. France and Belgium 1915* Volume I (London: Macmillan, 1927), p.342.

Divisions across the field in the direction of Château Wood, but it failed to gain any ground beyond the trenches east of Witte Poort Farm. Connecting trenches were then dug between the trenches east of Cambridge Road and those held by men of the 1st Cavalry Division, who by then had been evicted from Hooge and were occupying a position in Zouave Wood, which you are now going to visit. The connecting trenches remained in British hands, although heavy casualties were sustained.

LOCATION 3 CANADALAAN

Return to the Menin Road and turn left then first right onto Canadalaan, which leads to a Canadian Memorial at Hill 62 (Chapter 18). Canadalaan was constructed after the war to give access to this memorial. Look out for Hooge Crater Cemetery on your left. Figure 9.5 was taken shortly after entering Canadalaan, and gives a good view across to the cemetery, with Hooge beyond and Château Wood behind and to the right of Hooge. Sanctuary Wood is on the far right.

Continue until you get the same view shown in Figure 9.6. You can see Hooge Crater Cemetery and Hooge, which are clearly visible. Railway Wood is on the skyline to the far left. Witte Poort Farm is just out of the photograph

Figure 9.5 Hooge Crater Cemetery. Hooge is behind the cemetery and Château Wood is behind and to the right of Hooge. Sanctuary Wood is the large wood on the far right.

Figure 9.6 Hooge Crater Cemetery and Hooge. Zouave Wood was between your position and the cemetery. Railway Wood is on the far left. Witte Poort Farm is out of the picture on the left.

to the left, but you should make a point of spotting it. After the battle on 25 May, the British front-line trench passed along the margin of Railway Wood close to Cambridge Road, through the field to the right of Witte Poort Farm and parallel to the road. The connecting trench from there crossed the Menin Road and joined a trench running across the ploughed field in front of you (Figure 9.6), where it passed into Zouave Wood (Figure 9.8). No longer present, Zouave Wood was approximately midway between your position and the bottom end of Hooge Crater Cemetery. From Zouave Wood, the line then passed through Sanctuary Wood. Men from the 1st Cavalry Division were forced from Hooge into Zouave Wood as mentioned above.

The next place to visit is Hooge Crater Cemetery, but before you go, you might want to read the section entitled 'Diversionary attack at Hooge, 25 September 1915' (see below), before making your way to the bottom of the cemetery, and looking up towards Hooge (Figure 9.7).

LOCATION 4: HOOGE CRATER CEMETERY

Figure 9.7 Hooge Crater Cemetery. Hooge is beyond the top of the cemetery and Château Wood behind and to the right.

A night-time counter-attack on 25 May by the 1st Cavalry Division from Zouave Wood dislodged Germans from Hooge opposite the top of the cemetery, giving the British a small foothold extending across the Menin Road into the grounds of Hooge Château. Attacking from Zouave Wood, they would have passed over the ground where you stand in Hooge Crater Cemetery on their way to the village ahead.

The Battle of Bellewaarde Ridge on 24–25 May resulted in a further contraction of the Ypres Salient, with Hooge at the furthermost point from Ypres. The short section of British front line on the far side of the Menin Road was a dangerous and isolated position to hold.

There had been heavy fighting since 22 April. The British were very short of artillery ammunition, with practically nothing but shrapnel left. Fortunately, the Germans were exhausted by their efforts and stopped fighting. Their step-by-step advances had accomplished nothing decisive, despite having overwhelming superiority in heavy artillery, and despite repeated infantry attacks preceded by the release of chlorine gas. Total British losses for the period 22 April–31 May 1915 amounted to 2,150 officers and 57,125 other ranks. German losses too were heavy, and were given as 860 officers and 34,073 other ranks.[2]

---

2   Ibid., p.356.

EVENTS AROUND HOOGE, MAY–SEPTEMBER 1915

Several important events took place around Hooge and Bellewaarde in the months following the Second Battle of Ypres. The British were determined to improve their position at Hooge, while the Germans tried very hard to remove them. While you stand in Hooge Crater Cemetery, you may consider what happened. On 16 June, men of the British 3rd Division launched an attack between Railway Wood and Hooge in an effort to recapture Bellewaarde Ridge, but were unsuccessful. On 19 July, they detonated a mine beneath a German position within the grounds of Hooge Château on the far side of the Menin Road, gaining a few yards of ground on either side of the mine crater, which was fiercely contested with much loss of life. On 30 July, the Germans used flame-throwers, sending survivors from the mine crater and adjacent trenches running down through the site of Hooge Crater Cemetery to Zouave Wood. Figure 9.8 shows the approximate position of the front lines after this German attack.

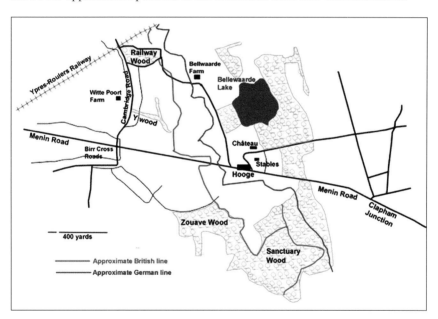

Figure 9.8 This shows the approximate positions of the British and German lines after the German flamethrower attack on 30 July 1915.

After several poorly organised and unsuccessful attempts had been made to regain lost ground, on 9 August the British 6th Division attacked Hooge with a much more effective artillery barrage and recaptured lost ground. For what it was worth, the crater within the grounds of Hooge Château was reoccupied by the British.

DIVERSIONARY ATTACK AT HOOGE, 25 SEPTEMBER 1915

On 25 September, an attack was launched against Hooge and Bellewaarde Ridge to coincide with the Battle of Loos, aimed at tying up German forces and preventing them from being moved to Loos as reinforcements. Other diversions were made by III Corps and the Indian Corps north of the La Bassée Canal. The French commander, General Joffre, was insistent that the British cooperate with a "large powerful attack" at Loos while French forces attacked German positions at Vimy Ridge and further south in Champagne. Standing in Canadalaan looking in the direction of Hooge (Figure 9.6), the front to be attacked was approximately a mile in length between Hooge and Bellewaarde Ridge, with the 14th Light Division on the left and the 3rd Division on the right. The British advance on 9 August (see above) had given them back the mine crater north of the Menin Road.[3] South of the Menin Road, the Germans held a deadly redoubt in the corner of Sanctuary Wood, from which they had poured enfilade fire against the British right flank in the August action (Figure 9.8).

The attack was due to start at 0400, preceded by a heavy artillery bombardment of the German lines which started at 0350 and lasted for half an hour. At 0419, two large mines were exploded near Hooge and a further two detonated in the same area 30 seconds later. This was the signal for men to advance across no man's land, where they encountered much undamaged barbed wire and came under heavy machine-gun fire. One battalion taking part was the 4th Battalion Gordon Highlanders, a Territorial battalion which included a company of men from the University of Aberdeen, the only university to have its own company in the British Army. Some of the 4th Gordon Highlanders managed to find gaps in the barbed wire and made progress, fighting their way through the German third trench line, accompanied by a few men from the 1st Gordon Highlanders. The following account is taken from the War Diary of the 4th Gordon Highlanders:

> 4.10a.m. ½ of D Coy and ½ of C Coy advanced and the other half advanced from our second line trenches.
>
> 4.18a.m. Our 1st and 2nd line got into German trenches with little loss. Found many Germans in it most of whom bolted.
>
> 4.20a.m. 3rd line advanced over this trench and along with second line, advanced to objective. Certain amount of confusion; Germans met with in considerable numbers in the open and in the trenches and a good bit of rifle fire and hand to hand fighting but all were soon captured, killed or escaped.

---

3   Hammerton, J.A., *A Popular History of the Great War* Volume 2 (London: Amalgamated Press Ltd, 1933), p.393.

Reports gradually got back saying the objective had been gained.

At the same time 1 off and 9 RE attached and 25 Battalion pioneers under Lt Waddell started to work on CT from Appendix to German line, but after a short time had to stop owing to heavy fire from artillery several of the pioneers being killed. They went forward to help consolidate the furthest line taken by us.

Germans started heavy bombardment of captured trenches in redoubt, reports came back telling of this and asking for shovels and sandbags to strengthen trenches. Some were sent up but did not arrive owing to shelling.

It was almost impossible to get up bombs etc to the furthest line held by us as the German CTs were blocked by shell fire and anyone coming out into the open was fired at by rifle and machine gun fire coming from North of the Menin Road.

4.50–12noon. Our men retired to the Royal Scots trenches and across the open through the wood to Appendix 2 B 8 where they were collected and lined the parapet of Appendix C1 and B8. They were well handled by 2Lt Bain. The Germans 4 times tried to advance from their own front line into C1 and Appendix but each time were stopped by accurate fire of these men.

The men of C and D Coys who were in the German 3rd line were cut off and are missing.

The remainder of A Coy were at once sent for to reinforce and hold our old front line [and] all this time the Germans were accurately shelling our trenches with field guns, inflicting several casualties.

Despite their best efforts they were forced to retire into the German first-line trenches where they fought off German counter-attacks, sustaining many casualties. The Germans directed artillery fire onto hastily dug communication trenches so that they could not be resupplied or reinforced. The War Diary indicates that C and D companies were cut off and never seen again.

Heavy casualties were sustained by both attacking divisions without any gain in territory. The attack had failed and 4,000 men had become casualties. Losses sustained by the 4th Battalion Gordon Highlanders were particularly heavy. Only a handful of the University of Aberdeen's own company, which was part of D company, remained. The Reverend A.M. McLean, who was with these men, returned to Aberdeen in March 1916 to tell the story of what happened, because he felt that he must. He said "I have come to Aberdeen to discharge what is a very sacred duty." He was conscious of military secrecy and that people were ignorant of what had happened. His descriptions revealed the horror of what had taken place:[4]

> We saw the red surge of war breaking out on the trenches from Hooge to La Bassée and the roar of the guns was like the thunder of the Hebridean seas ... I saw the stabling flashes of our guns suddenly extinguished and a huge mushroom of red flame leaping to the sky along the German lines where our mines were sprung; and I prayed that God might be with my boys and show His mercy to those passing into His presence. Along the lines of the trenches a continuous band of lurid fire showed the intensity of the German artillery resistance; it seemed no living thing could cross that unbroken zone of death ...But there the tragedy began. For some reason or other the maze of barbed wire in front of the remaining Company [of Gordons] and an English regiment on their left remained intact ... The Englishmen reached the wire and finding it insuperable wisely retired to their trenches. Not so the Gordons. On to the wire they surged, tried to get over it, tried to get under it, to get through it, and there on the wire they died, but they would not go back. Captain Menteith was shot in the arm as he cleared the parapet. He bound the wound up and went on. For the third time he went out, reached the wire, and there too, he died.

Following the diversion at Hooge on 25 September, Brigadier General A.R. Hoskins DSO, of 8 Brigade, wrote to Sir Alexander Lyon, Deputy Lord Lieutenant of Aberdeen, former Lord Provost of the city of Aberdeen and President of the Aberdeen Territorial Army Association. The words he used to describe the action were very different from those employed by the Reverend McLean.

> Dear Lyon,
> We had such strenuous times after the 25th September till I left that I did not have a chance of seeing the 4th Gordons in the Rest Area. I much wanted to do so that I could congratulate them personally on the very fine work which all ranks did on the 25th. There are few Battalions which could have done it, could have shown such dash or could have held on so tenaciously under most trying conditions. If the situation on your left flank had been a bit better you would have been there now, and much more would have been heard of the fine attack you had made. I shall try to see you someday when you are out of

---

4   McConachie, J., *The Student Soldiers* (Elgin: Moravian Press Ltd, 1995).

the Trenches, but meanwhile I wish you all the best of luck, and hope that I may have the good fortune to have the 4th Gordons under my command again or to be fighting alongside them.

Yours sincerely,

(sgd) A.R. Hoskins.[5]

The attack failed to take any territory, but did it achieve its other objective, which was to prevent the Germans sending reinforcements to Loos? Sir John French's dispatch to the Secretary of State for War on15 October 1915 suggested that it had done so.

> At the same time a secondary attack, designed with the object of distracting the enemy's attention and holding his troops to their ground, was made by the 5th Corps on Bellewaarde Farm, situated to the east of Ypres ... The object of the secondary attack was most effectively achieved, for not only was the enemy contained on that front, but we have reason to believe that reserves were hurried toward that point of the line. The attack was made at daybreak by the 3rd and 14th Divisions, and at first the greater part of the enemy's front line was taken; but, owing to the powerful artillery fire concentrated against them, the troops were unable to retain the ground, and had to return to their original trenches toward nightfall.

The reality was expressed by one of the men who was there, who felt it had made no difference at all,[6] and it is hard to reconcile Sir John French's interpretation of events and those of Brigadier General Hoskins with the facts.

---

5 GHPB146.15 Copy of typed letter (2 pages) from Brig.- Gen. A.R. Hoskins to Sir Alexander Lyon, concerning action of 25.9.1915. Courtesy Gordon Highlanders Museum.
6 Falls, C., *Gordon Highlanders in the First World War* (Uckfield, East Sussex: Naval and Military Press, 2014, reprinted).

Chapter 10

THE THIRD BATTLE OF YPRES: BATTLE OF PILCKEM RIDGE, 31 JULY 1917

This chapter deals with the Battle of Pilckem Ridge on 31 July 1917, although other important events which took place in the area to be described during the four years of the war are mentioned. The Battle of Pilckem Ridge was the first phase of the Third Battle of Ypres, which had the strategic aim of breaking free from the confines of the Ypres Salient and capturing the channel ports of Ostend and Zeebrugge, thereby denying their use to the Germans as U-Boat bases. It was not simply a localised attack aimed at capturing Pilckem Ridge. It was fought over the entire length of the Ypres Salient, to push outwards and capture German positions on the high ground at the perimeter of the Salient. Figure 10.1 shows the British line before the battle began, along with the objectives and the times expected to reach them. Unfortunately, things did not go as well as expected for the Allies, and as it turned out, the most significant gain was made in the northern part of the Salient when the British advanced from Boesinghe over Pilckem Ridge to a stream called the Steenbeek, close to the village of Langemarck.

Boesinghe is a village predominantly on the west bank of the Yser Canal, an important waterway which formed a natural defensive barrier of great importance during the war. Pilckem is a hamlet 1.24 miles from Boesinghe along the road between Boesinghe and Langemarck, while the Steenbeek crosses beneath the Boesinghe to Langemarck road a short distance before Langemarck. The Ypres to Staden railway line was a divisional boundary for the fighting. It ran roughly parallel to and 100 yards to the north of the road. Now closed as a railway, it has been converted into a good walking and cycling track, which leads the visitor towards Langemarck. This chapter takes you from the banks of the Yser Canal at Boesinghe to the Steenbeek, covering ground followed by men of the Guards and 38th (Welsh) Divisions during the Battle of Pilckem Ridge.

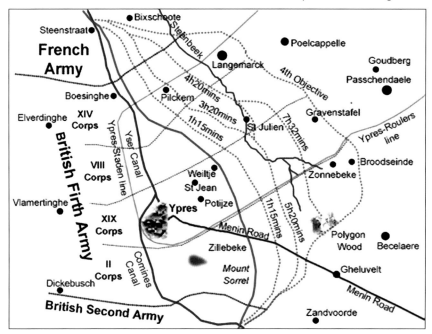

Figure 10.1 British positions at the commencement of the Battle of Pilckem Ridge on 31 July 1917 are shown, together with the proposed advances to be made over the Ypres Salient to capture the high ground round Ypres.

Boesinghe can be reached from Ypres by going along the Dixmuidseweg, but if you are cycling, then the path on the bank of the Yser Canal provides a more pleasant alternative (Figure 10.2). To reach the canal from the Grote Markt in Ypres, go along the Diksmuidsestraat until you reach a T-junction with the Brugseweg. Turn left onto the Brugseweg, which becomes continuous with the Dixmuidseweg. The canal can be seen a short distance to the right.

After reaching Boesinghe, cross the canal at traffic lights, which is also where the canal path emerges onto the Langemarkseweg, and then turn first right onto the Oostkaai. Stop when you reach the canal bank. Look across the canal towards Boesinghe, where you can reflect on events which took place here during the war (Figure 10.3).

Figure 10.2 The Yser Canal; the cyclists are travelling south towards Ypres from Boesinghe, on the west bank of the canal. Boesinghe is 1.25 miles north of their position. The canal marked the base of the northern part of the Ypres Salient, which was at a variable distance beyond the east bank of the waterway. In April 1918, the British evacuated the Salient and the Germans gained a foothold on the west bank where the cyclists are.

Location 1: The East Bank of the Yser Canal

Figure 10.3 The east bank of the Yser Canal. Germans in this vicinity abandoned their forward positions before the start of the Battle of Pilckem Ridge. Boesinghe Church spire is visible.

Summary of events at Boesinghe

- On 22 April 1915, French colonial troops retreated in disarray to the west bank of the Yser Canal at Boesinghe after fleeing from their front line in the northern part of the Ypres Salient following the first German gas attack. The Germans then held the east bank at Boesinghe where you stand (Chapter 6).
- On 27 July 1917, the east bank of the canal was regained by the Guards Division prior to the Battle of Pilckem Ridge on 31 July. This was an important manoeuvre, because the canal would otherwise have been a major barrier at the start of the battle.
- Boesinghe on the west bank of the Yser remained behind Allied lines until April 1918, when the Salient was evacuated, the Germans crossed the Yser and Boesinghe became incorporated into the front line (Chapter 17).
- On 28 September 1918, a final Allied advance drove the Germans back to Langemarck in a single day.

PRELIMINARY ACTION BY GUARDS DIVISION CROSSING THE YSER CANAL AT BOESINGHE, 13–21 JULY 1917

The canal bank where you stand was regained by men of the Guards Division following sustained shelling of German positions, both in the forward area where you stand and in rear areas, particularly around the Steenbeek three miles to the east. In addition, numerous raids covered by 'box barrages'[1] were carried out. German defences were shelled with lachrymatory (tear) gas and lethal gas shells on 13/14 July and again on 20/21 July. German morale was badly affected, and on 25 July, patrols reported that they could walk into the German front line in some places. With the help of air observation, it was established that German trenches on the east bank of the Yser were empty. During the afternoon of 27 July, patrols from the Guards Division crossed the canal and occupied German forward positions on a front of 3,000 yards to a depth of 500 yards.[2] The successful occupation of the east bank of the canal made things easier on 31 July, when men from the Guards Division and 38th (Welsh) Division, fighting with the British Fifth Army, went forwards to begin the Battle of Pilckem Ridge. They were assisted by the French First Army on the left flank of the Guards, which moved forwards simultaneously from Steenstraat towards Bixschoote (Figure 10.1). The ground that was actually captured on 31 July can be seen in Figure 10.4.

---

1   A box barrage is an artillery barrage on three sides of a given area to prevent escape or reinforcement of the enemy or to cover the front and flanks of a friendly force.
2   Edmonds, J.E., *History of the Great War Based on Official Documents by Direction of the Historical Section of the Committee of Imperial Defence. Military Operations. France and Belgium 1917* Volume 2 (London: HMSO, 1948), pp.139–40.

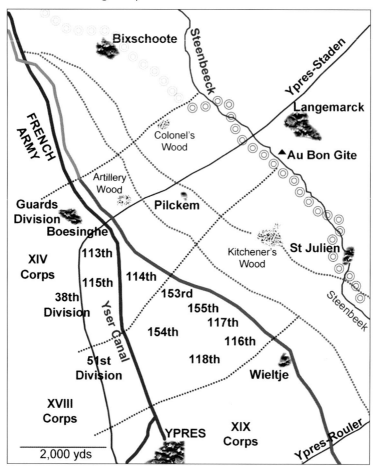

Figure 10.4 Map of the Battle of Pilckem Ridge, 31 July 1917, showing the attack made by the Guards and 38th Divisions (of XIV Corps). The 51st (Highland) Division (of XVIII Corps) was on the right flank of the 38th Division. Success for the 38th Division depended on the satisfactory progress of the 51st on its right. The line reached by these divisions is marked by the circles. Note the position of this line in relation to the Steenbeek.

THE BATTLE OF PILCKEM RIDGE, 31 JULY 1917

Retrace your steps to the Langemarkseweg, turn right and go towards Langemark over the ground captured by the Guards and 38th (Welsh) Divisions. There is a steady upward incline, scarcely perceptible in a car, but on a bicycle it is a notable ascent. You are following in the footsteps of men after they went over the top at 0350 on 31 July. Figure 10.5 was taken looking

Figure10.5 The ascent from Boesinghe onto Pilckem Ridge is relatively steep by the standards of the Salient. The church spire of Boesinghe is visible. Men from the 38th Division would have been coming towards your position, while the Guards were over to your right beyond the old Ypres to Staden railway line.

back towards Boesinghe and gives an idea of the relatively steep incline from the village onto Pilckem Ridge.

As you travel in the direction of Pilckem, the Guards Division would have been over to your left. There is a signpost to Artillery Wood Cemetery. Stop and reflect on what happened here on 31 July 1917.

Location 2: Road to Artillery Wood Cemetery

The Guards encountered machine-gun fire from strongholds in Artillery Wood and from within a copse of trees known simply as Wood 15 a little further on. Sergeant R. Bye (1st Welsh Guards) won a VC in Wood 15, and the citation for his award may help you to understand what conditions were like:

No. 939 Sergeant Robert Bye, Welsh Guards (Penrhiwceiber, Glamorgan). For most conspicuous bravery. Sergeant Bye displayed the utmost courage and devotion to duty during an attack on the enemy's position. Seeing that the leading waves were being troubled by two enemy blockhouses, he, on his own initiative, rushed at one of them and put the garrison out of action. He then rejoined his company and went forward to the assault of the second objective. When the troops had gone forward to the attack on the third objective, a party was detailed to clear up a line of blockhouses which had been passed. Sergeant Bye volunteered to take charge of this party, accomplished his object, and took many prisoners. He subsequently advanced to the third objective, capturing a number of prisoners, thus rendering invaluable assistance to the assaulting companies. He displayed throughout the most remarkable initiative.

London Gazette No. 30, 272, 4 September 1917

The morning of 31 July was misty, with a westerly breeze which drove low clouds over the battlefield. This meant that an extensive programme for air cooperation was cancelled.[3] At zero hour, a creeping barrage began, resting on German forward positions for some minutes before moving forwards at a distance of 100 yards every four minutes. Figure 10.6 shows the way men of the 38th (Welsh) Division would have gone on both sides of the road as they made their way up the steady incline towards Pilckem a short distance ahead. One can imagine the scene as men focussed on the grim task as they advanced behind the protective curtain of fire which would have lifted two or three times before they reached the next corner (Figure 10.6). German retaliation at this stage was relatively light, so the Welshmen made good progress.

German resistance stiffened once Pilckem was reached, 1.24 miles from Boesinghe. Pilckem is a small group of houses around a crossroads between the Boesinghe to Langemarck road and the Pilkemseweg, which leads to the N38 near Wieltje to the right and Bixschoote to the left. There were several concrete machine-gun emplacements here which inflicted heavy casualties on the advancing British (Figure 10.7).

Location 3: Pilckem

Two VCs were won during the fighting at Pilckem.

One was Corporal J.L. Davies of the 13th Royal Welch Fusiliers:

He advanced through the barrage and single-handed attacked a machine-gun emplacement which was causing serious losses, bayoneted one of the crew and brought in another with the captured gun. Although wounded, he then led a bombing party to assault a defended house. He died of wounds received during the engagement.[4]

---

3   Ibid., p.149.
4   Ibid., p.161.

Figure 10.6 Ascending Pilckem Ridge. Pilckem is a short distance beyond the corner in the distance.

Figure 10.7 Approaching Pilckem, machine-gun emplacements and pillbox fortifications held up progress here.

Meanwhile, over to the left beyond the railway line, Private T. Whitham (1st Coldstream Guards) was also awarded the VC. His citation reads:

> On his own initiative, he worked round an enemy machine gun which was enfilading the battalion on the right. Moving from shell-hole to shell-hole under heavy fire, he captured it, including an officer and two other ranks. His action saved many lives and enabled the advance to be continued.[5]

If you turn left at the crossroads where the cyclist is standing in Figure 10.7, walk a few yards to where the old railway line crosses the road and look in the direction of Langemarck, you will see a memorial plaque along the railway line there commemorating Private Whitham, which explains the actions taking place in the adjacent field where he won his VC (Figure 10.8).

Figure 10.8 Looking along the old Ypres to Staden railway line in the direction of Langemarck, the position of the memorial plaque to Private Whitham is 50 yards along the track. He won his Victoria Cross in the field to the left.

---

5   Ibid., p.161.

GERMAN DEFENCES ON 31 JULY 1917

Men of the 38th and Guards Divisions were opposed by soldiers of the German Fourth Army, employing defences which had evolved considerably from a single linear defensive line, characteristic of the Battle of the Somme in 1916. The principle which had evolved by 1917 was to defend in depth, with reserves ready to counter-attack quickly when necessary. The Germans had organised their defences into three zones, each 2,000–3,000 yards deep. These were called (i) a forward zone, (ii) a battle zone and (iii) a rearward zone, the backs of which were marked by what was called respectively the Second, Third and Flandern I Line (Figure 10.9).

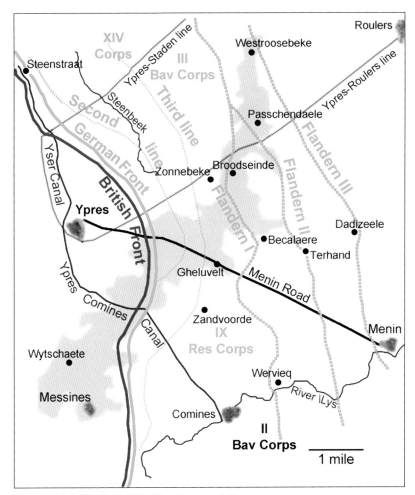

Figure 10.9 Flanders 1917: The German defences.

The forward zone was thinly held to avoid heavy casualties during an enemy attack and offered relatively little resistance. This perhaps explains why rapid progress was made initially by the Guards and the Welsh Divisions. The second line was reinforced by protective artillery, behind which reserves were positioned to counter-attack when needed. The main fighting was normally expected to take place in the battle zone between the Second and Third lines, where German resistance stiffened. Germans here were part of Group Ypres, comprising the 38th, 235th and 3rd Guard Divisions. Figure 10.9 shows the German positions, where it can be seen that the Steenbeek was an important part of the German Second Line. This is why British artillery had targeted German positions behind the Steenbeek in the preliminary barrage.

As you make your way from Pilckem towards the Steenbeek, it might help to link events over four years by considering what happened here during those years. Stop at the entrance of Cement House Cemetery (Figure 10.10).

Location 4: Cement House Cemetery

In 1914, men from the British 1st Division mustered near Pilckem on their way to defend Langemarck on 21 October (Chapter 2). You can see the church spire of Langemarck from your position at the cemetery. On 22 April 1915, French Colonial troops fled past here during their retreat from Langemarck to the Yser Canal (Chapter 6). Now, on 31 July 1917, men of the Welsh (38th) Division and Guards Division made their way in the opposite direction to reclaim the lost territory. As they advanced, they would have passed where Cement House Cemetery is to be found today. This cemetery remains open to bury the remains of soldiers uncovered in the Salient wherever land is excavated for building projects. Some of those buried here were men who came this way during the attack on 31 July 1917.

The Steenbeek was reached at 0953[6] and successfully forded. You should stop at the bridge over the Steenbeek, with the outskirts of Langemarck visible ahead. Look towards the open ground to your right (Figure 10.11).

Location 5: The Steenbeek

After fording the Steenbeek, a German stronghold close to the bank was captured. Two German officers and 30 other ranks were taken prisoner. The stronghold was a ruined roadside inn called 'Au Bon Gite', which had been reinforced by a pillbox. Two adjacent strongpoints were also taken.[7] This

---

6   Ibid., pp.160–63.
7   Ibid., p.161.

Figure 10.10 These cyclists have come steadily uphill from the Yser Canal at Boesinghe and have passed the hamlet of Pilckem. They are stopping for a welcome break at Cement House Cemetery on their way to the Steenbeek a short distance ahead. The old Ypres to Staden railway is 100 metres over to their right and marked the divisional boundary between the 38th and Guards Divisions.

Figure 10.11 The Steenbeek. On the near bank there is a heavy steel strut sticking out of the ground, which may be all that remains of a German blockhouse located here. The edge of the Langemarck to Boesinghe road can just be seen on the right of the photograph. Men from the 38th Welsh Division would have come up the road towards this position from Pilckem, and also across the adjacent field, until they reached the Steenbeek.

action won Sergeant I. Rees of the 11th South Wales Borderers a VC. His citation read as follows.

> Sergeant Rees gained his VC when he worked round the flank of and rushed from 20 yards a machine gun which was inflicting many casualties, shot one of the team and bayoneted another. He then bombed a large concrete shelter, killing 3 and capturing 30 prisoners, including 2 officers, in addition to an undamaged machine gun.[8]

Figure 10.12 'Au Bon Gite' would have been close to the position from which this photograph was taken on the left bank of the Steenbeek.

Now look further along to the right, where men of the 51st Highland Division would have been visible moving beyond the right flank of the 38th (Welsh) Division (Figure 10.12). Sergeant G. McIntosh of the 6th Gordon Highlanders won a Victoria Cross when he rushed across the Steenbeek to neutralise a German machine-gun position. His citation reads:

> No. 265579, George McIntosh, Private, 1/6th Battalion, the Gordon Highlanders (Buckie, Banffshire). For most conspicuous bravery when,

---

8   Ibid., p.161.

during the consolidation of a position, his company came under machine gun fire at close range.

Private McIntosh immediately rushed forward under heavy fire, and reaching the emplacement, he threw a Mills grenade into it, killing two of the enemy and wounding a third. Subsequently, entering the dug-out, he found two light machine guns, which he carried back with him.

His quick grasp of the situation and the utter fearlessness and rapidity with which he acted undoubtedly saved many of his comrades, and enabled the consolidation to proceed unhindered by machine gun fire.

Throughout the day the cheerfulness and courage of Private McIntosh was indomitable, and to his fine example in a great measure was due the success which attended his company.

London Gazette (Supplement) No. 30, 272, p.9, 260,
4 September 1917

GERMAN COUNTER-ATTACKS

Between 1430 and 1500, waves of German infantry counter-attacked from the direction of Langemarck a short distance away, towards the Steenbeek, attacking men from the 38th Division and the adjacent 51st Highland Division. At approximately 1700, the bridgehead at 'Au Bon Gite' was abandoned, the garrison withdrawing to the line already established west of the stream.[9] The 51st Division successfully beat off the German counter-attack, turning it into a disorderly flight.[10] Elsewhere, the impact of the German counter-attacks was very keenly felt, and much hard-fought-over ground was lost (Chapter 11 and Figure 10.13).

An advance of approximately 3,000 yards was made here. This opening phase of the Third Battle of Ypres was judged a success, although the striking power of German counter-attacks using fresh soldiers had been underestimated. There were 31,850 British casualties for three days' fighting between 31 July and 2 August.

General Sir Douglas Haig wrote in his diary:

Tuesday 31st July 1917
Our troops established themselves beyond the Steenbeek and the French had taken Bixschoote and Cabaret Kortekeer, which was so frequently attacked in October and November 1914 [Chapter 2]. This was a fine day's work. Gough thinks he has taken over 5,000 prisoners

9   Ibid., p.174.
10   Ibid., p.174.

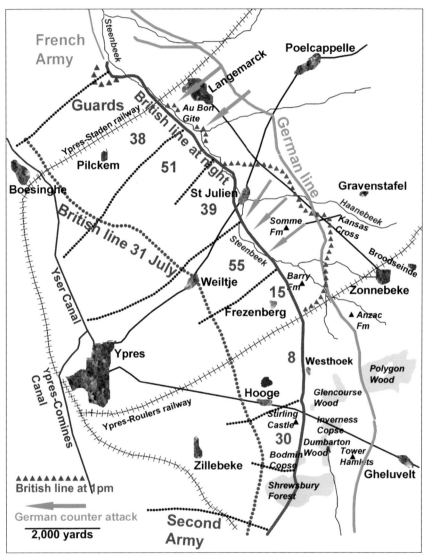

Figure 10.13 Ground lost following the German counter-attack on 31 July 1917.

and 60 guns or more. The ground is thick with dead Germans, killed mostly by out artillery. I sent Alan Fletcher and Colonel Ryan round the Casualty Clearing Stations. Wounded are very cheery indeed. Some 6,000 wounded had been treated in ten hours up to 6pm.[11]

Heavy rain began on the evening of 31 July, which over the following weeks and months frequently transformed the battlefield into a quagmire. Haig recorded that it had begun to rain in the afternoon of 31 July. Aeroplane observation was impossible and the going was very bad because the ground had been badly cut up, hampering further progress and robbing the attacking soldiers of much of their advantage. On Wednesday, 1 August, Haig wrote:

Glass fell a tenth after midnight. Heavy rain began to fall about 3am and continued all day ... a terrible day of rain. The ground is like a bog in this low lying country. The light railways and roads are steadily being pushed forward. Still, in view of the terrible wet, I judge that we are fortunate not to have advanced to the extreme 'Red Line'[12] because it would not have been possible to supply our guns with ammunition. Our troops would thus have been at the mercy of a hostile counter-attack.[13]

By the evening of 31 July, soldiers who were exhausted by their efforts took what shelter they could in positions close to where you stand near the Steenbeek. They prepared themselves for incoming shellfire from German guns and for the ever-present risk of counter-attacks. The first phase of the Third Battle of Ypres was over. The next phase, the Battle of Langemarck, was launched on 16 August, when British soldiers advanced across the Steenbeek to capture the ruins of this village.

11 Blake, R., *The Private Papers of Douglas Haig 1914–1919* (London: Eyre and Spottiswoode, 1952), p.250.
12 The 'Red Line' was the projected final position (Figure 10.1, 4th objective).
13 Blake, R., op cit.

Chapter 11

THE THIRD BATTLE OF YPRES: BATTLE OF LANGEMARCK, 16 AUGUST 1917

The Battle of Langemarck on 16 August 1917 was the second phase of the Third Battle of Ypres. While bearing the name Langemarck, the main thrust was directed towards the Menin Road as the British attempted to push further onto the Gheluvelt Plateau. Langemarck was close to the northern flank of the attack near Bixschoote, where the French First Army advanced adjacent to British forces. As things turned out, the sole British successes were around Langemarck and St Julien, or what remained of these villages after previous fighting (Figure 11.1). There were no gains on, or around, the Menin Road.

Location 1: Bridge over the Steenbeek

The starting position for the Battle of Langemarck is where Chapter 10 finishes. If you are going directly from Ypres, then go to the roundabout at 'Hell Fire Corner', take the fifth exit and go straight on at the next roundabout at Potijze. Keep going until you reach a T-junction at St Jean, then turn right onto the N313 (Brugseweg) and go past Wieltje. The road joins the N38 towards Poelcappelle. Pass through St Julien, and after a mile you will reach the hamlet of Keerselare, where the Canadian Memorial stands adjacent to the staggered crossroads with the Zonnebeke to Langemarck road. Go to Langemarck, and turn left at the traffic lights. Just after you leave the outskirts of Langemarck, you cross the Steenbeek.

Stand on the bridge over the Steenbeek facing in the direction of Langemarck. Boesinghe is 2.3 miles behind you. Turn to your left and you will see an industrial complex ahead (Figure 11.2). The Steenbeek winds round the left side of this complex. Once past it, the stream runs in a north-westerly direction. The old Ypres to Staden railway line is adjacent to the near side of the complex, and was a divisional boundary on 16 August 1917.

The 20th Division, fighting with the Fifth Army, commanded by General Sir Hubert Gough, occupied trenches between where you stand and the railway line, while the 29th Division was beyond the railway line. Their starting

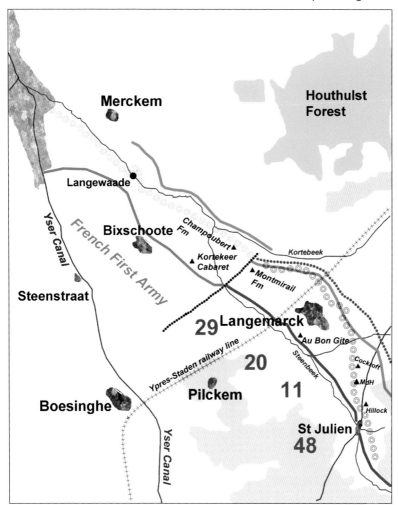

Figure 11.1 The Battle of Langemarck, 16 August 1917, the northern flank. The solid green line shows the German Third Line; the dotted red line shows the British objective; and red circles show ground actually gained by British, with blue circles the ground gained by the French. MdH stands for Maison du Hibou.

line was the left bank of the Steenbeek as you look, reached by the Guards Division on 31 July during the Battle of Pilckem Ridge (Chapter 10). Today, the Steenbeek is an insignificant stream, but in August 1917 it was a swollen quagmire as a result of heavy rain and persistent shelling. Local actions on 11, 12, and 14 August 1917 established outposts on the opposite bank, except at

Figure 11.2 The Steenbeek near Langemarck passes beneath the Boesinghe to Langemarck road, before flowing to the left of the industrial complex. The old Ypres to Staden railway line (now a cycle and walking track) is in front of the complex as you look towards it.

the German strongpoint of Au Bon Gite (Chapter 10).[1] These outposts would have been on the grassy bank to the right of the Steenbeek as you look towards the complex (Figure 11.2) and to the left of the Steenbeek as you look in the opposite direction on the other side of the road.

It rained very heavily on the days before 16 August. The ground was extremely muddy and trenches along the Steenbeek were waterlogged. Plank roads, duckboards and mule tracks were laid between the Yser Canal (2.3 miles away at Boesinghe) and the front line to facilitate movement of men and materials. Pack animals often blocked and damaged the tracks, and were frequently driven 'across country' between shell craters. Small steel shelters were provided for sleeping accommodation, and every use was made of old German concrete pillboxes. Water was brought up in water carts and petrol tins until pipe lines could be laid.[2]

---

1   Edmonds, J.E., *History of the Great War Based on Official Documents by Direction of the Historical Section of the Committee of Imperial Defence. Military Operations. France and Belgium 1917* Volume 2 (London: HMSO, 1948), p.199.
2   Ibid., pp.198–202.

One can only try to imagine how appalling conditions must have been as men waited here to advance on 16 August. At 0445, an artillery barrage opened up and men of the 20th Division left their front-line trenches around your position as far as the railway line, and advanced towards Langemarck. The *Official History of the Great War* states:

> The whole area, a mile wide, between the stream and the objective, the worst patch on the battlefield, was a muddy waste, pitted with water-filled shell holes and the assaulting groups quickly split into small parties, picking their way in single file, many men sinking up to their knees.[3]

Clean rifles were passed forward to replace weapons which had become clogged with mud, and to facilitate this, armourers' positions were established well forward. The ground between the Steenbeek and the rubble of what remained of Langemarck was a water-covered swamp.

Sergeant E. Cooper of the 12th KRRC won a VC when he rushed forward to a German blockhouse and fired his revolver into the opening. He captured the garrison of 45 Germans as well as seven machine guns. Private W. Edwards of the 7th KOYLI also won a VC by attacking a blockhouse and throwing hand grenades through loopholes, capturing 36 prisoners. Their citations read:

> No. R.2794 Sjt. Edward Cooper, KRRC (Stockton).
> For most conspicuous bravery and initiative in attack. Enemy machine guns from a concrete blockhouse, 250 yards away, were holding up the advance of the battalion on his left, and were also causing heavy casualties to his own battalion. Sjt. Cooper, with four men, immediately rushed towards the blockhouse, though heavily fired on. About 100 yards distant he ordered his men to lie down and fire at the blockhouse. Finding this did not silence the machine guns, he immediately rushed forward straight at them and fired his revolver into an opening in the blockhouse. The machine guns ceased firing and the garrison surrendered. Seven machine guns and forty-five prisoners were captured in this blockhouse. By this magnificent act of courage he undoubtedly saved what might have been a serious check to the whole advance, at the same time saving a great number of lives.
> *London Gazette* (supplement) No. 30, 284, 14 September 1917

---

3   Ibid., p.199.

Private W Edwards 7th Battalion KOYLI
When all the company officers were lost, Private Edwards, without hesitation and under heavy machine-gun and rifle fire from a strong concrete fort, dashed forward at great personal risk, bombed through the loopholes, surmounted the fort and waved to his company to advance. Three officers and 30 other ranks were taken prisoner by him in the fort. Later he did most valuable work as a runner and eventually guided most of the battalion out through very difficult ground. Throughout he set a splendid example and was utterly regardless of danger.

London Gazette (supplement) 14 September 1917

Beyond the Ypres to Staden railway line as you look towards the industrial complex, men of the 29th Division advanced in a north-easterly direction (Figure 11.1). Those on the right flank attacked over ground where the industrial complex now stands. Their direction of attack took them towards where Langemarck German Cemetery is today, which you will pass shortly. Further to the left, soldiers encountered machine-gun fire from blockhouses near a position called Montmirail Farm (Figure 11.1) which inflicted heavy casualties. Montmirail Farm was approximately 0.9miles north-west of your present position, and was roughly in line with the right margin of the industrial complex. This fortified ruin was a strongpoint close to the German Third Line (Gheluvelt to Langemarck Line on British maps), which was closely linked to a stream called the Kortebeek. There is a German blockhouse one mile due north of your position, which was on the German Third Line and which you are going to visit. Its approximate direction is beyond the right margin of the industrial complex. If you look at the map (Figure 11.1), you will see that the German Third Line was partly north and partly south of the Kortebeek, which formed an integral part of the defence.

If you are in a car, go into Langemarck, passing a memorial to the 20th Division on your left. Turn left at traffic lights, go past the church and out through the village in the direction of Langemarck German Cemetery. You will cross a cobbled section of road, just after which you will see the old Ypres to Staden railway line on both sides of the road. This is very useful because it shows you of the direction of the British attack, which was to the north-east. It was also the boundary between the 20th and 29th Divisions.

If you are on a bicycle, there is a more interesting way. Go in the direction of Boesinghe for 200 yards and turn right towards the industrial complex. You reach the old railway line on your right, crossing the Steenbeek as you join the track. You are now on the front line of the 29th Division on 16 August. Go along the railway line for approximately 2,000 yards, passing Langemarck Church to your right as you negotiate a roundabout and cross the road you would have reached had you gone by car. Keep going until you have travelled 2,000 yards from your starting point. You are now on the new front line position for the right flank of the 29th Division and left flank position of the 20th Division, abutting against the German Third Line (Figure 11.1). Turn around and look back towards Langemarck German Cemetery. The restored blockhouses in the cemetery are part of the German defensive line. Go back to the road and turn right, passing the cemetery and the Visitors' Centre, and then take the first turning to the left onto a road called the Beekstraat. As you enter the Beekstraat, you cross the Kortebeek. Now look at Figure 11.1, where you can see that the British advanced to within a short distance of this stream, partly capturing the section of the German Third Line south of the Kortebeek. Now proceed along the Beekstraat. As you go, you will see the Kortebeek immediately adjacent to the left side of the road. You can imagine men of the 29th Division advancing on 16 August 1917. They would have been coming through the fields from your left from their front line at the Steenbeek, which is almost parallel to the Kortebeek, capturing German pillboxes as they made their way towards the Kortebeek and the German Third Line.

Figure 11.3 German pillbox on the Langemarck to Gheluvelt line north of the Kortebeek. The stream is a few feet behind the position from which the photograph was taken. The British crossed the Kortebeek to attack the defenders here.

Location 2: German Pillbox, German Third Line (Figure 11.3)

The pillbox you are going to visit is 300 yards ahead on the right side of the road. It was probably captured on 9 October 1917 during the Battle of Poelcappelle, about which more will be said later.

A memorial in front of the pillbox commemorates Royal Artillery and Royal Engineers attached to the 34th Division. There are defects in the pillbox and large protruding pieces of twisted metal caused by direct hits from shell fire. The damage gives cause for reflection on what it must have been like inside its confined space during a heavy bombardment. One can only wonder how many British and German soldiers were killed or wounded here. In contrast, the pillboxes in nearby Langemarck German Cemetery give the appearance of never having been subjected to an artillery barrage. They must either have been extensively repaired or reconstructed between 1931 and 1932, when the cemetery was landscaped.

Turn around and face away from the pillbox. You are looking across fields over which the 29th Division advanced on 16 August. You can see the industrial complex on the far side of the fields (Figure 11.4). Location 1 is beyond the complex, one mile due south of your position at Location 2. Montmirail Farm would have been a short distance within the field to your right.

Figure 11.4 Looking towards the tall building of the industrial complex from the pillbox on the German Third Line. On 16 August 1917, men of the 29th Division attacked from the Steenbeek on the far side of the complex towards the German Third Line here.

THE BATTLE OF POELCAPPELLE, 9 OCTOBER 1917

After the Battle of Langemarck on 16 August, no significant progress was made where you stand until 9 October, when men of the 29th Division advanced to begin the Battle of Poelcappelle. An overview of this battle is given in Chapter 16, where a glance at Figure 16.6 will show that the only significant gain on 9 October was a distance of 1.4 miles from Langemarck towards Houthulst Forest, 2.5 miles to the north east.[4] Private F.G. Dancox won a VC here, or near here, on 9 October. His citation reads:

> For most conspicuous bravery and devotion to duty in attack at Boesinghe Sector on the 9th of October, 1917. After the first objective had been captured and consolidation had been started, work was considerably hampered, and numerous casualties were caused by an enemy machine gun firing from a concrete emplacement situated on the edge of our protective barrage. Private Dancox was one of a party of about ten men detailed as moppers-up. Owing to the position of the machine gun emplacement, it was extremely difficult to work around a flank. However this man with great gallantry worked his way round through the barrage and entered the 'pill-box' from the rear, threatening the garrison with a Mills bomb. Shortly afterwards he reappeared with a machine gun under his arm, followed by about 40 enemy. The machine gun was brought back to our position by Private Dancox, and he kept it in action throughout the day. By his resolution, absolute disregard for danger and cheerful disposition, the morale of his comrades was maintained at a very high standard under extremely trying circumstances.
>
> *London Gazette*, 26 November 1917

You may now visit a third location which will contribute to your understanding of the Battle of Langemarck on 16 August, and also add to your knowledge of some aspects of the Battle of Pilckem Ridge on 31 July concerning German counter-attacks (Chapter10). It places you in the heart of the village of St Julien, captured by the British on 16 August. As you go, specific locations of importance will be pointed out. Retrace your steps past the German cemetery and proceed through Langemarck to the traffic lights. Go straight ahead along the Langemarck to Zonnebeke road. There was a German strongpoint called 'The Cockcroft' on the left side of the road 500 yards before you reach Keerselare. For the time being, note its name. You will soon reach the staggered crossroads at Keerselare. Kansas Cross, discussed in previous chapters, is 1.4 miles

---

4   Ibid., p.336.

Figure 11.5 The Poelcappelle to St Julien road at Keerselare; there were three important German strongpoints near here. The tractor is heading towards St Julien. On 20 August 1917, seven tanks moved along this road in the opposite direction to destroy these strongpoints (see text).

ahead on the road to Zonnebeke. You should turn right and go along the road towards Ypres, stopping at St Julien 0.6 miles ahead (Figure 11.5).

There were a further two German strongpoints you should note on the Poelcappelle to St Julien road. The first on the right was 'Maison du Hibou', 500 yards to the south-west of Keerselare, and the second was 'Hillock Farm', on the left side of the road 500 yards towards St Julien (Figure 11.1). Their importance will soon become apparent. The church in the centre of St Julien is 0.6 miles from the spot from which Figure 11.5 was taken. You should stop 50 yards beyond the church.

Location 3: St Julien Church (Figure 11.6)

Look towards the church. The Steenbeek passes beneath the main street of St Julien where you are standing. Inspect the map in Figure 11.1, where you will see its course. As you stand over the Steenbeek, you will remember that St Julien was lost to the Germans on 24 April 1915 during the Battle of St Julien (Chapter 7), and remained in their hands for more than two years, until the Third Battle of Ypres.

On 31 July 1917, in the Battle of Pilckem Ridge, St Julien was captured by men of the 39th Division, who would have come from behind you and

Figure 11.6 St Julien Church.

by 0800 had consolidated a position along the Steenbeek before continuing. You will see from Figure 11.7, that by 1300 they had reached the crossroads at Keerselare, having successfully crossed the Steenbeek in force. The 55th Division to their right had reached the German Third Line at Kansas Cross 1.1 miles to the east of your position. An intense German artillery bombardment and counter-attack forced the men to withdraw, and their hard won positions (on the Langemarck to Gheluvelt line) at Kansas Cross were lost, as was the entire village of St Julien. If you had been here all day on 31 July, you would have seen the 39th Division withdrawing to a position to the west of St Julien (Figure 11.7). Events in St Julien give you some idea of the impact German counter-attacks had, at least during the initial phases of the Third Battle of Ypres.

On 16 August 1917 at the Battle of Langemarck, the 48th (South Midland) Division captured St Julien, and overcame significant German opposition. For example, in one strongpoint which offered particular resistance, forty Germans and a machine-gun were captured. The advance through the village met with heavy cross-fire from ground two hundred yards beyond the Steenbeek; in other words beyond the church as you look towards it. Further attempts to advance beyond the village were met with machine gun fire, especially from the aforementioned three strong points, one on either side of the road between St Julien and Keerselare ahead of you and the third on the road between Langemarck and Keerselare.

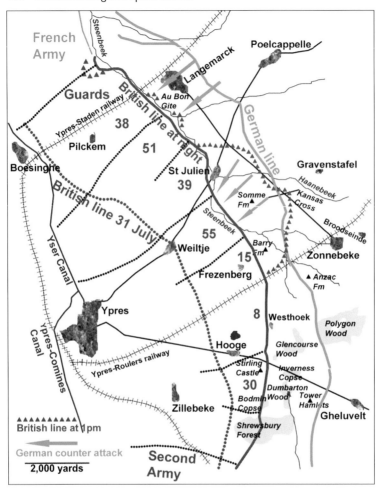

Figure 11.7 Progress of Fifth Army on 31 July 1917.

On 20 August, after a few fine days with a drying wind, seven tanks moved along the St Julien to Poelcappelle road. The tanks, protected by a smoke and shrapnel barrage, captured the three strongpoints that had held up the 48th Division on 16 August.

On 16 August, the only significant British gains were made around Langemarck, and to a lesser extent at St Julien. The British failed to make any ground on the Gheluvelt Plateau.

Chapter 12

THE THIRD BATTLE OF YPRES: BATTLES ON THE MENIN ROAD AND GHELUVELT PLATEAU, 31 JULY–20 SEPTEMBER 1917

This chapter focuses on efforts made by the British during the Third Battle of Ypres to defeat the Germans on the Menin Road and surrounding Gheluvelt Plateau. The strategic aim was to break out from the Ypres Salient and occupy the Channel ports of Ostend and Zeebrugge, thereby denying their use to the Germans as U-Boat bases. There were German defensive positions the length and breadth of the plateau, making its capture a very difficult proposition.

THE BATTLE OF PILCKEM RIDGE

The opening phase of the Third Battle of Ypres on 31 July 1917 became known as the Battle of Pilckem Ridge, and whilst the most notable success that day was on Pilckem Ridge to the north (Chapter 10), fighting took place along the entire length of the Salient. Figure 12.1 shows the projected gains around the Menin Road, where the British plan was to capture Gheluvelt Plateau and Polygon Wood before reaching final objectives at Zonnebeke and the Broodseinde Ridge beyond. Figure 12.1 also shows the divisions taking part in the southern part of the battlefield, where the ground gained was considerably less than anticipated. This chapter begins by explaining the actions of the 8th and 30th Divisions.

From the Grote Markt in Ypres, go through the Menin Gate and turn right onto the Menin Road (N8 or Meenseweg). Go straight across the roundabout at 'Hell Fire Corner' towards Hooge. Take the second turning to the right, which is Canadalaan. Go along it until you get a good view of Hooge and Hooge Crater Cemetery, and stop there. Look in the direction of the cemetery (Figure 12.2).

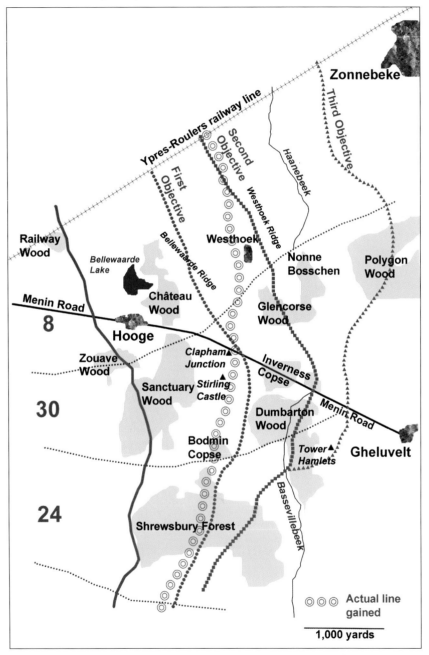

Figure 12.1 Battle of Pilckem Ridge, 31 July 1917, around the Menin Road. The ground gained, denoted by the circles, was much less than had been planned.

Location 1: Canadalaan

Figure 12.2 Looking from Canadalaan towards Hooge Crater Cemetery. Hooge is behind the cemetery and Château Wood beyond; Sanctuary Wood is to the right.

On 31 July, the British front line ran through the near side of Sanctuary Wood to your right, before passing across the fields in front of you roughly halfway between your position and the bottom of Hooge Crater Cemetery. Men of the 8th Division attacked up the hill to capture Hooge and Château Wood, behind and to the right of the village. The right flank of the 8th Division extended as far as the remnants of Zouave Wood, below the lower boundary of where Hooge Crater Cemetery is today. There it linked with men on the left flank of the 30th Division, tasked with capturing Sanctuary Wood and a strongpoint beyond it called Stirling Castle, which you will visit later.

Go further along Canadalaan until you get a view similar to that in Figure 12.3. You are closer to Sanctuary Wood and looking back towards Hooge Crater Cemetery. You can see Railway Wood on the crest of Bellewaarde Ridge. The British front line on 31 July was towards the right side of Railway Wood, and came down through the field before crossing the Menin Road and running across the fields in front of you. The Ypres to Roulers railway line was beyond Railway Wood, and was the divisional boundary with the 15th (Scottish) Division.

Figure 12.3 Railway Wood is visible on the far left, on the far side of the Menin Road and on Bellewaarde Ridge. The left flank of the 8th Division attacked Bellewaarde Ridge and Château Wood from the north side of the Menin Road, while the right flank attacked Hooge and Château Wood from the south side of the road.

After capturing Hooge and Château Wood, the 8th Division should have passed to the left of Glencorse Wood and Polygon Wood (Figure 12.1) before finishing at a position on Broodseinde Ridge beyond Zonnebeke (Figure 10.1). As you follow the men of the 8th Division, it will become clear that their progress was hindered by the failure of the adjacent 30th Division to capture its designated objectives.

Leave Canadalaan and return to the Menin Road. Turn right and go the short distance up the relatively steep incline to Hooge. Look back towards Ypres, and you will appreciate that the Germans held a very commanding position here (Figure 12.4).

Location 2: Hooge Crater Cemetery

Go into Hooge Crater Cemetery and look towards Zouave Wood, which was beyond the bottom wall of the cemetery. At 0350 on 31 July, men of the 8th Division left their trenches and many came through the cemetery behind a protective creeping barrage, before crossing the Menin Road behind you on their way to Hooge and Château Wood beyond (Figure 12.5).

Figure 12.4 From Hooge, the Germans had an excellent view of the British trenches in the flat basin round Ypres, which can be seen ahead.

Figure 12.5 Looking from Hooge Crater Cemetery in the direction of Zouave Wood. Men on the right flank of the 8th Division attacked across the ground of Hooge Crater Cemetery on 31 July 1917 on their way to Hooge.

Go to the bottom of the cemetery and look towards Hooge to appreciate the final yards covered by soldiers as they approached the village. Many must have died as they made their way up the incline of the cemetery and across the Menin Road (Figure 12.6). As they advanced through Château Wood beyond, they experienced difficulty because the creeping barrage was lost when they became ensnared in a tangle of barbed wire and tree stumps.[1]

Figure 12.6 View from the bottom of Hooge Crater Cemetery. Hooge is at the top of the incline and Château Wood is behind and to the right.

With your back to Hooge, go to the left perimeter fence and look across towards Sanctuary Wood (Figure 12.7). In the foreground is the field through which others of the 8th Division advanced on their way to Château Wood, while beyond them men of the 30th Division fought their way through Sanctuary Wood. The latter was a very difficult task, all the more so because beyond Sanctuary Wood was the German strongpoint of Stirling Castle, which had to be overcome before further progress could be made.

Stirling Castle was adjacent to Clapham Junction, which you will visit later. Men on the left flank of the 30th Division lost their way and veered off across the Menin Road into Château Wood. They thought they had entered

1   Edmonds, J.E., *History of the Great War Based on Official Documents by Direction of the Historical Section of the Committee of Imperial Defence. Military Operations. France and Belgium 1917* Volume 2 (London: HMSO, 1948), pp.156–57.

Figure 12.7 The edge of Sanctuary Wood to the left. Men of the 30th Division experienced difficulty and were held up as they took German positions within the wood. Some veered off course, went up the field in the foreground and crossed the Menin Road into Château Wood.

Glencorse Wood, which was part of their remit. The Germans poured artillery fire into Château Wood and Sanctuary Wood, inflicting many casualties and creating a complete breakdown of communications.

As you will see, the 30th Division was brought to a halt at Clapham Junction. It should have advanced to take Glencorse Wood, Nonne Bosschen and Polygon Wood, allowing the 8th Division to advance alongside it towards Zonnebeke, but this proved to be impossible. Figure 12.1 will make this clear.

Leave the cemetery and proceed to the next location. For the time being, attention will focus on the 8th Division, and the fortunes of the 30th Division at Clapham Junction will be dealt with later. Turn left and go down the Menin Road, passing Canadalaan. Go along a minor road opposite it called Begijnenbosstraat. A signpost at the bottom directs you to the Royal Engineers Grave. This road was called Cambridge Road during the war. Stop after a short distance.

Location 3: Cambridge Road

Figure 12.8 The farm on the left was called Witte Poort. It played an important role in the Second Battle of Ypres (Chapter 9). Railway Wood is beyond the farm. The Royal Engineers Grave is in front of the trees at the top of the ridge to the right.

Figure 12.9 The British front line was a short distance into the field in front of the camera. Hooge and Château Wood are visible on the skyline in the centre. Sanctuary Wood is on the far right.

Look straight up the road in the direction of Railway Wood, which you can see beyond Witte Poort Farm on the left (Figure 12.8). The British front line was towards the right of Railway Wood, and continued beyond the far side of the wood to the divisional boundary with the 15th (Scottish) Division at the Ypres to Roulers railway line (Figure 12.1). Look to your right (Figure 12.9). The British front line was within the field in front of you. You can see the ground to be attacked at Hooge, Château Wood and Sanctuary Wood.

Go round Railway Wood, looking across towards the Royal Engineers Grave as you go. Beyond the trees surrounding the RE Grave, and not visible from where you stand, is Bellewaarde Farm. Château Wood is just visible to the far right (Figure 12.10).

Figure 12.10 The Royal Engineer Grave is visible in front of the trees in the foreground. Bellewaarde Farm is over the rise immediately beyond and is out of sight. Château Wood is just visible beyond and to the right of the Cross of Sacrifice of the RE Grave.

The minor road skirting round Railway Wood is called Oude Kortrijkstraat. Follow this road until you are level with Bellewaarde Farm, captured by men of the 8th Division. Figure 12.11 is a photograph of the farm taken from three-quarters of a mile away near Westhoek and will help you to orientate yourself.

Figure 12.11 Bellewaarde Farm with Château Wood beyond. The photograph was taken from three-quarters of a mile away on Westhoek Ridge. Men of the 8th Division emerging from Château Wood would have been coming towards the direction from which the photograph was taken.

Location 4: Close to Bellewaarde Farm

You are standing less than 200 yards from Bellewaarde Farm. It is to your right and it has just come clearly into view after you have skirted round Railway Wood, leaving the trees surrounding the Royal Engineers Grave behind you. Château Wood is ahead of you to your right. Men on the left flank of the 8th Division would have been passing your position, moving across the ground seen in Figure 12.11. Some would have come through Bellewaarde Farm, capturing it on their way. Others to their right would have made their way through the trees of Château Wood. They would all have been moving across the fields in the general direction from which Figure 12.11 was taken near the top of Westhoek Ridge (see below). Their advance was taking them towards their next objective, the village of Westhoek, which is behind the camera.

Figure 12.12 puts you back in your actual position. Bellewaarde Farm is out of the photograph to the right. Château Wood is ahead on the right. Glencorse Wood is in the distance on the left. Château Wood extended to the Menin Road, and while men on the left flank of the 8th Division captured the part of the wood you see here, those on the right flank attacked and captured the remainder of the wood from the Menin Road, having first taken Hooge. The

Figure 12.12 Close to Bellewaarde Farm. Château Wood is in the foreground to the right; Lake Wood surrounds Bellewaarde Lake and is continuous with Château Wood. Glencorse Wood is in the distance to the left of the photograph.

advance should then have taken the 8th Division past the left side of Glencorse Wood and Polygon Wood beyond it towards Zonnebeke and Broodseinde (Figure 12.1). The 30th Division should have captured Glencorse Wood and Polygon Wood, but failed to do so. As a result, men of the 8th Division encountered heavy machine-gun fire from intact German machine-gun positions in Glencorse Wood and from the village of Westhoek ahead, and were forced to take up position in front of the village, having achieved as much as they could.

Location 5: Westhoek

Leave Bellewaarde Farm and continue on the Oude Kortrijkstraat till you reach a fork in the road, where there is a memorial to the Princess Patricia's Canadian Light Infantry (Chapter 8). Take the left fork, the Princess Patriciastraat, which leads to a crossroads at Westhoek. Stop when you reach the upward incline to the village and look ahead (Figure 12.13). You are standing in the approximate position reached by the 8th Division on 31 July. They could make no further progress because the 30th Division had failed to take its objectives. You will soon make for the Menin Road at Clapham Junction to understand why.

Figure 12.13 Westhoek village on Westhoek Ridge. Men of the 8th Division had to halt near the front of the village.

Go to Westhoek and cross the Frezenbergstraat at a crossroads. Stop when you reach the road on the other side. Look ahead and you will see Zonnebeke, with Broodseinde Ridge beyond. These were the projected final objectives for the 8th Division on 31 July (Figures 10.1 and 12.14).

Return to the Frezenbergstraat and turn left for about 300 yards, until you reach another crossroads. Turn left, stand on the road and look ahead towards Zonnebeke. On 20 September 1917, during the Battle of the Menin Road, which was the third phase of the Third Battle of Ypres (see below), the Australian 1st and 2nd Divisions attacked German positions to the north of the Menin Road. The Australian 2nd Division advanced on either side of the road you are standing on for a distance of approximately 1,200 yards, in a corridor between Polygon Wood and Zonnebeke (Figure 12.15). The Australian action will be explained fully later in the chapter, but it is worth noting this as you pass.

Go back to the Frezenbergstraat and turn left. You will see Glencorse Wood to your left. When you reach a road junction, turn right to reach the Menin Road, where you should turn left. You will see the 18th Division Memorial at Clapham Junction (Figure 12.16).

Figure 12.14 The downward slope of the Westhoek Ridge, taken from the roadway. Zonnebeke Church is visible to the right of the central telegraph pole; Broodseinde Ridge is beyond. The 8th Division should have advanced to Zonnebeke on 31 July 1917.

Figure 12.15 The Australian 2nd Division advanced on either side of this road, which leads towards Zonnebeke, on 20 September 1917. Polygon Wood is on the far right. Zonnebeke Church can just be seen close to the left side of the photograph.

Location 5: Clapham Junction

Figure 12.16 The 18th Division Memorial at Clapham Junction serves as a guide to Stirling Castle, which was within the wooded area to the right.

Stand opposite the memorial (Figure 12.16). There is a wood to the right, within which was the fortified position called Stirling Castle. After emerging from Sanctuary Wood, men of the 30th Division encountered fierce resistance from Stirling Castle, which they eventually captured at heavy cost. Look along the Menin Road in the direction of Gheluvelt (Figure 12.17). There was a huge pillbox a short distance ahead which commanded the main approach route along the Menin Road from Hooge. Efforts to capture it by the 30th Division were in vain. The pillbox contained an anti-tank gun which destroyed no fewer than 17 tanks taking part in the battle. This area would become known as the tank graveyard. The *Official History of the Great War* states:

> The failure of the 30th Division to capture the strongpoint east of Clapham Junction was most unfortunate. Approaching tanks had been knocked out one after another by an anti-tank gun within it. Seventeen derelict tanks soon dotted the ground in this area.[2]

2   Ibid., p.157.

The 30th Division attack finished here and Glencorse Wood remained in German hands. This stopped any further advance of the 8th Division, which met with stiff resistance from German positions in Westhoek. As you stand at Clapham Junction, there are three further attacks to consider before you move on. The first was on 10 August and resulted in the capture of Westhoek. The second on 16 August became known as the Battle of Langemarck (Chapter 11). The third on 20 September was the Battle of the Menin Road.

ATTACK ON 10 AUGUST 1917

A further attempt to take more of the Gheluvelt Plateau was made on 10 August by the 18th Division, which was instructed to advance 800 yards and capture Glencorse Wood on the north side of the Menin Road and Inverness Copse at the approximate position of the wooded areas ahead of you on both sides of the Menin Road. The 25th Division was given the job of capturing Westhoek, which it carried out successfully.

Inverness Copse was entered, but heavy machine-gun fire prevented any further progress by the 18th Division up the Menin Road. The 7th Queen's, one of the battalions in the division, came under intense fire:

Figure 12.17 Looking up Menin Road from Clapham Junction towards Inverness Copse, from which heavy fire impeded the progress of 18th Division on 10 August 1917. Inverness Copse was on either side of the Menin Road. That part on the south (right) side of the road became continuous with Dumbarton Wood.

Held up at the start by machine-gun fire from an intact strongpoint at the south-western corner of the copse, it could make no further progress. The men had been seen by German sentries crossing the crest of the Stirling Castle Ridge in bright moonlight, about 1.30 am, to their starting line. They suffered heavy losses, including most of their officers, from artillery and machine-gun fire before zero hour. Threatened with envelopment, the Queen's fell back. Renewed efforts to advance were in vain.[3]

Soon after 1700, the Germans launched a counter-attack from Inverness Copse, driving the British back to their starting line near Clapham Junction.

BATTLE OF LANGEMARCK, 16 AUGUST 1917

The Battle of Langemarck was the second phase of the Third Battle of Ypres While the battle was conducted over the length of the Ypres Salient, its only impact was near the villages of Langemarck and St Julien (Chapter 11). No progress was made around the Menin Road.

BATTLE OF THE MENIN ROAD

This was the third phase of the Third Battle of Ypres. Figure 12.18 shows the divisions involved in this attack. The main thrust was made by the 1st and 2nd Australian Divisions fighting to the north of the Menin Road. The 23rd and 41st Divisions fought on this, the south side of the Menin Road. The 23rd Division attacked from close to your position at the 18th Division Memorial and captured Inverness Copse ahead of you. Four tanks providing assistance were unable to negotiate the broken ground ahead.

The 41st Division reached the base of a fortified position called the Tower Hamlets Spur, approximately half a mile beyond your present position to the right of the road as you look towards Gheluvelt. Gheluvelt was not reached, and would only be recaptured in late September 1918; almost four years after the British were forced out of the village on 31 October 1914.

Leave Clapham Junction to follow the Australian 1st and 2nd Divisions. Go down the Menin Road towards Ypres for 50 yards and turn right onto the Oude Kortrijkstraat. Continue until you reach open ground with farm buildings to your left and a wooded area ahead (Figure 12.19). Stop when you get a clear view.

---

3   Ibid., p.187.

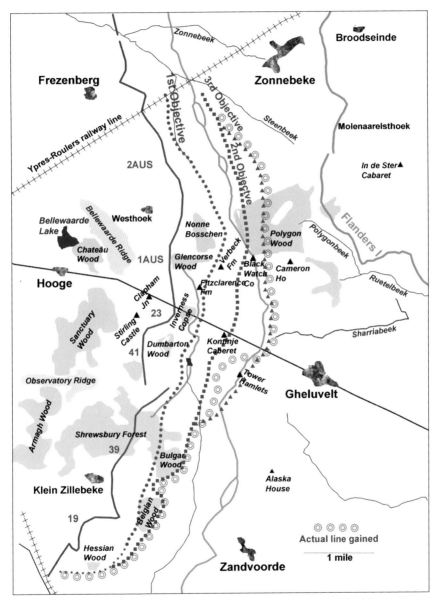

Figure 12.18 The Battle of the Menin Road; the Australian 1st and 2nd Divisions formed the spearhead of the attack.

Location 6: Looking towards Glencorse Wood

Figure 12.19 Glencorse Wood, ahead to the left of the road, was captured by the Australian 1st Division on 20 September 1917. Westhoek is on the ridge to the far left.

Glencorse Wood was full of water-filled shell craters and broken tree trunks. It was attacked and occupied on 10 August by the 18th Division, but was easier to reach than to hold. The Germans bombarded the line between Stirling Castle and Westhoek, boxing in the assaulting battalions of the 18th Division and cutting them off from reinforcements and supplies. German counter-attacks forced the evacuation of Glencorse Wood, but Westhoek was retained by the 25th Division. No progress was made during the Battle of Langemarck, and it was not until 20 September that the Australian 1st Division recaptured Glencorse Wood. Australians would have been moving in the same direction as you towards their first objective. The ground conditions had improved because the weather during the first three weeks of September had been good. Massive artillery support was provided and advancing soldiers were screened to a depth of 1,000 yards. Extensive counter-battery preparations had also been made.[4]

4   Ibid., p.253.

THE ADVANCE OF THE 1ST AND 2ND AUSTRALIAN DIVISIONS

The two Australians divisions advanced over a 2,000-yard front north of the Menin Road and captured the Third German Line (Figure 12.18). The 1st Australian Division captured Glencorse Wood in spite of stiff German opposition emanating from concrete shelters at the northern end of the wood which caused many casualties:

> Machine-gun fire from the roof of one of these shelters swept and temporarily checked the advance, with many casualties, until support groups, moving in close reserve, quickly surrounded the area and, after a savage encounter, numbers of Germans who emerged from the shelters were killed or taken prisoner.[5]

The 1st Division went on to capture Nonne Bosschen beyond (Figure 12.1). Nonne Bosschen was a wasteland of water-filled shell holes, which Australians crossed by keeping to the lips of water-filled craters. They finally reached Black Watch Corner and the western margin of Polygon Wood. Meanwhile, the right flank of the Australian 1st Division made good progress along the Menin Road (Figure 12.18).

Men of the Australian 2nd Division were on the left flank of the 1st Division. They advanced on both sides of the Westhoek-Zonnebeke road, as already explained when you passed through Westhoek on your way to Clapham Junction. The 1st Australian Division advanced to Polygon Wood and the 2nd Division kept in line with it (Figure 12.18).

Go past Glencorse Wood and Nonne Bosschen. You will soon reach a bridge over the motorway and see Polygon Wood beyond. Cross the bridge and stop at Black Watch Corner (Figure 12.20).

Location 7: Black Watch Corner

Look beyond the memorial along the southern margin of Polygon Wood. Black Watch Corner was captured by the Australian 1st Division, along with a group of German pillboxes south of the corner in the field to the right. There was a strongpoint called Cameron House, which inflicted casualties on the Australians.[6] Cameron House was within the field ahead and was roughly level with the mid-point of the southern margin of Polygon Wood.

---

5 Ibid., p.257.
6 Prior, R., and Wilson, T., *Passchendaele, The Untold Story* (New Haven: Yale University Press, 2002), p.119.

Figure 12.20 Black Watch Corner was captured by men of the Australian 1st Division. The southern margin of the wood is shown here (see text and Figure 12.18).

Figure 12.21 The western margin of Polygon Wood, within which was the German Third Line. The cyclist in the foreground is proceeding towards Black Watch Corner.

The captured pillboxes were on the German Third Line as it continued beyond the western margin of Polygon Wood (Figures 12.18 and 12.21). The *Official History of the Great War* states:

> The objective along the western edge of Polygon Wood, recognisable only by a thin growth of saplings among the shell craters was gained, the pillboxes and concrete shelters in the Third Line being rushed or surrounded.[7]

Retrace your steps and cross the motorway. Take the first turning to the right along Nonnebossenstraat, going through Nonne Bosschen, captured by the Australian 1st Division. Men would have been moving left to right as you make your way along this road. Once clear of Nonne Bosschen, you are on ground taken by the Australian 2nd Division, as they too advanced from left to right. Keep going until you reach the Grote Mollenstraat, where you should turn left. Men from the Australian 2nd Division attacked on either side of this road in the direction of Zonnebeke, and would have been coming directly towards you. Keep going, and you will soon reach the position near the top of Westhoek Ridge from which Figure 12.15 was taken. Stop and turn around.

Location 8: Westhoek Ridge looking towards Zonnebeke and Polygon Wood

As you look down the road towards Zonnebeke, you are looking at the ground over which Australians of the 2nd Division advanced on 20 September until they were level with the Australian 1st Division within the western margin of Polygon Wood. The remaining part of the wood was still in German hands after completion of the fighting on that day. German counter-attacks were launched between 1200 and 1900 on 20 September, but were unsuccessful, thanks to strong Australian artillery support. One Australian officer said that his men simply sat back and laughed when they saw the opportunity they had been praying for (to kill counter-attacking Germans) snatched away at the last minute by the guns; they knew the Germans would be unable to pass through such a barrage, and in fact no further sign of movement was seen that evening.[8] While this artillery support was certainly welcome to these Australian soldiers, it also implied that their own artillery had not been required to advance, because the gains had been relatively small. German gun positions

---

7   Edmonds, J.E., *History of the Great War Based on Official Documents by Direction of the Historical Section of the Committee of Imperial Defence. Military Operations. France and Belgium 1917* Volume 2 (London: HMSO, 1948), p.257.
8   Ibid., p.274.

had not been over-run and large numbers of prisoners had not been taken. The two Australian divisions sustained many casualties on 20 September, numbering 947 killed and 3,283 wounded, of whom 114 later died.[9] This makes the following statement from the *Official Australian History* (Vol. IV, p.761), and reproduced in *The Official Australian Medical History of the War*, somewhat difficult to comprehend:

> The Battle of Menin Road is easily described inasmuch as it went almost precisely in accordance with plan. The advancing barrage won the ground; the infantry merely occupied it.[10]

BATTLE POLYGON WOOD, 26 SEPTEMBER 1917

It is convenient to consider the attack made by the 4th Australian Division on 26 September at this point; otherwise it would mean returning to this location unnecessarily at a later time. You are referred to Chapter 13 for a full explanation of the Battle of Polygon Wood on 26 September. As you look in the direction of Zonnebeke and Polygon Wood, the 2nd Australian Division attack on 20 September took its front line approximately a mile forward and level with the 1st Division's position within Polygon Wood. The 4th Australian Division attack on 26 September continued along the same corridor, between Zonnebeke on the left and Polygon Wood on the right (Figure 12.15). The 4th Division captured part of the village of Zonnebeke, while the 5th Division advanced through Polygon Wood to its east side, capturing the Flandern I Line. A full explanation of this is given in Chapter 13.

9   Butler, A.G., *Official History of the Australian Army Medical Services, 1914–1918 Volume II – The Western Front* (Canberra: Australian War Memorial, 1940), pp.204–05.
10   Ibid., p.204.

Chapter 13

THE THIRD BATTLE OF YPRES: BATTLE OF POLYGON WOOD, 26 SEPTEMBER 1917

This chapter deals with the Battle of Polygon Wood on 26 September 1917. Chapter 12 explains how the Australian 1st and 2nd Divisions achieved their objectives during the Battle of the Menin Road on 20 September, when the 1st Division captured that part of the German Third Line which ran from north to south within the western side of Polygon Wood, through Black Watch Corner at the south-west corner of the wood and on to the Menin Road between Hooge and Gheluvelt, approximately half a mile from the latter (Figure 13.1).

Although the western part of Polygon Wood was captured, the eastern part remained in German hands. The Battle of Polygon Wood resulted in the complete capture of the wood and that part of the Flandern I Line which ran along its eastern margin (Figure 13.2). The Australian 5th and 4th Divisions replaced the 1st and 2nd Divisions respectively to carry out the attack on 26 September.

Location 1: Opposite Black Watch Corner

If you are coming from Ypres, take the Menin Road (N8 or Meenseweg) at 'Hell Fire Corner' towards Menin, and just before Clapham Junction turn left onto the Oude Kortrijkstraat, passing Glencorse Wood and Nonne Bosschen. Just before you reach a bridge which crosses the motorway, turn sharp right along a narrow road which runs parallel to, and close to, the motorway for the first few hundred yards. Stop after 200 yards and look towards Black Watch Corner, which is at the south-west corner of Polygon Wood on the far side of the motorway (Figure 13.3).

You can see the west margin of Polygon Wood to the left of Black Watch Corner, and the south margin to the right. The German Third Line was within the west side of the wood. Look straight across the motorway. You are facing towards the German Third Line as it continued in a southerly direction to the Menin Road less than three-quarters of a mile away (Figure 13.1). The ruins

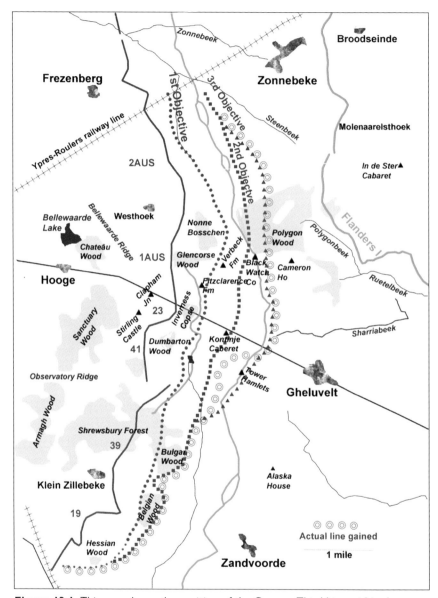

Figure 13.1 This map shows the position of the German Third Line within the western edge of Polygon Wood and the gains made on 20 September 1917 during the Battle of the Menin Road.

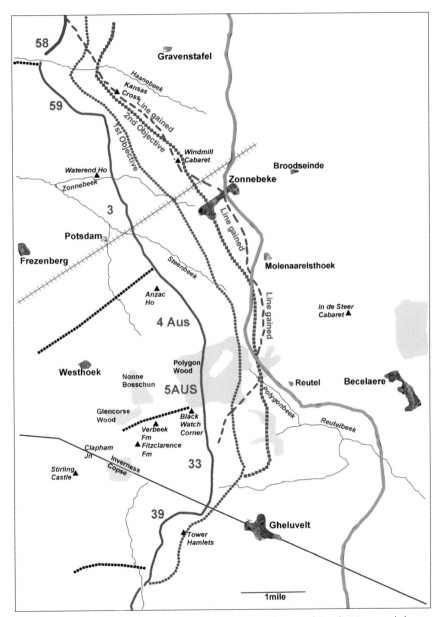

Figure 13.2 The Battle of Polygon Wood, showing the attacking divisions and the ground gained.

Figure 13.3 Looking towards Black Watch Corner in the centre of the photograph at the south-west corner of Polygon Wood. To the right is the south margin of the wood and to the left is the western edge which contained the heavily fortified Third German Line, which passed approximately in a north-south direction.

of pillboxes would have been scattered along and behind that line. If you continue along the minor road you are on, it takes you south onto the Menin Road a short distance from Gheluvelt, following roughly the direction of the German Third Line.

The Germans launched a determined counter-attack on 25 September between Polygon Wood and the Menin Road, in an attempt to recapture their Third Line. The British 33rd Division was moving into position on the right flank of the Australian 5th Division, which had replaced its 1st Division within Polygon Wood. Men of the 33rd Division would have been taking their places in the front line across from where you stand in preparation for the battle next day (Figure 13.2). Their job was to advance outside and parallel to the south margin of Polygon Wood, keeping pace with men of the Australian 5th Division who would advance within it, and whose task it was to capture the remainder of Polygon Wood and the German Flandern I Line beyond, approximately 0.9 miles away. The 33rd Division was subjected to a heavy artillery bombardment during this counter-attack. At 0530 on 25 September, large numbers of Germans approached between the south margin of the wood and the Menin Road, moving towards you in a westerly direction. Men of the Australian 5th Division within Polygon Wood formed a protective flank along the part of the wood they held to prevent the Germans penetrating their positions. Fortunately for the 33rd Division, the Australians in Polygon Wood poured machine-gun and mortar fire onto the advancing Germans, forcing them to take cover. Owing to disruption in the preparations of the 33rd Division caused by the fighting on 25 September, General Plumer restricted its participation in the forthcoming battle to a single brigade (98th) instead of two. Leave your position and cross the motorway by the bridge. Stop at Black Watch Corner and Memorial (Figure 13.4).

Location 2: Black Watch Corner

The main thrust of the attack on 26 September was made by the 4th and 5th Australian Divisions of I Anzac Corps. The 5th Division captured the remainder of Polygon Wood, while the 4th Division captured part of Zonnebeke 1.5 miles north of your position. The 4th Division attack stopped just short of the Third German Line which ran through the village (Figure 13.2). The Australian 4th Division was supported on its left by the British 3rd Division, which contributed to the partial capture of Zonnebeke, while next to the 3rd Division, the 59th Division captured and held the German strongpoint at Kansas Cross, a position taken and lost on 31 July 1917. You are referred to Chapters 7 and 11 if you have not yet come across Kansas Cross, important because the German Third Line ran through it.

Figure 13.4 Men of the Australian 5th Division formed a protective flank within the south margin of Polygon Wood on 25 September 1917 (see text) and came to the assistance of the weakened 33rd Division the following day.

As you look along the south margin of Polygon Wood (Figure 13.4), the depleted 33rd Division was unable to provide the Australian 5th Division with sufficient support as men advanced away from you through the field adjacent to the wood. Some Australians came to their assistance by emerging from the wood and capturing ground which should have been taken by the 33rd Division.

Leave Black Watch Corner and go along the west side of Polygon Wood. The captured German Third Line was within the trees to your right and was a good base for the Australian 5th Division to make preparations for the forthcoming attack. Australian front-line trenches were approximately 300 yards in front of the German Third Line (Figure 13.2).

At 0550 on 26 September, men advanced behind five belts of an artillery barrage which was 1,000 yards deep. You can imagine the sights and sounds coming from the wood to your right. It is often thought that soldiers fought up to their knees in mud for the entire Third Battle of Ypres. In fact it had not rained for many days and mud had dried, leaving the ground bone hard, as the following description from the *Official History of the Great War* conveys:

The ground was so powdery dry that the bursts of the high explosive shell raised a dense wall of dust and smoke, and a morning mist adding to the obscurity, direction had to be kept by compass bearing; but so closely did Australians follow the dust cloud that most of the German machine-gun detachments were rushed or out-flanked before they could fire a shot. Bursts of fire from a few isolated places along the 2,000 yard frontage, however, caused considerable casualties before these centres of resistance could be quelled.[1]

When you reach the end of the west margin of Polygon Wood, turn right onto the Lange Dreve, where the northern edge of the wood is to your right. Continue until you reach the entrance to Butte Military Cemetery, which is within Polygon Wood. Go into the cemetery. You will see a 5th Australian Division Memorial ahead of you (Figure 13.5). Each of the five Australian divisions has a memorial at a place of special significance for that division. The other four are in France as follows: 1st Division Memorial at Pozières, 2nd Division Memorial at Mont St Quentin, 3rd Division Memorial at Sailly-le-Sec and 4th Division Memorial at Bellenglise.

---

1   Edmonds, J.E., *History of the Great War Based on Official Documents by Direction of the Historical Section of the Committee of Imperial Defence. Military Operations. France and Belgium 1917* Volume 2 (London: HMSO, 1948), p.284.

Figure 13.5 The Australian 5th Division Memorial on the Butte, which was a rifle range for the Belgian Army before the outbreak of the Great War. There were German dugouts on the left side of the Butte, where soldiers sheltering would have been protected from incoming Australian artillery fire.

Location 3: Australian Memorial, Butte Military Cemetery

Go to the far end of the cemetery, where there is a New Zealand Memorial to the Missing. Look back towards the Butte (Figure 13.6). The Australian 5th Division captured the Butte, which had been turned into an observation position by the Germans. The *Official History of the Great War* described what happened.

> It had captured in its stride the important German observation station on the Butte in Polygon Wood, some of the garrison running away, and about sixty surrendering from the dugouts in its back slope.[2]

The trees had been completely destroyed by 26 September, and consequently the Butte was an important observation point from which the Germans could see everything that was going on about them. You can imagine Australian soldiers attacking towards the Butte behind a protective barrage as they clambered through the twisted remnants of the wood and across the ground which now houses the cemetery.

---

2 Ibid., p.285.

Figure 13.6 Looking towards the Butte from the far end of Butte Military Cemetery. From the Butte, the German defenders would have had a very good view of the approaching Australian Division.

Having captured the Butte, the Australians advanced over it and around it to the east side of Polygon Wood a very short distance ahead, and which you can see beyond the Butte. They were subjected to machine-gun fire from the Flandern I Line just beyond the trees. The German defenders, however, had been subjected to the intense Australian artillery barrage and were unable to prevent the Australian infantry from taking this position (Figure 13.2). Leave the cemetery and turn right. The road leads round to the east side of the wood. A moderately steep hill and a Z-bend lead onto the Spilsstraat. Go up it for 100 yards or so, and then turn around and look back towards the Butte and Polygon Wood (Figure 13.7).

Location 4: Looking towards east side of Polygon Wood

You are now looking towards the east side of the wood, within which you can see the 5th Australian Division Memorial. The Flandern I Line passed north to south close to its margin, and you have crossed it to reach your present position. You can easily imagine the fighting here as the Australian soldiers smashed through, overwhelming the German defenders. The *Official History of the Great War* states:

Figure 13.7 Looking towards the east side of Polygon Wood; the Flandern I Line was close to, and parallel to, the wood. The Australian 5th Division Memorial can be seen within the wood.

The backbone of the new line consolidated by the division was formed by the captured German shelters of the Flanders I Line, east of Polygon Wood.[3]

AUSTRALIAN 4TH DIVISION ATTACK ON 26 SEPTEMBER 1917

The Australian 4th Division was to the left of the Australian 5th Division (the right as you look) and attacked towards Zonnebeke, which you can see approximately 0.9 miles to your north-west. You can see open ground between Polygon Wood and Zonnebeke, over which the Australians attacked. Further explanation of the 4th Division attack is given in Chapter 12, to which you are referred.

Following the battle, the Germans launched a counter-attack, which failed, just as it had on 20 September. An effective protective barrage came down very quickly, so that the counter-attack did not materialise and German losses were very heavy. The Australian 4th and 5th Divisions sustained 1,529 and 3,723 casualties respectively, while the adjacent British 3rd Division lost 4,032 killed, wounded and missing.

---

3   Ibid., p.285.

Chapter 14

THE THIRD BATTLE OF YPRES: BATTLE OF BROODSEINDE, 4 OCTOBER 1917

The Battle of Broodseinde on 4 October 1917 was fought between Langemarck in the north and the Menin Road in the south (Figure 14.1). This chapter sets out to explain how men from the Australian 1st and 2nd Divisions and British 7th Division recaptured the high ground of the Broodseinde Ridge to the east of Zonnebeke, from which the British had been forced to withdraw in May 1915 during the Second Battle of Ypres (Chapter 7). The Battle of Broodseinde is also dealt with in Chapters 11, 15 and 16, where engagements of those divisions fighting further north are explained.

Broodseinde Ridge is on the perimeter of the Ypres Salient, and is continuous with Passchendaele Ridge to the north and Gheluvelt Plateau to the south. It overlooks Ypres, which lies within a flat basin to the west (Figure 14.2). From Broodseinde Ridge on a clear day, good views may be had of Ypres six miles away.

Your starting point is the same as the final location for the Battle of Polygon Wood (Chapter 13). If you are making a specific visit to Broodseinde Ridge, then here are directions how to get here. Take the Menin Road (N8 or Meenseweg) at 'Hell Fire Corner' towards Menin, and just before Clapham Junction turn left onto the Oude Kortrijkstraat, passing Glencorse Wood and Nonne Bosschen. Cross the motorway, turn left along the western edge of Polygon Wood, then right along the north margin. You will pass Polygon Wood Cemetery on your left before turning a corner and going up an incline. Stop 100 yards after a sharp Z bend and turn around, looking back towards the Australian 5th Division Memorial within Polygon Wood (Figure 14.3).

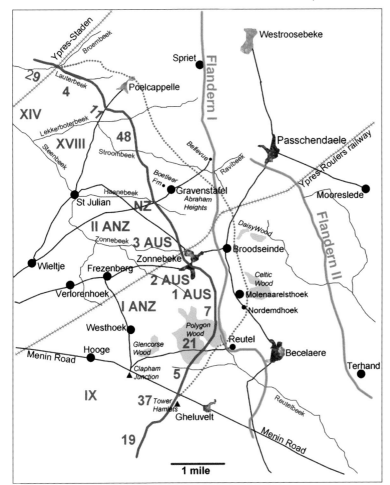

Figure 14.1 Battle of Broodseinde, 4 October 1917. The dotted line denotes ground gained.

Location 1: The German Flandern I Line at Polygon Wood

You are standing on a road called the Spilstraat between Polygon Wood and the village of Molenaarelsthoek, which is behind you and to your right. The road leads to a crossroads with the Beselarestraat, the main road between Passchendaele and Becelare. Nordemdhoek was a hamlet on the ridge behind you, south of Molenaarelsthoek. You will not find it on present day maps. The 5th Australian Division Memorial is ahead on the Butte in Polygon Wood (Chapter 13).

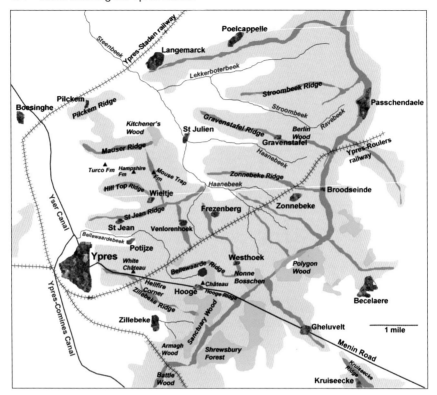

Figure 14.2 Relief map of the Ypres Salient.

On 26 September 1917, at the Battle of Polygon Wood, Australians of the 5th Division captured Polygon Wood and part of the German Flandern 1 Line along the east side of the wood in front of you, while the Australian 4th Division to your right and British 3rd Division further to your right captured much of Zonnebeke (Chapter 13) one mile away. If you look right you can see Zonnebeke (Figure 14.4).

Australians spearheaded the attack at the Battle of Broodseinde on 4 October, when they completed the capture of Zonnebeke and occupied Broodseinde Ridge in the fifth phase of the Third Battle of Ypres. As you look towards the Butte (Figure 14.3), the 2nd Gordon Highlanders of the 7th Division occupied trenches in front of you that day approximately midway between your position and the Butte. The 1st Australian Division was on their left (your right). According to P.D. Thomson, it was by mutual request that

Figure 14.3 Looking towards the position of the German Flandern I Line on the east side of Polygon Wood. The Australian 5th Division Memorial is on the Butte within the trees straight ahead. The Butte became Regimental HQ for the 2nd Battalion Gordon Highlanders on 4 October 1917.

Figure 14.4 Looking towards Zonnebeke from Location I (see text).

the Gordon Highlanders fought side-by-side with the Australians.[1] Thomson described the attack:

> After enduring a heavy enemy bombardment, at zero [hour] the 2nd Gordons swept forward with the main assault, reaching their first objective by 7am. At 7.50, they advanced again under the creeping barrage, and drove everything before them, inflicting heavy losses on the enemy. Strong-points and pill-boxes gave little trouble, and the final objective on the ridge at Nordemdhoek was under their feet by 9am.[2]

The regimental diary of the 2nd Battalion Gordon Highlanders makes it clear that the Gordon Highlanders were in the second attacking wave:

> 4th October 1917
> At 3am the enemy shelled the forming up line and Companies were ordered to close on the 8th Devon Rgt if necessary. At 4:30 am the enemy began an intense fire which was answered by our artillery. At 6am the advance began behind a barrage which started 200 yards in front of the 8th Devon Rgt, who advanced up and got underneath it. The Battalion also advanced till the front-line got 400 yards beyond our front-tape. The Officers had great difficulty in preventing the men from moving forward with the 8th Devon Rgt. It was ultimately ascertained that a number of our men assaulted the 1st Objective with the Devons. About 7am the 1st Objective was taken and at 7:50am the Battalion moved forward to get close up to the barrage which had halted 200 yards in front of the 1st Objective. At 8:10am the barrage again moved forward, closely followed by the Battalion driving everything before it, inflicting very heavy casualties on the enemy. Strong points and concrete emplacements gave very little trouble and were easily mopped-up. The final objective 'On the RIDGE OF NORDEMDHOEK' was reached at 9am, with only 40 casualties. Reorganising and consolidating commenced at once.[3]

On their way, they captured 70 prisoners and three machine guns, as well as killing an estimated 130 of the enemy. Once they reached Nordemdhoek, they were subjected to intense German artillery fire:

---

1   Thomson, P.D., *The Gordon Highlanders* (Devonport: Swiss and Co. Military Printers, 1921), pp.120–21.
2   Ibid.
3   War Diary 2nd Battalion Gordon Highlanders, Gordon Highlanders Museum.

From this time the enemy commenced to shell heavily all along the line causing our casualties to increase considerably, the Battalion remained in the position captured and dealt with any of the enemy that showed themselves. At 7pm Battalion Head Quarters moved forward from the Butte and occupied a concrete pill box near the line of the 1st Objective. Rations were bought up around midnight under great difficulties; a number of the carrying part became casualties including three of the Coy ... Sergts.[4]

Over the next two days, the Gordon Highlanders had to withstand and beat off two German counter-attacks as they held onto their position. They did so without fresh water and with scanty rations, as these could not be brought up through furious shellfire:

6th October
The enemy continued shelling our line all day and I regret to say did much damage to our men. They made one or two attempts to counter attack which were stopped by our artillery fire, machine gun and rifle fire. In the distance Capt. JS Nobbie and 2nd Lt. AM Ogilvie were killed by a shell. The same shell killed the Coy Regt. Major of 'G' Company and wounded all the Company orderlies. At 7pm orders were received that the 12th Australian Battalion would take over part of our line, as during the advance the whole line had swerved slightly to the left and we had encroached on Australian territory. This relief was carried out; B & G Companies were withdrawn to a position in our front line prior to the attack. Battalion headquarters returned to the BUTTE. The rations were again brought up under great difficulties, no water arrived owing to the heavy hostile artillery fire, and the impossible task of bringing pack animals over the shell pitted country.[5]

They were finally relieved on the night of 7 October after four days of bitter fighting. Their casualties were 12 officers and 312 other ranks.[6]

The medical officer who dealt with the many of the casualties was Major D.W. Pailthorpe, whose Regimental Aid Post was a dugout in the far side of the Butte, which you see in front of you, and which was relatively sheltered from incoming German shell fire. Pailthorpe wrote:

4   Ibid.
5   Ibid.
6   Thomson, op.cit., pp.120–21.

October 4th

Many R.A.M.C. bearers with their loads were killed on the way down the duck board track where the shelling at times was more intense than further forward. The Gordons attacked at about 8a.m. and the attack was a success, only about 40 casualties occurring – I went up to see the position and found our front posts – a series of shell holes – I saw Dobbie sitting with his Coy. Sergeant Major and an orderly in a small shelter which had some elephant iron but faced the wrong way – he asked me what I thought of it – I looked round and could not see anything better so said he might as well stay there – I wish I had advised him to be content with a shell hole. Unfortunately some of our men started moving about as it was very quiet – it was diffi-cult to make men understand the necessity for no movement but the Australians who were on our left understood it – a Bosche aeroplane came over flying low and our men in shell holes looked up at it – the Australians lay as if they were dead. Soon afterwards the Bosche having learnt what he wanted to know, i.e., where our men were and his own – started shelling very heavily and there were many casualties amongst the Gordons – by now the drizzle which had started at dawn had turned to heavy rain and the whole area grew more waterlogged than before. We had some bearers hit and that reduced the number of our squads. All that day we kept having steady casualties and by night owing to the R.A.M.C. casualties many of them still remained at the Butte – I started sending some of my bearers back on the Hooge track to help the R.A.M.C. whose job was nigh hopeless.[7]

He continued:

October 5th

At dawn a party of Manchester Pioneers were sent up from Brigade to assist in the removal of casualties – there were about 60 men – they were brought up in two parties instead of in driblets – a shell burst near one of these parties and they had twelve casualties nearly all stretcher cases so we were as badly off as before. A chaplain whom I knew slightly attached to another Battalion had come up – I had advised him not to as he was over 14 stone. He was soon hit and then there was 14 stone to be carried 4 or 5 miles to Hooge. During the day the Bosche started getting direct hits on the back of the mound where the men were dug in – there was no cover anywhere else and no trenches near and the

7   PB375: 'With the Highlanders by a Sassenach', the First World War diary of Major D.W. Pailthorpe. Courtesy Gordon Highlanders Museum.

only dugout was a mob of wounded and Battalion Headquarters. A 5.9 fell on top of a 'bivvy' in which 6 machine gunners were sitting – they were all blown to pieces – the M.O. of the Manchesters who was in the entrance way to the dugout was killed by the same shell – he was a specialist in Dermatology and was to have gone to a Base Hospital in November. We continued having casualties both from the trenches and the shell holes in front and at the Butte itself.[8]

You should now ascend the Spilstraat, moving in the same direction as the advancing Gordon Highlanders on 4 October until you reach the crossroads with the main Passchendaele to Becelaere road, which runs north to south along the summit of the ridge. Once you have reached the main road, pause for a few moments. The Gordons reached Nordemdhoek on the summit close to where you stand. Turn left and continue beyond Molenaarelsthoek. Stop when you reach a memorial to the 7th Division (Figure 14.5).

Location 2: 7th Division Memorial

Figure 14.5 Close to the 7th Division Memorial on Broodseinde Ridge looking towards Zonnebeke. The German Flandern I Line was on the rising ground in the foreground leading up to the ridge.

8   Ibid.

Broodseinde is approximately 200 yards ahead and Molenaarelsthoek twice that distance behind you. If you look beyond the memorial, you can see Zonnebeke (Figure 14.5) and on a clear day you may catch a glimpse of Ypres from within a few yards of your position (Figure 14.6). The two Australian divisions captured what was left of the eastern part of Zonnebeke closest to the ridge where you stand, and then ascended the rising ground in front of you to capture the Flandern I Line (Figure 14.1).

Men from the Australian 1st Division were in front of you and to your left, while those of the Australian 2nd Division were further along the ridge towards Broodseinde, which you can see if you look to your right. The first objective was a line of pillboxes on the Flandern I Line, which lay on a natural terrace just below the crest as you look towards Zonnebeke (Figure 14.1). Unbeknown to the Australians, the Germans were just on the point of launching a counter-attack to regain previously lost ground. At 0520, intense German artillery fire fell on the front line of the two Australian divisions in Zonnebeke, and also on the 3rd Australian Division and New Zealand Division of II Anzac Corps to their left, and your right (Chapter 15). Many casualties were inflicted by the German bombardment. When the British barrage opened at 0600, high explosive shellfire rained down on German positions crowded with troops, before Australians soldiers went over the top. The following account from the *Official History of the Great War* gives an idea of what it was like here for men of the Australian 1st Division:

> Before the leading companies had crossed No Man's Land, they saw in the dim light, close ahead, lines of men rising up from shell-holes. Some were already on the move forward with bayonets fixed, and the Australians opened fire. The assault was only momentarily delayed. As the Australians advanced, they found Germans in every shell-hole waiting for the signal to advance.[9]

Australian artillery support on 4 October was not as strong as on 26 September. Nevertheless, the Australians quickly gained control of the situation. The account continues:

> Many of the enemy would not face the onslaught and fled back, risking the barrage, whilst numerous sharp and merciless encounters took place with any survivors who offered resistance. The area was soon

---

9   Edmonds, J.E., *History of the Great War Based on Official Documents by Direction of the Historical Section of the Committee of Imperial Defence. Military Operations. France and Belgium 1917* Volume 2 (London: HMSO, 1948), p.304.

Figure 14.6 Looking towards Ypres in the distance from the 7th Division Memorial. When Australian soldiers looked in this direction on 4 October 1917, there was nothing but mud to be seen for as far as the eye could see.

littered with German dead, and the large number who bore bayonet wounds was evidence of the bitterness of the encounter.[10]

The Australians reached the Flandern I Line in front of you. One Australian captured 31 prisoners from a single blockhouse, and the garrison of another surrendered three machine guns. German machine-gunners, who were in a number of pillboxes in marshy ground near Molenaarelsthoek to your left, inflicted heavy casualties on the advancing soldiers. The Australians would have come past your position, pursuing Germans who were fleeing across the road. The routed Germans were chased over the crest towards the final objective some 400 yards beyond. When the Australians reached where you stand, they saw undamaged fields and trees ahead, while behind there was nothing but mud extending all the way to Ypres.

Look to your right in the direction of Broodseinde. During the Australian 2nd Division attack, Germans who resisted were killed in the same way as those who opposed the advance of the Australian 1st Division. There was an area of water-filled marshland a couple of hundred yards wide called Zonnebeke Lake within the ruins of Zonnebeke, which was by-passed. Heavy resistance was put up by German machine-gun teams amongst the ruins

10 Ibid., p.305.

Figure 14.7 The cyclist is approaching Broodseinde on his way towards Passchendaele. Australians advanced across the entire length of this section of road from left to right.

before the advancing Australians made their way up the gentle slope to the summit of the ridge, where they were met by withering machine-gun fire as they topped the crest. German defenders also had four anti-tank guns on the far side of the ridge firing at point-blank range.

Leave the 7th Division Memorial and go through Broodseinde. The cyclist in Figure 14.7 is approaching the village and is travelling in the direction of Passchendaele, the centre of which is 1.9 miles beyond Broodseinde.

To the north of Broodseinde, the ridge flattens out. There was a position called Daisy Wood close to the right of the road (Figure 14.1). Partly because of fire coming from Daisy Wood, and partly because the lie of the ground was suitable for defence, Australians here consolidated their position in an old trench line 200 yards short of their final objective. This old trench system had formed part of the British front line over the winter of 1914–15. The *Official History of the Great War* states that as the Australians dug in, they found scraps of khaki uniforms belonging to British soldiers who had died in these trenches three years earlier. They probably also found the remains of soldiers, although there is no mention of that.[11] Australian losses for the Battle of Broodseinde totalled 2,448 for the 1st Division and 2,174 for the 2nd Division.

---

11 Ibid., p.307

Chapter 15

THE THIRD BATTLE OF YPRES: BATTLES OF BROODSEINDE, POELCAPPELLE AND FIRST PASSCHENDAELE, 4–12 OCTOBER 1917

This chapter explains actions of the New Zealand Division and the 3rd Australian Division of II Anzac Corps at the Battle of Broodseinde on 4 October 1917 and at the First Battle of Passchendaele on 12 October. It also describes the engagement of the 49th (West Riding) and 66th (East Lancs) Divisions, both attached to II Anzac Corps, at the Battle of Poelcappelle on 9 October. These battles were part of efforts made to remove the Germans from Broodseinde Ridge and the village of Passchendaele. The Battle of Broodseinde was the fifth phase of the Third Battle of Ypres and was fought over a broad front (Figure 14.1). The Australian 1st and 2nd Divisions of I Anzac Corps captured Broodseinde Ridge near Zonnebeke (Chapter 14), while the Australian 3rd Division and the New Zealand Division fought over the ground to be described in this chapter.

The Canadian Memorial at the hamlet of Keerselare is a suitable starting point. The memorial is adjacent to a staggered crossroads between the St Julien to Poelcappelle and the Langemarck to Zonnebeke roads, where important events took place in 1915 (Chapter 6). Go in the direction of Zonnebeke. You will soon reach a minor road on the left, with a windmill clearly visible near the summit of a gentle incline. This road passes over Gravenstafel Ridge to a New Zealand Memorial, about which more will be said later. Look at the windmill and Figure 15.1 as you pass.

Continue towards Zonnebeke until you come to a crossroads. Turn left, and after approximately 100 yards turn around and stop (Figure 15.2).

Location 1: Kansas Cross

The crossroads was the approximate site of a German strong-point called Kansas Cross. Behind your position, the sGravenstafelstraat leads to

Figure 15.1 Gravenstafel Ridge from close to Zonnebekestraat. The New Zealand Division captured the ridge on 4 October 1917. The Canadian 1st Division was engaged in fierce combat on Gravenstafel Ridge during the Second Battle of Ypres on 24 April 1915, before being forced to withdraw (Chapter 7).

Figure 15.2 Kansas Cross, the strongpoint where the German Third Line intersected with the crossroads. The New Zealand Front Line on 4 October 1917 was behind the camera.

Gravenstafel and Passchendaele beyond. If you go to Gravenstafel from here, you will reach the New Zealand Monument at Gravenstafel Crossroads. The road straight ahead leads to Wieltje; Zonnebeke is approximately two miles to the left and Langemarck 2.5 miles to the right. The Third German Line passed close to where you stand through Kansas Cross in a north to south direction, and several pillboxes were in the vicinity. Kansas Cross was captured by men of the 55th Division on 31 July, but a German counter-attack forced a withdrawal along the road and through the fields straight ahead to a position west of St Julien several hundred yards away. Soldiers of the 59th Division captured Kansas Cross on 26 September during the Battle of Polygon Wood (Chapter 13).[1] Return to the main road and go towards Zonnebeke until you reach Dochy Farm Cemetery (Figure 15.3).

Location 2: Dochy Farm Cemetery

Stand with your back to the cemetery wall. Across the road to the right is a farm building. The ruins of Dochy Farm were near here in October 1917. The New Zealand front line was behind you, and the cemetery where you stand was in no man's land. The Australian 3rd Division attacked between Dochy Farm and the Ypres to Roulers railway line just over half a mile to your right at Zonnebeke (Figure 14.1).

Figure 15.3 Dochy Farm on the far side of the Langemarck to Zonnebeke Road. Zonnebeke is half a mile beyond the farm.

---

1   Carberry, A.D., *The New Zealand Medical Services in the Great War* (Auckland: Whitcombe and Tombs Ltd, 1924), p.329.

Look ahead towards a monument on a hillside in the middle distance (Figure 15.4). This is the New Zealand Memorial at Gravenstafel Crossroads, commemorating soldiers of the New Zealand Division who fought near here on 4 and 12 October 1917. To the right of the memorial is a ridge of elevated ground called Abraham Heights, which becomes continuous on the right with Broodseinde Ridge.

Figure 15.4 The New Zealand Memorial is visible towards the left of the photograph, with four tall poplar trees marking its position. The relatively high ground straight ahead to the right of the New Zealand Memorial is Abraham Heights, continuous with Gravenstafel Ridge on the left and Broodseinde Ridge on the right. The New Zealand Division advanced across the ground visible in this photograph.

The right flank of the New Zealand Division advanced on a front of 1,000 yards across the fields in front of you to attack German positions on Abraham Heights. The left flank attacked over Gravenstafel Ridge. The New Zealanders overcame all German resistance.

The 3rd Australian Division to the right of the New Zealand Division attacked Broodseinde Ridge, as did the Australian 1st and 2nd Divisions of I Anzac Corps (Chapter 14). Thus the three Australian divisions attacked Broodseinde Ridge, while the New Zealand Division attacked Abraham Heights and the adjoining Gravenstafel Ridge.[2]

2   Bean, C.E.W., *Anzac to Amiens* (Canberra: Australian War Memorial, 1946), pp.368–69.

Look to the right of Abraham Heights. Tyne Cot Cemetery can be seen, its position marked by tall poplar trees. Tyne Cot is on the slope of Broodseinde Ridge and the ground within which the cemetery stands was taken by the Australian 3rd Division on 4 October (Figure 15.5).

Figure 15.5 From Dochy Farm Cemetery, Tyne Cot Cemetery can be seen in the distance. The 1,500 yards of ground between the camera position and Tyne Cot was captured by the Australian 3rd Division. Its right flank was on Ypres to Roulers railway line (Figure 14.1).

The Australian 3rd Division captured the Flandern I Line, which passed across its front (Figure 14.1). Heavy casualties were inflicted by machine-gun fire from pillboxes on the Flandern I Line and from Tyne Cot immediately behind, as well as from machine guns on Abraham Heights. These machine-gun positions were outflanked and captured by daring exploits. Sergeant L. McGee of the 40th Australian Battalion was awarded a VC. His citation reads:

No.456, Sergeant Lewis McGee
40th Battalion, Australian Imperial Force
For most conspicuous bravery in action East of Ypres on October 4th 1917; in the advance to the final objective, Sergeant McGee led his platoon with great dash and bravery in spite of exceedingly heavy enemy opposition and shell fire. His platoon was suffering heavily and the advance of the company was stopped by Machine Gun fire from a

concrete 'pill-box'. Single handed, Sergeant McGee rushed the position armed only with a revolver. He shot some of the crew and captured the rest, and thus enabled the advance to proceed. He reorganised the remnants of his platoon and was foremost in the remainder of the advance, and during consolidation of the position did splendid work. This non-commissioned officer's coolness and bravery were conspicuous and contributed largely to the success of the company's operations. Sergeant McGee was subsequently killed in action on the 12th instant.[3]

London Gazette No. 30400, 23 November 1917

It is possible to visualise the attack of the Australian 3rd Division to the right, and the New Zealand Division to the left, from your position. Australian 3rd Division losses on 4 October were 1,810 killed, wounded and missing, while New Zealand losses were 1,643.[4]

Location 3: Tyne Cot Cemetery

You should now go to the entrance of Tyne Cot Cemetery by going to Zonnebeke, turning left onto the N332 and left again onto the Passendalestraat, continuing until a signpost directs you to Tyne Cot. If you are cycling, there is a better way. After reaching the outskirts of Zonnebeke, look for the old Ypres to Roulers railway on the left side of the road. This has been converted to a cycling track which passes to the south-east of Passchendaele (Figure 14.1), taking you close to Tyne Cot on the way. Men of the Australian 3rd and the adjacent 1st Divisions advanced on either side of the railway line, which was the divisional boundary.

Figure 15.6 looks from Tyne Cot towards the main entrance. Dochy Farm Cemetery is in the distance. There was a trench called Dab Trench in the field in front of Tyne Cot which was part of the German Third Line, and which had to be overcome. There are strategically positioned pillboxes around you, with a command bunker beneath the Cross of Sacrifice which exercised control over surrounding pillboxes.

Turn to your right and go to the north wall of the cemetery. Look towards high ground on the far side of a valley (Figure 15.7). There is a tiny stream at the bottom of the valley called the Ravebeek, which you cannot see from your

---

3   Sergeant McGee is buried in Tyne Cot Cemetery, grave reference Plot XX, Row D, Grave I.
4   Edmonds, J.E., *History of the Great War Based on Official Documents by Direction of the Historical Section of the Committee of Imperial Defence. Military Operations. France and Belgium 1917* Volume 2 (London: HMSO, 1948), p.309.

Figure 15.6 Tyne Cot Cemetery looking back towards Dochy Farm. The Australian 3rd Division attacked directly towards Tyne Cot. The New Zealand Divisions attacked Abraham Heights to the right. Dab Trench would have been in the field in the foreground (see text).

present position but will visit soon. Scarcely noticeable today, the Ravebeek was an impenetrable quagmire many yards wide in October 1917 as a result of frequent shelling. It would have been impossible to go from Tyne Cot Cemetery to the far side of the valley without sinking and drowning in mud many feet deep.

The high ground on the far side is the Bellevue Spur, on which sits the tiny hamlet of Bellevue between Gravenstafel and Passchendaele. The Bellevue Spur is part of the Stroombeek Ridge which joins the Passchendaele Ridge north of Passchendaele (Figure 14.2).

Go past the visitor centre and find a location where you can see Passchendaele Church. Figure 15.8 shows the upward incline towards the village. The church steeple can be seen one mile away. The Australian 3rd Division reached your approximate position on 4 October. Two further battles can be explained here; the Battle of Poelcappelle (9 October) and the First Battle of Passchendaele (12 October). These may be considered together, since their outcomes were similar.

Figure 15.7 Looking from Tyne Cot across to the high ground on the far side of the Ravebeek Valley. The Ravebeek cannot be seen from this position.

Figure 15.8 Passchendaele church from Tyne Cot, showing the upward incline from the shoulder of the ridge to the summit where men from the 66th (East Lancs) Division made their abortive attack on Passchendaele on 9 October 1917, and men from the Australian 3rd Division their equally unsuccessful assault on the village on 12 October.

THE BATTLE OF POELCAPPELLE, 9 OCTOBER 1917

After the Battle of Broodseinde on 4 October, Generals Plumer and Gough, commanders of the British Second and Fifth Armies, wanted to end the Third Battle of Ypres. Persistent rain, which began late on 4 October, reduced the battlefield to a quagmire. Sir Douglas Haig was keen to persist until the Germans were driven from Passchendaele, where the higher and better-drained ground would provide better conditions for the British over the winter months.[5]

The Battle of Poelcappelle on 9 October was fought on a front between Langemarck and Broodseinde, although a barrage was laid down over the entire Ypres Salient to simulate a general offensive. The Battle of Poelcappelle is also discussed in Chapters 11 and 16, where engagements around Langemarck and Poelcappelle are considered, but the main thrust was to be towards Passchendaele. The 49th Division, fighting with II Anzac Corps, replaced the New Zealand Division following the latter's successful capture of Gravenstafel Ridge on 4 October. Its job was to capture Bellevue Spur. The 66th Division replaced the Australian 3rd Division and was tasked with attacking to within 700 yards of Passchendaele. Figure 15.8 shows the ground over which men of the 66th Division advanced. The starting line extended from the Ravebeek Valley on the left to the Ypres to Roulers railway line on the right (Figure 15.9). There were many ruined farm buildings ahead which the Germans had fortified. Conditions were so bad that it proved impossible to move artillery pieces into position. Consequently, the supporting barrage was ineffective. Some battalions were late for zero hour at 0530 because it had taken so long to struggle across the boggy ground to the front line. A few soldiers reached their final objective 700 yards short of Passchendaele, and one patrol even reached the outskirts of the village before being raked by machine-gun fire and forced to withdraw to the starting position.

THE ATTACK ON 12 OCTOBER 1917, THE FIRST BATTLE OF PASSCHENDAELE

A further attempt to capture Passchendaele was made by the Australian 3rd Division and the New Zealand Division on 12 October, in what would become known as the First Battle of Passchendaele. The Australians were tasked with capturing Passchendaele from close to your present position, whilst men of the New Zealand Division attempted to take the Bellevue Spur on the opposite side of the Ravebeek Valley on their way towards the village. Australians

---

5   Ibid., p.325.

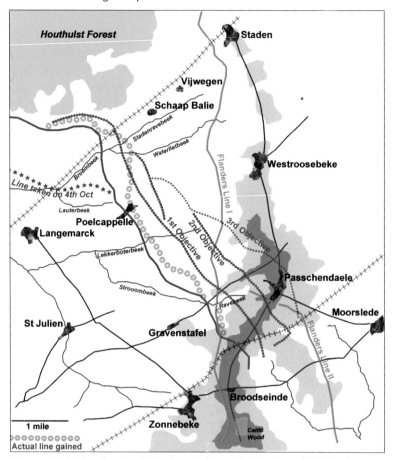

Figure 15.9 First Battle of Passchendaele on 12 October 1917. The dotted line shows the small advances made.

struggled towards Passchendaele as they made their way up the hillside ahead of you, which was dotted with pillboxes similar to the ones in Tyne Cot.

The following account is based on an extract from the 34th Australian Infantry Battalion Diary and gives an impression of the conditions. Men had assembled for the attack by 0245, and until zero hour were subjected to heavy fire. At 0525, the Australian barrage came down, but it was weak, and it was sometimes difficult to tell if the barrage came from Australian or German guns. It was hard to keep up with what little barrage there was, and the greatest obstacle to the advance was the appalling state of the ground, particularly on the left flank towards the valley of the Ravebeek. Many men were lost in this bog, and others had to be helped after they had sunk into

Figure 15.10 The Ypres to Roulers railway line. German machine guns near here beyond the Australian right flank inflicted heavy casualties on Australians advancing up the gentle incline towards Passchendaele.

shell holes and were unable to extract themselves. The centre of the attack was held up by a strongpoint with two concrete pillboxes, until Captain C.S. Jeffries organised a bombing party and successfully rushed and captured the strongpoint. Four machine guns and 35 prisoners were taken, and the advance continued. Machine-gun fire from Bellevue on the other side of the Ravebeek caused many casualties, as did fire from machine guns on the Australian right flank close to the Ypres to Roulers railway line (Figure 15.10). Jeffries organised another bombing party to deal with this latter threat, but was killed in the operation.[6]

Captain Jeffries won a Victoria Cross for his actions. Thanks largely to his efforts, a few Australians reached the outskirts of Passchendaele. The citation for his VC reads:

> With a small party of his company, he captured a pillbox from which a machine-gun was holding up the advance, taking 4 machine guns and 35 prisoners. Later, he organised another successful attack on

---

6   A short diversion will take you to the location of the machine-gun fire coming from the Ypres to Roulers railway line. Go to the Passchendaele to Broodseinde road and go a short distance towards Passchendaele. The railway crosses the road at Defy Crossing (Figure 15.10). Look across the road along the track. Machine guns here fired on advancing Australians.

214 Understanding the Ypres Salient

an emplacement, capturing 2 machine guns and 30 more prisoners, subsequently leading his company forward under heavy artillery and machine-gun fire to the objective. The gallant officer was killed later in the day, after his inspiring influence and his initiative had prevented the centre of the attack from being held up to the objective.[7]

After reaching Passchendaele, men were raked by fire from machine guns and snipers, and pounded by shellfire from German field guns, with gunners firing over open sights, meaning they could physically see their targets. Facing annihilation, the survivors withdrew to their starting position close to where you stand.

Jeffries' body was not recovered and subsequently could not be found. In July 1920, his father, Joshua Jeffries, travelled to the battlefield to try find his son's remains, but could not. Shortly after the father's visit, the remains were found on 14 September 1920 and were re-interred in Tyne Cot Cemetery behind the German blockhouse to the front left of the cemetery as you look towards Ypres (Plot XL, Row E, Grave 1). Correspondence in the Service Record for Captain Jeffries suggests that his father did make the trip to Flanders from Australia again in the mid 1920s and visited his son's grave.

Australians on the left flank advanced along the slope of the ridge close to the Ravebeek, where those closest to the morass became completely bogged down. Enfilade fire raked these men and they sustained very heavy casualties as they floundered helplessly in the mud. The First Battle of Passchendaele cost the Australians 3,000 casualties.[8] Before leaving Tyne Cot, it is worth looking back towards Ypres, where the spires of the city can be seen easily on a clear day (Figure 15.11). The Third Battle of Ypres began on 31 July 1917 with the aim of breaking free from the Ypres Salient and capturing the ports of Zeebrugge and Ostend. Nearly three months later, the British had barely advanced five miles. There would be no breakout, and the sole aim now was to capture the ruins of Passchendaele.

Leave Tyne Cot through the main entrance at the front of the cemetery and turn right onto the Tynecotstraat. Continue to a crossroads with Canadalaan and go straight across. After a couple of hundred yards, you cross a small stream, the Ravebeek. Stop, and look in the direction of Passchendaele Church (Figure 15.12).

7 Edmonds, J.E., *History of the Great War Based on Official Documents by Direction of the Historical Section of the Committee of Imperial Defence. Military Operations. France and Belgium 1917* Volume 2 (London: HMSO, 1948), p.342.

8 Bean, C.E.W., *Anzac to Amiens*. (Canberra; Australian War Memorial, 1946), pp.373–74.

Figure 15.11 Looking from Tyne Cot back towards Ypres.

Figure 15.12 The Ravebeek, looking towards Passchendaele. Many soldiers perished in the quagmire here during the Battles of Poelcappelle and First and Second Passchendaele.

Location 4: The Ravebeek

The Ravebeek today is so insignificant that it is easily missed. In 1917 it was impassible. Men drowned in the mud here, or were shot by snipers as they floundered helplessly. The left flanks of the attacks made by the 66th Division on 9 October and 3rd Australian Division on 12 October met similar fates in this treacherous trap. Continue uphill towards the sGravenstafelstraat. Just before reaching it, stop and look back the way you have come (Figure 15.13).

Figure 15.13 The Ravebeek is in the bottom of the valley 250 yards ahead. The poplar trees are within Tyne Cot Cemetery. Men on the left flank of the 66th Division on 9 October 1917, and Australian 3rd Division on 12 October, were strung out along the hillside ahead on a line extending towards the Ravebeek Valley, moving from right to left. Those who were unfortunate enough to be near the Ravebeek became bogged down in mud, where they were easy targets and often drowned.

Location 5: Gravenstafel Crossroads

Turn left and keep going until you reach the New Zealand Memorial, where you should stand and face the main road. Passchendaele is to your left and Kansas Cross to your right. Straight ahead, the Schipstraat goes along Abraham Heights until it joins Broodseinde Ridge. Men of the New Zealand Division stormed Abraham Heights on 4 October 1917 and continued in the direction of Passchendaele. Beyond them, Australians of the 3rd Division attacked towards Broodseinde Ridge. Behind your position at the memorial, there is a

Figure 15.14 Gravenstafel Ridge was captured by men of the New Zealand Division on 4 October, 1917. The cyclist is travelling towards a modern farm which is on the approximate site of Boetleer's Farm, a German strongpoint. Passchendaele Church steeple is visible in the distance to the left. The New Zealanders would have been advancing in the direction of Passchendaele.

minor road which takes you over Gravenstafel Ridge. Follow this road towards its flat summit. You can imagine New Zealand soldiers coming towards you. You may also reflect that the Canadian 1st Division was involved in heavy fighting here on 24 April 1915 during the Second Battle of Ypres (Chapter 7). When you have reached the top, turn around and retrace your steps. Before rejoining the main road, you will pass a farm building at the approximate location of Boetleer's Farm, a fortified German position captured by men of the New Zealand Division as they made their way across Gravenstafel Ridge. Boetleer's Farm was also an important location during the Second Battle of Ypres (Figure 15.14).

You can follow in the New Zealanders' footsteps after they overcame German resistance on Gravenstafel Ridge and Abraham Heights. Turn left towards Passchendaele, and as you go along, the road goes down into a small valley with a tower on the left side of the road. Stop and look along the road beyond the tower (Figure 15.15).

Figure 15.15 The Ravebeek passes through boggy ground to the right of the road in the trees at the foot of Bellevue Spur, before passing beneath the road, emerging on the left side of the road where its course is marked by the three trees in the field on the left. The upward incline ahead leads to Bellevue Spur.

Location 6: Looking towards Marsh Bottom with Bellevue Spur beyond

The Ravebeek crosses diagonally beneath the road close to the tower, changing its name to the Stroombeek as it does so. Beyond the Ravebeek was an area called Marsh Bottom, after which the road goes up a short incline onto the Bellevue Spur, where the German Flandern I Line ran north-south a short distance beyond (Figure 15.15). New Zealand soldiers sustained heavy casualties in the quagmire around Marsh Bottom, where their advance on 4 October was brought to a standstill.

THE BATTLE OF POELCAPPELLE 9 OCTOBER 1917

At the Battle of Poelcappelle on 9 October, the task of the 49th Division was to advance through Marsh Bottom onto the Bellevue Spur ahead. As men made their way to the front line on 8 October, there was torrential rain as they moved in single file on slippery duckboards which were pounded by German artillery. One soldier wrote:

It was an absolute nightmare. Often we would have to stop and wait for up to half an hour, because all the time the duckboards were being blown up and men being blown off the track or simply slipping off ... It had taken us more than twelve hours to get there. The Colonel had led the battalion up the track. And he said to me 'Get them into the attack.' I passed it on to the NCOs, who gave the orders: 'Fix bayonets. Deploy. Extended order. Advance!'[9]

In pouring rain, men scrambled and floundered with great difficulty through the clinging mud of Marsh Bottom. Some used the road ahead, which in 1917 was much narrower than today. It was easier to move over, but German machine guns were trained on the road, and when men appeared over the crest of the incline onto the Bellevue Spur ahead, they were cut down by machine-gun fire from positions on the German Flandern I Line beyond (Figure 15.9). A few isolated groups sheltered in water-filled craters as best they could and the dead lay all around. The attack was a complete failure.

On 12 October, men from the New Zealand Division were confronted by the same terrible conditions, starting from the same front line. One soldier who entered the front-line position on 11 October wrote:

It was a terrible night. We dug in as best we could at the bottom of the Bellevue Ridge, but the idea of digging in was ridiculous. You can't dig water ... As we started up the road we were being caught by enfilade fire from big pill-boxes in the low ground to our right. People were dropping all the way. Then, as we turned the corner on top of the rise, we saw this great bank of barbed wire ahead, maybe a hundred yards away. The bombardment should have cut the wire but it hadn't even dented it.[10]

The thick band of unbroken barbed wire described by this soldier was protecting the Flandern I Line (Figure 15.9). Now turn first left up the Ravestraat, easily recognizable because of the tower at the bottom of the road. Go along for a couple of hundred yards and turn around.

Location 7: Ravestraat

Using Figure 15.16, you can see a line of stubby trees going obliquely away from the tower to the right marking the course of the Stroombeek, the

---

9 MacDonald, L., *They Called it Passchendaele* (London: Macmillan Publishers Ltd, 1983), pp.197–98.

10 Ibid., pp.205–06.

Figure 15.16 The New Zealand front line on 12 October 1917 was in the field to your right. The line of short trees to the immediate right of the cows marks the position of the Stroombeek. The new front line moved only a short distance to within the field on the left side of the road.

Ravebeek having changed its name as it passes beneath the road. There was a wooden bridge nearby, where the Stroombeek could be crossed to reach the front line within the field. If you turn round and look behind you, there is a farm on the left side of the road. This is the approximate location of a fortified ruin which in 1917 was called Peter Pan. The slope of the Bellevue Spur is across the road from Peter Pan.

It is impossible to imagine what it must have been like here on 9 and 12 October. Conditions were appalling, and it proved very difficult to bring supporting artillery pieces into position. Many guns became completely bogged down in the mud. There was very little time for counter-battery work, and German pillboxes on Bellevue Spur remained undamaged. Machine guns in two pillboxes close to Peter Pan were particularly destructive.[11] On both 9 and 12 October, supporting artillery fire was poor and sporadic, and became progressively more feeble as first the 49th Division and then the New Zealand Division attempted to advance up the slope of Bellevue Spur. It was so muddy that howitzer shells buried themselves in the mud, merely splashing

11 Cave, N., *Passchendaele, the Fight for the Village* (London: Leo Cooper, 1997), pp.19–30.

German pillboxes with fountains of muddy water. There were broad belts of unbroken wire entanglements which were completely impenetrable. As the New Zealanders attacked on 12 October, they tried to advance through a hail of machine-gun bullets past the dead bodies of men killed on 9 October. Soon, the bodies of New Zealand soldiers lay beside them. The New Zealand Division made a tiny gain where you stand, the front line going from one side of the road to the other. Withering fire from German positions on the Flandern I Line caused many casualties and arrested the attack. The Battles of Poelcappelle and First Passchendaele were costly failures. There were 5,704 casualties in the 49th and 66th Divisions on 9 October,[12] and 6,000 soldiers from Australia and New Zealand became casualties on 12 October. The four divisions which made up the Canadian Corps were next given the task of capturing Passchendaele. They finally achieved in three stages what II Anzac had failed to do in one.

---

12 Edmonds, J.E., *History of the Great War Based on Official Documents by Direction of the Historical Section of the Committee of Imperial Defence. Military Operations. France and Belgium 1917* Volume 2 (London: HMSO, 1948), p.334.

Chapter 16

THE THIRD BATTLE OF YPRES: FIGHTING AROUND POELCAPPELLE, 4 OCTOBER 1917 AND 9 OCTOBER 1917

Poelcappelle is a village on the periphery of the Ypres Salient between Langemarck and Passchendaele. It is 2.4 miles from the centre of Langemarck and twice that distance from Passchendaele. Like most towns and villages in the Ypres Salient, the easiest way to distinguish it from others, in an otherwise bland and featureless landscape, is by the shape of its church and steeple (Figure 16.1). It is difficult enough today to navigate ones way around the Salient. It must have been much worse during the war after all the buildings had been completely destroyed by shellfire. The *Official History of the Great War* commented on how difficult it had become by October 1917, when it stated:

> It must be emphasised that in all that vast wilderness of slime, hardly tree, hedge, wall or building could be seen. As at the Somme no landmarks existed, nor any scrap of natural cover other than mud-filled shell-holes.[1]

Poelcappelle was held by the Germans for the first three years of the war. On 22 April 1915, they released chlorine gas between Poelcappelle and Langemarck against unsuspecting French Colonial troops, an action which marked the beginning of the Second Battle of Ypres (Chapter 6). It was not until the Battle of Broodseinde on 4 October 1917 (Chapter 14) that most, but not all, of the village of Poelcappelle was captured by the British. On 9 October, a further effort was made to get closer to Passchendaele, an engagement which became known as the Battle of Poelcappelle. This chapter takes

---

1   Edmonds, J.E., *History of the Great War Based on Official Documents by Direction of the Historical Section of the Committee of Imperial Defence. Military Operations. France and Belgium 1917* Volume 2 (London: HMSO, 1948), p.330.

Figure 16.1 Poelcappelle, with its distinctive church and church steeple. This photograph was taken from a point approximately midway between Poelcappelle and Passchendaele. If you note the shape of churches and their steeples, it helps you to identify towns and villages as you travel around the Ypres Salient.

you to locations around Poelcappelle to appreciate the fighting which took place there.

BATTLE OF BROODSEINDE, 4 OCTOBER 1917

Figure 16.2 shows that on 4 October 1917 Poelcappelle was attacked by the 11th Division, while the 4th Division attacked to its left and the 48th Division to its right. A small stream, the Lekkerboterbeek, crosses the road between St Julien and Poelcappelle, and this is a landmark to look out for on your journey.

Poelcappelle may be reached from Ypres by following the N8 (Meenseweg) to the roundabout at 'Hell Fire Corner', from which you should take the fifth exit, and go straight on at the next roundabout through Potijze. Turn right at a T-junction at St Jean onto the N313 (Brugseweg) and past the village of Wieltje. The road joins the N38 towards Poelcappelle. Go through St Julien and the hamlet of Keerselare, where the Canadian Memorial stands. Keep going towards Poelcappelle. Approximately halfway to the village you cross the Lekkerboterbeek. It is easy to stop if you are on a bicycle, but impossible in a car because of heavy traffic. There is a signpost, however, marking

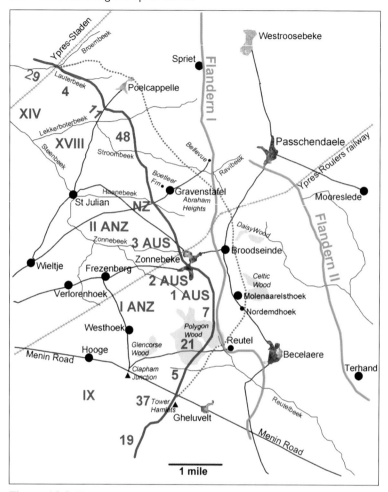

Figure 16.2 The attacking divisions at the Battle of Broodseinde, 4 October 1917; the 11th Division attacked Poelcappelle, with the 4th Division to the left and 48th Division to the right.

its position. There is a low wall set back from the road on each side which helps. On 4 October 1917, the British front line was approximately 300 yards beyond the Lekkerboterbeek (Figure 16.2). As you continue towards the village, you are travelling in the direction that men of the 11th Division took during their attack on 4 October 1917. They would have been on the road and in the fields to either side. Keep going until you see a roundabout close to the entrance of the village with the statue of a stork in the middle (Figure 16.3). This is a memorial to the French pilot Georges Guynemer, who was 21 when

Figure 16.3 Approaching Poelcappelle from the direction of St Julien. The roundabout with the statue of a stork is visible, with the church in the background. Men of the 11th Division advanced along this road on 4 October 1917 during the Battle of Broodseinde.

he started flying in 1915. As his tally of kills began to mount up, he became a favourite with the French people. He was promoted to be the leader of a squadron known as 'The Storks', hence the design of the memorial. He was shot down somewhere near Poelcappelle on 11 September 1917. His body was never found. The roundabout is a good place to stop and reflect on events which took place at Poelcappelle on 4 October 1917.

Location I: Roundabout at Poelcappelle

As you stand at the roundabout, look in the direction of St Julien and imagine you had been on this spot on 4 October 1917. At 0600, men of the 11th Division would have advanced towards your position from their front line a short distance in front of the Lekkerboterbeek (Figure 16.2). They were well supported by tanks as they advanced towards Poelcappelle. They were met by machine-gun fire from many fortified positions in the village, but the tanks of 1 Tank Brigade helped to overcome German resistance. The St Julien road was macadamised, and although cratered as a result of shell fire, was in sufficiently good condition to enable the tanks to use it.

Generally speaking, the use of tanks in the Ypres Salient was limited for a number of reasons. The weight of the tank mitigated against use in heavily shelled ground, over which its speed was only 10 yards a minute. The driver usually experienced difficulty in maintaining direction because of limited visibility, while heat exhaustion of crews frequently made conditions unbearable. On a hot day, the temperature inside a tank could rise to almost 50°C. It was realised that to use tanks on poor ground which was soft and covered with water-filled craters was to throw them away.[2] Their successful use here was attributable to the reasonably good road surface. By the end of the battle on 4 October, men of the 11th Division had fought their way through most of the village around you, but had not captured the eastern part, which remained in German hands. The maximum distance advanced was approximately 0.75 miles (Figure 16.2).

You can now look at territory gained by the 48th and 4th Divisions during the Battle of Broodseinde. Leave the roundabout and proceed in the direction of the Lekkerboterbeek. If you are on a bicycle, stop when you reach it and look to your left. The Lekkerboterbeek runs west to east here, and by using Figure 16.2 you can work out where the British front line was. You can see the windmill on Gravenstafel Ridge further to the right (Figure 16.4). The ridge was attacked by the New Zealand Division on 4 October (Chapter 15). On that day, men of the 48th Division advanced between the 11th Division and the New Zealand Division. They would have been advancing across the fields in front of you from right to left as you look towards the windmill.

Now cross the road and face towards Langemarck Church. Langemarck was captured by the 20th Division on 16 August 1917 (Chapter 11). The starting position for the 4th Division on 4 October would have been out to the right of Langemarck Church (Figure 16.5). The front line would then have run approximately in a south-east direction diagonally across the field in front of you to cross the road you are on (Figure 16.2).

Go to Gravenstafel Ridge. Make your way to the staggered crossroads with the Langemarck to Zonnebeke road and turn left onto the Zonnebekestraat. Take the first turning left onto Gravenstafel Ridge, using the windmill as a landmark. Go past the windmill and keep going until you get to the 'summit' of the ridge, with a good view of Poelcappelle to the north (Figure 16.6). You will recognise it from its church steeple and distinguish it from Langemarck Church, which you can also see.

2   Ibid., p.319

Figure 16.4 Looking towards Gravenstafel Ridge. The windmill in the centre is a good landmark for the ridge. Men of the 48th Division advanced from right to left between the 11th Division, astride the road from which the photograph was taken, and the New Zealand Division, advancing across Gravenstafel Ridge.

Figure 16.5 Langemarck was captured on 16 August 1917, and the front line of the 4th Division was to the right of Langemarck Church on 4 October, extending as far as the Ypres to Staden railway line (Figure 16.2).

Location 2: View of Poelcappelle from Gravenstafel Ridge

Figure 16.6 Poelcappelle from Gravenstafel Ridge. The attack on 4 October 1917 captured the ground seen in this photograph. In the foreground, men of the New Zealand Division advanced over Gravenstafel Ridge (Chapter 15), while beyond them the 48th Division attacked from left to right, passing the near side of Poelcappelle and fanning out across the fields in front of the camera, reaching a position level with the far right of the village.

Look towards Poelcappelle Church. Men from the New Zealand Division would have been advancing from left to right in the foreground. Beyond them, men of the 48th Division would have been attacking between the New Zealanders and the village of Poelcappelle, while the 11th Division fought its way through the village, capturing most of it. The 48th Division kept in line with them on the near side of the village.

Return to the roundabout in Poelcappelle and take the road to Langemarck. Stop after half a mile when you reach a position where you get as good a view through the fields to your right as growing crops will allow. This varies depending on the time of year (Figure 16.7).

Location 3: Looking across fields on Poelcappelle to Langemarck Road

Figure 16.7 The 4th Division attack took men across these fields in the Battle of Broodseinde. Poelcappelle Church is visible.

Look across the fields with Poelcappelle Church to your right. Langemarck village is out of sight to your left. Imagine the front line swinging across the fields in front of you, passing from the far (north) side of Langemarck to the near (south) side of Poelcappelle, and then crossing the Poelcappelle to St Julien road near the Lekkerboterbeek, from where the 11th Division attacked (Figure 16.2). Men of the 4th Division advanced across the fields in front of you behind a creeping barrage and came under heavy machine-gun fire. The creeping barrage was described in the *Official History of the Great War* as ragged. They were raked by machine-gun fire from Poelcappelle which stopped their advance.[3]

---

3   Ibid., p.311.

BATTLE OF POELCAPPELLE, 9 OCTOBER 1917

This was the sixth phase of the Third Battle of Ypres. The aim of the battle was to drive the line outwards ever closer to Passchendaele. On their way to the front line on 8 October, men had to traverse boggy ground on unstable duckboards to reach their jump-off positions, and anyone falling off was likely to drown in thick mud. The *Official History of the Great War* describes the conditions. You can imagine them as you look across these fields.

> The roads and tracks across the battle area had gravely deteriorated. Three months of persistent shelling had blocked the watercourses and the mass of shell-holes frustrated every effort of the water to drain away. Conditions in certain areas became impossible. The entire valley of the upper Steenbeek and its tributaries was a porridge of mud.[4]

The main thrust of the Battle of Poelcappelle on 9 October was intended to push the front line closer to Passchendaele, and was carried out by the 66th and 49th Divisions, which were attached to II Anzac Corps. This attack, explained in Chapter 15, failed completely. The 4th, 11th and 48th Divisions, which attacked around Poelcappelle, and which had been relatively successful on 4 October, failed to make any progress at all and the part of Poelcappelle not captured on 4 October remained in German hands.

The dreadful ground conditions meant that artillery pieces could not be moved, and most were forced to remain west of the Steenbeek (Figure 16.2) and were ineffective. Any attempts to move the guns further forward resulted in them getting bogged down in mud. There was no spotting by aircraft between 5–9 October, and consequently counter-battery work was blind. Men were exhausted before they began after their long march to get to the front line on the night of 7/8 October, and were not in a fit state to attack. Men of the 4th Division in front of you had to make their way knee-deep in mud across these fields, over a landscape pockmarked with water-filled shell holes to get to their front line. They were raked by machine-gun fire from the outset. It is not at all surprising that their attack failed.

The only part of the Battle of Poelcappelle where there was some success was in the northern part near Langemarck (Figure 16.8). This fighting is explained in Chapter 11.

---

4   Ibid., p.327.

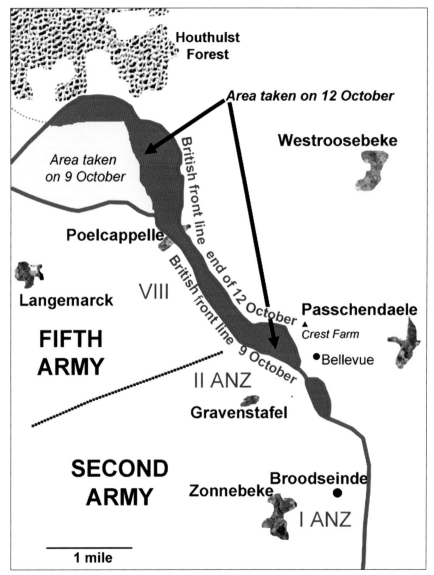

Figure 16.8 Map showing the gains on 9 October (Battle of Poelcappelle) and 12 October 1917 (First Battle of Passchendaele, Chapter 15).

Chapter 17

THE THIRD BATTLE OF YPRES
THE SECOND BATTLE OF PASSCHENDAELE,
26 OCTOBER–10 NOVEMBER 1917

This chapter sets out to explain how the village of Passchendaele was finally captured between 26 October and 10 November 1917. A previous attack by the New Zealand and 3rd Australian Divisions of II Anzac Corps had failed during the First Battle of Passchendaele on 12 October (Chapter 15). They were replaced by the four divisions of the Canadian Corps, which continued in spite of appalling ground conditions. General Sir Douglas Haig decided that the village must be captured before halting the offensive so that the British could occupy the higher ground at Passchendaele over the winter months.

The Canadians were commanded by General Sir Arthur Currie, who delayed his attack to begin the Second Battle of Passchendaele until 26 October, allowing time for supporting artillery to be moved forward and positioned as advantageously as ground conditions permitted. The Canadian 3rd and 1st Divisions attacked Passchendaele along Bellevue Spur (part of Stroombeek Ridge) on one side of the Ravebeek Valley, and the 4th and 2nd Divisions

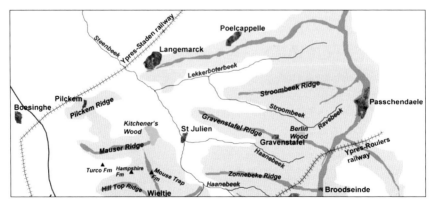

Figure 17.1 The Canadians advanced along the high ground on either side of the Ravebeek. Mud in the vicinity of the Ravebeek made ground conditions impossible.

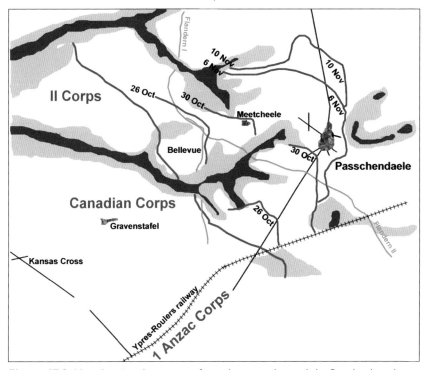

Figure 17.2 Map showing the extent of marshy ground round the Ravebeek and Stroombeek. The darker blue shows the marshiest of ground immediately adjacent to the stream. Men had to pick their way over higher and therefore drier ground on either side.

along Passchendaele Ridge on the other (Figure 17.1). The Ravebeek Valley was so marshy that movement here was impossible (Figure 17.2).

Currie planned to capture Passchendaele in three steps, unlike the First Battle of Passchendaele, where the intention was to capture it in one effort. Figure 17.3 shows Canadian positions on 26 October, 30 October and 6 November.

Make your way from the Grote Markt in Ypres to 'Hell Fire Corner'. Take the final roundabout exit through Potijze and St Jean before turning right past Wieltje, from where you join the road to Poelcappelle. Go through St Julien and turn right at the Canadian Memorial. After approximately 1.3 miles, turn left onto the sGravenstafelstraat. Go past the New Zealand Memorial (Chapter 15), and after half a mile you will pass a tower adjacent to a road called the Ravestraat, before going through a depression in the road called 'Marsh Bottom' (Chapter 15). As you go through Marsh Bottom, look to your right and you will see trees, within which is a small pond. The Ravebeek,

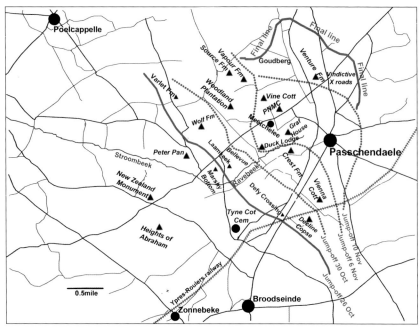

Figure 17.3 Canadian positions on Bellevue Spur and Passchendaele Ridge for attacks between 26 October and 10 November 1917. Connecting lines between the two areas of high ground have been drawn in to show the link between these attacks, but it was impossible to occupy the Ravebeek Valley in the centre.

Figure 17.4 The Ravestraat is just beyond the tower on the left. Marsh Bottom is at the foot of the upward incline beyond the tower which leads onto Bellevue Spur. The Ravebeek crosses beneath the road from the clump of trees on the right to the line of trees in the foreground on the left.

which comes from Passchendaele, passes through this pond before crossing beneath the road, emerging on the other side behind the tower, changing its name to the Stroombeek (Figure 17.1). Go up an incline onto Bellevue Spur (Figure 17.4).

You will see scattered farm buildings straight ahead which constitute Bellevue. Stop at a road on the right called Tynecotstraat and look towards Passchendaele.

Location 1: Entrance to Tynecotstraat

Figure 17.5 View of Passchendaele from Tynecotstraat. Passchendaele Church is just over one mile away. The farm building in front of the trees to the right is the approximate location of a fortified German position known as Duck Lodge.

Men of the Canadian 3rd Division attacked along Bellevue Spur on 26 October. They began a short distance behind you and stopped short of the farm building which you can see on the right in Figure 17.5. The amount of ground gained was small. Turn right and look along the Tynecotstraat. You can see a farm adjacent to the road on the left. This was the position of a fortified German position called Laamkeek (Figure 17.6).

While men of the Canadian 3rd Division advanced along Bellevue Spur on 26 October, the Canadian 4th Division attacked along Passchendaele Ridge, which is a continuation of Broodseinde Ridge (Figure 17.6). Machine-gunners in Laamkeek inflicted casualties on both 3rd and 4th Divisions.

Figure 17.6 Laamkeek is immediately adjacent to the road on the left. German machine-gun teams in Laamkeek inflicted many casualties as Canadians of the 3rd Division advanced from right to left past the cyclist. Broodseinde Ridge is on the skyline.

Location 2: Peter Pan

Return to the Ravestraat, go up it and stop when you reach the first farm on your left. This is close to the ruins of a farm called 'Peter Pan', which held up the New Zealand Division during the First Battle of Passchendaele (Chapter 15). Face right towards Bellevue Spur. The Canadian front line was a short distance into the field in front of you. Dead from the failed attacks of the British 49th Division (attached to II Anzac Corps) on 9 October during the Battle of Poelcappelle, and by the New Zealand Division on 12 October during the First Battle of Passchendaele, still lay in these fields (Figure 17.7).

The attack began at 0540. There were intact pillboxes scattered across the hillside, which were full of Germans who poured fire into the Canadians. By 0630, men of the Cameron Highlanders of Winnipeg (43rd Battalion) were on the skyline around the pillboxes directly in front of you. To your right, between your position and the sGravenstafelstraat, men from the Central Ontario Battalion (58th Battalion) were visible from Laamkeek and were cut down by machine-gun fire. By 0800, an intense German artillery and machine-gun barrage inflicted many casualties and brought the Central Ontario Battalion to a standstill. It was pouring rain, and a repetition of the failures on 9 and 12 October was feared. The Manitoba (52nd) Battalion was sent to reinforce

Figure 17.7 Bellevue Spur from Peter Pan. The Canadian 3rd Division attacked up the hillside here on 26 October 1917. The hillside was dotted with pillboxes which poured machine-gun fire into advancing Canadians.

the part of the crest which had been taken, and together with the Cameron Highlanders of Winnipeg, they attacked to their right and outflanked the German pillboxes on the crest which were holding up the attack of the Central Ontario Battalion. Two Victoria Crosses were won in the field in front of you, the first by Captain C.P.J. O'Kelly of the Manitoba Battalion, whose citation reads:

> For most conspicuous bravery in an action in which he led his company with extraordinary skill and determination. After the original attack had failed and two companies of his unit had launched a new attack, Capt. O'Kelly advanced his command over 1,000 yards under heavy fire without any artillery barrage, took the enemy positions on the crest of the hill by storm, and then personally organised and led a series of attacks against 'pill-boxes', his company alone capturing six of them with 100 prisoners and 10 machine guns. Later on in the after-noon, under the leadership of this gallant officer, his company repelled a strong counter-attack, taking more prisoners, and subsequently during the night captured a hostile raiding party consisting of one officer, 10 men and a machine gun. The whole of these achievements

were chiefly due to the magnificent courage, daring and ability of Capt. O'Kelly.

London Gazette, No. 30, 471, 11 January 1918

The second VC was won by Lieutenant R. Shankland of the Cameron Highlanders of Winnipeg. His citation reads:

For most conspicuous bravery and resource in action under criti-cal and adverse conditions. Having gained a position he rallied the remnant of his own platoon and men of other companies, disposed them to command the ground in front, and inflicted heavy casualties upon the retreating enemy. Later, he dispersed a counter-attack, thus enabling supporting troops to come up unmolested. He then person-ally communicated to Battalion Headquarters an accurate and valu-able report as to the position on the Brigade frontage, and after doing so rejoined his command and carried on until relieved. His courage and splendid example inspired all ranks and coupled with his great gallantry and skill undoubtedly saved a very critical situation.

London Gazette, No. 30, 433, 18 December 1917

Continue along the Ravestraat and when you reach a fork in the road, take the road to the right, which is the Wallemolenstraat. There is a farm which marks the start of a Z bend ahead. As you go towards this farm, the Canadian front line crossed the road from the field on your right to that on your left (Figure 17.3). Go round the Z bend and as you emerge there is a farm on your right marking Wolf Farm, a German strongpoint close to where the present day building stands. Stop beyond Wolf Farm and look towards it (Figure 17.8).

Location 3: Wolf Farm

Men of the 4th Canadian Mounted Rifles on the left flank of the Canadian 3rd Division attacked here on 26 October. They were pinned down by machine-gun fire until Private T. Holmes ran across no man's land and destroyed two German machine-gun positions and overwhelmed the defenders of a pillbox in the vicinity of Wolf Farm, allowing the attack to proceed. Holmes was awarded a Victoria Cross, and his citation reads:

For most conspicuous bravery and resource when the left flank of our attack was held up by heavy machine-gun and rifle fire from a 'pill-box' strong point. Heavy casualties were producing a critical situ-ation when Pte. Holmes, on his own initiative and single-handed, ran forward and threw two bombs, killing and wounding the crews of two

Figure 17.8 Wolf Farm on the right; the Canadian front line is a short distance further out to the right. The trees on the skyline are on the crest of Bellevue Spur. Passchendaele Church is just visible in the distance to the left of the trees.

machine guns. He then returned to his comrades, secured another bomb, and again rushed forward alone under heavy fire and threw the bomb into the entrance of the 'pill-box', causing the nineteen occupants to surrender. By this act of valour at a very critical moment Pte. Holmes undoubtedly cleared the way for the advance of our troops and saved the lives of many of his comrades.

London Gazette, No. 30, 471, 11 January 1918

The 3rd Division advanced approximately 500 yards towards Passchendaele. Retrace your steps to the sGravenstafelstraat and go along the road towards Passchendaele, passing the Tynecotstraat and hamlet of Bellevue. You will reach a crossroads where a yellow signpost directs you to Varlet Farm along a road called the Bornstraat. Stop at the crossroads to consider events on 30 October 1917. Face the road to the right (Figure 17.9).

Location 4: sGraventafelstraat to Bornstraat Crossroads

Figure 17.9 The farm building on the right is in the vicinity of Duck Lodge, a fortified German position. The Canadian front line on 30 October was in the field to the right of Duck Lodge. The Ravebeek is at the bottom of the hill. The line of trees beyond and to the left of the farm gives an indication of its position. Passchendaele Ridge is beyond on the skyline.

Men of the Princess Patricia's Canadian Light Infantry (PPCLI) on the right flank of the 3rd Division attacked from here on 30 October. One of them, Major Talbot Papineau, came from a prominent French Canadian family and was an aspiring politician. He had won a Military Cross following a trench raid at St Eloi in February 1915, and fought at the Battle of Frezenberg in May 1915 (Chapter 8). In late 1915, suffering from battle fatigue, he was invalided out and took a staff officer post. He missed Canadian fighting at the Battle of Mount Sorrel in June 1916 (Chapter 18) and at Vimy Ridge in April 1917. Believing that his safe staff officer post would hinder his future political career, he returned to the PPCLI in May 1917. Papineau was blown in half by a German shell just after the attack began. Some days later, a pair of legs was found implanted in the ground. The puttees on the legs were noted to be reversed, which was how Papineau applied his. On digging up these remains, the top half of the body was missing. An examination of the trouser pockets confirmed the identity of the corpse to be that of Papineau, which was buried under a wooden cross, but when the battlefield was cleared subsequently,

Figure 17.10 Looking along sGraventafelstraat towards the tiny hamlet of Meetcheele. The PPCLI attacked across the field in the foreground towards the buildings ahead on 30 October 1917. The water tower on the right is in Passchendaele.

nothing was found beneath the cross. Papineau's name is on the Menin Gate (Panel 10).[1]

Face along the sGravenstafelstraat towards Passchendaele. A few houses ahead denote the position of Meetcheele (Figure 17.10). At 0550, the PPCLI attacked, but were held up by machine-gun fire from a pillbox close to where the houses stand today. A machine-gun team would have had a commanding view over the attack. Lieutenant H. MacKenzie of the Canadian Machine Gun Corps led a diversionary frontal attack on this pillbox, while Sergeant G. Mullin of the PPCLI led an enveloping action and personally captured the pillbox. MacKenzie was killed and his body never found. Both were awarded the Victoria Cross, and MacKenzie's citation reads:

> For most conspicuous bravery and leading when in charge of a section of four machine guns accompanying the infantry in an attack. Seeing that all the officers and most of the non-commissioned officers of an infantry company had become casualties, and that the men were hesitating before a nest of enemy machine guns, which were on

1   Christie, N.M., *For King and Empire: The Canadians at Passchendaele* (Ottawa, Ontario: CEF Books, 1999), pp.38–39.

commanding ground and causing them severe casualties, he handed over command of his guns to an NCO, rallied the infantry, organised an attack, and captured the strong point. Finding that the position was swept by machine-gun fire from a 'pill box', he himself was killed while leading the frontal attack. By his valour and leadership, this gallant officer ensured the capture of these strong points and so saved the lives of many men and enabled the objectives to be attained.
London Gazette, Supplement, No. 30, 523, p.2, 003, 13 February 1918

Mullin's citation reads:

For most conspicuous bravery in attack, when single-handed he captured a commanding 'Pill-box' which had withstood the heavy bombardment and was causing heavy casualties to our forces and holding up the attack. He rushed a sniper's post in front, destroyed the garrison with bombs, and, crawling on top of the 'Pill-box', he shot the two machine-gunners with his revolver. Sergeant Mullin then rushed to another entrance and compelled the garrison of ten to surrender. His gallantry and fearlessness were witnessed by many, and, although rapid fire was directed upon him, and his clothes riddled by bullets, he never faltered in his purpose and he not only helped to save the situation, but also indirectly saved many lives.
London Gazette, Supplement, No. 30, 471, 11 January 1918

Turn left along the Bornstraat. The Edmonton Battalion (49th) advanced across the road from their front line on the left towards the hillside on your right. The attack was halted by machine-gun fire. Private C. Kinross attacked a German machine-gun position and despite receiving wounds to the arm and head he saved the Edmonton Battalion from being wiped out. He too was awarded the Victoria Cross. His citation reads:

For most conspicuous bravery in action during prolonged and severe operations. Shortly after the attack was launched, the company to which he belonged came under intense artillery fire, and further advance was held up by a very severe fire from an enemy machine-gun. Private Kinross, making a careful survey of the situation, deliberately divested himself of all his equipment save his rifle and bandolier and, regardless of his personal safety, advanced alone over the open ground in broad daylight, charged the enemy machine-gun, killing the crew of six, and seized and destroyed the gun. His superb example and courage instilled the greatest confidence in his company, and enabled a further advance of 300 yards to be made and a highly important position to be established. Throughout the day he showed marvellous coolness and courage, fighting with the utmost aggressiveness against heavy odds until seriously wounded.

London Gazette, Supplement, No. 30, 471, 8 January 1918

Keep going along the road. The Canadian front line on 30 October was in the field to your left. It was close to, and roughly parallel to the road. An extensive area of very boggy flat ground ahead and to the right was called Woodland Plantation (Figure 17.11).

Figure 17.11 The Canadian front line was just to the left of the road. Woodland Plantation was ahead and to the right.

Location 5: Y Junction

You will soon reach a Y junction, where you should take the right fork and stop. Look to your right across Woodland Plantation. Houses visible in a cluster to the left are in the location of three ruined fortified farms called Vapour Farm, Vegetable House and Vine Cottage (Figure 17.12). Canadians attacking across this boggy ground were from the 5th Canadian Mounted Rifles, under the command of Major G. Pearkes. Their objectives were the aforementioned fortified ruins. Look beyond and to the right of these buildings, where you can see the tower in Passchendaele. To the left, farm buildings standing in isolation mark the location of a German position called Source Farm (Figure 17.12).

Figure 17.12 Looking across Woodland Plantation from LOCATION 5. The tower at the northern end of Passchendaele is seen, as are the positions of Vapour Farm, Vegetable House and Vine Cottage to the left of the tower. Source Farm is marked by the whitewashed wall to the far left.

The Paddebeek is a small stream close to Woodland Plantation, joining the Lekkerboterbeek near Source Farm, and contributing to the boggy nature of the ground. As Canadians advanced, their left flank came under heavy fire from Source Farm, which should have been taken by the adjacent British 63rd Division, advancing past where you stand, but it had made very slow progress. Major Pearkes despatched Lieutenant Otty to deal with the Germans at Source Farm. Otty captured the farm but was killed. Meanwhile, Pearkes captured Vapour Farm, which he successfully held despite German counter-attacks. His actions secured the Canadian left flank, for which he was awarded the Victoria Cross. His citation reads:

> Just prior to the advance Major Pearkes was wounded in the thigh. Regardless of his wound, he continued to lead his men with the utmost gallantry, despite many obstacles. At a particular stage of the attack his further advance was threatened by a strong point which was an objective of the battalion on his left, but which they had not succeeded in capturing. Quickly appreciating the situation, he captured and held this point, thus enabling his further advance to be successfully pushed forward. It was entirely due to his determination and fearless

personality that he was able to maintain his objective with the small number of men at his command against repeated enemy counter-attacks, both his flanks being unprotected for a considerable depth meanwhile. His appreciation of the situation throughout and the reports rendered by him were invaluable to his Commanding Officer in making dispositions of troops to hold the position captured.

London Gazette, No. 30, 471, 11 January 1918

Now continue until you get closer to Source Farm, where you can clearly see the course of the Paddebeek, which was a major obstacle to the advance (Figure 17.13).

The left flank of the Canadian 3rd Division advanced approximately 1,000 yards from its starting position, while the right flank only reached Meetcheele, some 400 yards distance from the starting position, as you have already seen when considering the advance of the PPCLI on the sGravenstafelstraat.

From Source Farm, look across to Vapour Farm, Vegetable House and Vine Cottage. The attack on 6 November was launched by the Canadian 1st Division, replacing the 3rd Division. Corporal Barron of the Third Battalion singlehandedly destroyed a machine-gun position at Vine Cottage (Figure 17.3) and killed the crew, allowing the attack to continue towards Passchendaele. Barron was awarded the Victoria Cross and his citation reads:

Figure 17.13 Source Farm is to the left; the Paddebeek follows a straight line across the field in the foreground. The grass bank traversing the field gives its position. Vapour Farm, Vegetable House and Vine Cottage are amongst the trees to the right.

For conspicuous bravery when in attack his unit was held up by three machine-guns. Corporal Barron opened on them from a flank at point-blank range, rushed the enemy guns single-handed, killed four of the crew, and captured the remainder. He then, with remarkable initiative and skill, turned one of the captured guns on the retiring enemy, causing them severe casualties.

The remarkable dash and determination displayed by this N.C.O. in rushing the guns produced far-reaching results, and enabled the advance to be continued.

London Gazette, No. 30, 471, 11 January 1918

The Canadian 1st Division fought its way up to Passchendaele to join with the 2nd Division at the north end of the village, the latter having attacked through the village from the Passchendaele Ridge. You will soon follow the attacks made by the Canadian 4th and 2nd Divisions, but first you can visit Vindictive Crossroads, captured by the Canadian 2nd Division on 10 November.

Continue until you reach another Y junction. Take the right fork (Goudbergstraat) and go along it for approximately a quarter of a mile. You are now near the front line on the left flank of the Canadian 1st Division on 6 November as it attacked towards Passchendaele (Figure 17.3).

Figure 17.14 The cyclists are ascending Stroombeek Ridge and are approaching the furthest point reached on 10 November 1917 by men of the Canadian 2nd Division (Figure 17.3). Men on the Canadian front line were over to their right. The Germans were to their left.

Pass a few scattered houses on both sides of the road in the locality of Goudberg, which was attacked and captured during a final attack on 10 November by the Canadian 2nd Division (Figure 17.3). The aim was to consolidate the position on the ridge north of Passchendaele. As you proceed, you are passing to the left of the final Canadian front line after the attack on 10 November and are moving towards the furthest point reached by the Canadians (Figure 17.3). The cyclists in Figure 17.14 have passed through Goudberg and are on their way to this furthest point. Men of the 2nd Canadian Division's left flank would have been over to their right under very different circumstances from the cyclists, who were here on a peaceful summer's day. They would have been consolidating the Canadian left flank against German counter-attacks, while the central thrust was directed towards Vindictive Crossroads and beyond.

Continue on the Goudbergstraat until you reach a junction with the Haringstraat. You are now very close to the furthest point reached during the Third Battle of Ypres. You have climbed the fairly steep slope of Stroombeek Ridge which joins Passchendaele Ridge north of the village (Figure 17.1).

Turn right and continue to the sGraventafelstraat, where you should turn left to reach Vindictive Crossroads. The front line reached on 6 November was roughly halfway between where you rejoined the sGraventafelstraat and the crossroads ahead.

Location 6: Vindictive Crossroads

Position yourself facing north in the direction of Westroozebeke (Figure 17.15). The Canadian line after fighting on 10 November crossed the road to Westroozebeke just over half a mile ahead of you, before curving back round the field to your right (Figures 17.3 and 17.15). You may wonder why the battle on 10 November was fought. While it may have provided a firmer foothold on the ridge, it created a vulnerable salient.

From Vindictive Crossroads, you may now visit key locations on Passchendaele Ridge where attacks were launched on 26 and 30 October by the Canadian 4th Division and on 6 November by the Canadian 2nd Division. Go through Passchendaele until you reach an industrial complex on your left approximately one and a quarter miles from the centre of the village. The old Ypres to Roulers railway line crosses the road just before you reach it (Figure 17.16). This was called Defy Crossing. Go to the track on the right side of the road and look directly across to the other side (Figure 17.16).

Figure 17.15 Vindictive Crossroads, captured by Canadian 2nd Division on 10 November 1917, looking north towards Westroozebeke. The sGraventafelstraat is the road to the left; the road to the right is the Grote Roeselarestraat.

Location 7: Defy Crossing

Figure 17.16 The old Ypres to Roulers railway line at Defy Crossing, The centre of Passchendaele is just over a mile to the left. Broodseinde is approximately a mile to the right. Decline Copse (see text) is close to where the line disappears around the corner at the wooded section ahead.

The railway line was the divisional boundary between the Canadian 4th Division and the Australian 1st Division. As you look across the road and along the railway line, Canadians advanced through the field on your left, while Australians supporting the Canadian right flank advanced where the industrial complex stands today. The front line on 26 October passed through Defy Crossing, from where the Canadians advanced approximately 400 yards towards Passchendaele (Figure 17.3). Heavy casualties were sustained by both Canadians and Australians from German positions around the railway, particularly Decline Copse which straddled the railway line a short distance ahead of your present position. Neither the Canadians nor the Australians had been given responsibility for dealing with the Germans occupying Decline Copse, and consequently neither dealt with them effectively. Fighting at Decline Copse continued until 27 October, when it finally fell to the Canadians.

Cross the road to the other side of the line. Look towards Passchendaele, where you can see a memorial to the Nova Scotia Highlanders ahead, marking the approximate position of the front line on 30 October (Figure 17.17).

Go towards Passchendaele and turn into the grassy path which takes you through a field to the Nova Scotia Highlanders Memorial. Stop when you reach it.

Figure 17.17 Memorial to Nova Scotia Highlanders ahead on the skyline in the centre, a useful marker for the distance advanced by Canadian 4th Division on 26 October 1917 and the starting position for the attack by the same division on 30 October.

Location 8: Memorial for Nova Scotia Highlanders

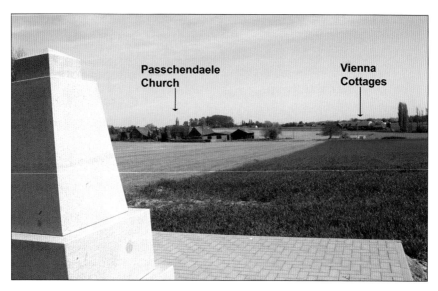

Figure 17.18 Memorial to Nova Scotia Highlanders facing north towards Passchendaele Church, which is visible less than a mile away in the centre of the photograph. Vienna Cottages are the farm buildings to the right.

The Nova Scotia Highlanders advanced from near here at 0550 on 30 October. The memorial commemorates the 13 officers and 135 other ranks killed that day. Look in different directions from the Nova Scotia Highlanders Memorial to spot important positions. First, look towards Passchendaele (Figure 17.18). Houses in the village can be seen to the left, as can Passchendaele Church. The farm buildings ahead are close to where the ruins of Vienna Cottages were in 1917. The advance on 30 October took the Canadian 4th Division beyond Vienna Cottages. Look to the right of Vienna Cottages. The wooded area in Figure 17.19 marks the position of the old Ypres to Roulers railway line. Look back towards your previous location at Defy Crossing (Figure 17.20).

Now go to Tyne Cot Cemetery by going along Tynecotstraat near Defy Crossing, make your way to the rear of the cemetery and find a suitable location beyond the visitor centre which provides a view towards Passchendaele.

Figure 17.19 Vienna Cottages to the left. The old Ypres to Roulers railway line is in the trees to the right. Passchendaele village is now out of sight to the left.

Figure 17.20 From the Nova Scotia Highlanders Memorial looking towards Defy Crossing. The trees and grass verge adjacent to the industrial complex mark the position of the railway line which crosses the road a short distance beyond.

Location 9: Rear of Tyne Cot Cemetery

Figure 17.21 The Canadian front line on 26 October 1917 was close to this location before crossing the summit of Passchendaele Ridge close to the old Ypres to Roulers railway line at Defy Crossing.

Look towards Passchendaele Church (Figure 17. 21). The front line on 26 October was a short distance away, and close to that from which the failed attacks on 9 and 12 October were launched (Chapter 15). At 0540, the South Saskatchewan Battalion (46th) covered the distance to its objective towards Passchendaele, keeping close behind the protective barrage. The Germans launched two counter-attacks from the direction of Passchendaele. The survivors of the 46th Battalion were forced to pull back to within 100 yards of their starting line. Reinforcements from the 44th and 47th Battalion gave support and the ground was regained.[2] You can visualise Canadians crossing the hillside ahead past the dead from previous battles, moving towards Passchendaele and overcoming German defenders in pillboxes and in heavily fortified ruins of farm houses (Chapter 15).

---

2   Edmonds, J.E., *History of the Great War Based on Official Documents by Direction of the Historical Section of the Committee of Imperial Defence. Military Operations. France and Belgium1917* Volume 2 (London: HMSO, 1948), p.349.

Figure 17.22 On the Tynecotstraat. The Ravebeek passes under a very small bridge from where the photograph was taken; the stream is so insignificant that it can easily be missed (Figure 15.12). Laamkeek is on the right of the road ahead, where German machine-gunners had an excellent view of advancing soldiers. The Ravebeek was an impassable morass in 1917, where many soldiers drowned or were easy targets for snipers as they floundered in the mud.

Leave the cemetery by the main entrance and turn right on the Tynecotstraat. Continue until you reach a right turn onto Canadalaan. If you were to go straight ahead, you would pass Laamkeek on your right before reaching the top of the Tynecotstraat and LOCATION 1 of your itinerary. You are going to turn right and make for Passchendaele, but before you do, proceed for a short distance to see the Ravebeek (also Chapter 15).

Return and go along Canadalaan. The Ravebeek is over to your left as you make your way. The ground over which you are travelling was extremely muddy in October 1917, while that even closer to the Ravebeek was impassable. Men could only advance towards their objectives on the higher ground to your right. You will soon pass a road to the left. Do not go along it, but stop briefly to face up the road. There is a farmhouse halfway up the hill beyond the Ravebeek which is the location of Duck Lodge (Figure 17.23). The Canadian front line on 30 October, from which the PPCLI on the right flank of the Canadian 3rd Division advanced, was in the field to the left of this farmhouse, as you have seen from LOCATION 4 at the top of the hill. You can appreciate how the advance of the Canadian 3rd Division on 30 October was on higher ground ahead, while the attack of the 4th Division was on the higher ground behind you. There was a break in the Canadian front line when it reached the impassable morass of the Ravebeek, before going up and across the ridge behind you in the direction of the Nova Scotia Highlanders Memorial. From close to where you are, the Seaforth Highlanders of Vancouver (72nd Battalion) of the 4th Division attacked and captured Crest Farm close to Passchendaele on 30 October. Keep going, and you will soon leave the lower ground close to the Ravebeek onto the higher ground as you approach Crest Farm (Figure 17.24).

The capture of Crest Farm put the Canadians within striking distance of Passchendaele. Figure 17.25 is the Canadian Memorial which marks the position of Crest Farm. It was taken from the road between the memorial and Passchendaele. Seaforth Highlanders of Vancouver would have been coming in your direction as they overcame German resistance at this fortified position.

Stand with your back to the memorial and look towards Passchendaele (Figure 17.26). It is a short distance to the church, but it required an attack by the Canadian 2nd Division on 6 November to capture this ground, while soldiers from the Canadian 1st Division captured the northern part of the village.

A German machine gun between Crest Farm and the village held up the attack. Private J. Robertson of the City of Winnipeg Battalion (27th) crossed the open ground in front of the German position and killed some of the crew,

Figure 17.23 Looking up past Duck Lodge. The PPCLI of the Canadian 3rd Division attacked from the higher ground of the ploughed field on the left. Location 4 is at the top of the road at its junction with the sGraventafelstraat. The cyclist is just crossing the Ravebeek, which passes diagonally beneath the road.

Figure 17.24 Approaching Crest Farm, with Passchendaele Church visible ahead. Crest Farm is a few yards around the corner ahead. The cyclists are climbing onto the higher ground of Passchendaele Ridge.

Figure 17.25 The site of Crest Farm, which was reached by the Seaforth Highlanders of Vancouver, Canadian 4th Division on 30 October 1917.

Figure 17.26 Passchendaele Church from Crest Farm.

while others fled. Robertson was killed later that day. He was awarded a post-humous Victoria Cross and is buried in Tyne Cot Cemetery (Plot LVIII, Row D, Grave 26). His citation reads:

> For most conspicuous bravery and outstanding devotion to duty in attack. When his platoon was held up by uncut wire and a machine gun causing many casualties, Pte Robertson dashed to an opening on the flank, rushed the machine gun and, after a desperate struggle with the crew, killed four and then turned the gun on the remainder, who, overcome by the fierceness of his onslaught, were running towards their own lines. His gallant work enabled the platoon to advance. He inflicted many more casualties among the enemy, and then carrying the captured machine gun, he led his platoon to the final objective. He there selected an excellent position and got the gun into action, firing on the retreating enemy who by this time were quite demoralized by the fire brought to bear on them.
>
> During the consolidation Pte Robertson's most determined use of the machine gun kept down the fire of the enemy snipers; his courage and his coolness cheered his comrades and inspired them to the finest efforts. Later, when two of our snipers were badly wounded in front of our trench, he went out and carried one of them in under very severe fire. He was killed just as he returned with the second man.
>
> *London Gazette*, Supplement, No. 30, 471, 8 January 1918

The following description has been taken from the *Official History of the Great War* and gives some idea of conditions on 6 November 1917:

> By 0710, the Canadians were streaming through, and past either side of Passchendaele, in large numbers, bayoneting Germans in the ruins and along the main street. Resistance from pillboxes and shell-holes, particularly at the northern exit, was at once engaged by covering fire of Lewis guns and rifle grenades, and then outflanked. By 0845, the entire objective along the eastern crest beyond the village had been gained.[3]

Table 17.1 shows the total number of casualties sustained by the four Canadian divisions between 26 October and 11 November 1917. No fewer than 521 officers and 12,403 other ranks became casualties, a very heavy price indeed to pay for the muddy wasteland that was Passchendaele.

Table 17.1 The total casualties sustained by the Canadian Corps during the period 26 October–11 November 1917. Edmonds, J.E., *History of the Great War Based on Official Documents by Direction of the Historical Section of the Committee of Imperial Defence. Military Operations France and Belgium, 1917* (Vol. 2) (London: HMSO, 1948), p.359.

	Killed		Wounded		Taken Prisoner		Gas (Fatal)		Gas (Non-fatal)		Totals	
	Off	OR	Off	OR	Off	OR	Off	OR	Off	OR	Off	OR
1st Division	42	871	63	1,746		5	1	6	10	242	116	2,870
2nd Division	34	924	71	1,715	2	3		6	6	201	113	2,849
3rd Division	58	1,171	88	1,964		3		2	16	229	162	3,369
4th Division	36	792	70	1,679		9		3	8	353	114	2,836
Canadian Corps Troops	6	94	9	298			1	1		86	16	479
Totals	176	3,852	301	7,402	2	20	1	18	41	1,111	521	12,403

POSTSCRIPT

On 21 March 1918, the Germans began the first of five major offensives in an effort to end the war quickly, before the almost unlimited resources of the United States of America could be brought to bear against them. It was launched from the Hindenburg Line against the British Third and Fifth Armies. Operation Georgette, the second major attack, began on 9 April

---

3   Ibid., p.356.

1918. The initial blow fell on a narrow front near Armentières and the River Lys, which gave its name to the battle. Sir Douglas Haig warned General Plumer, commander of the British Second Army, to make preparations for evacuating the Ypres Salient.[4] A strong assault was launched against General Plumer's Second Army defending Ypres. It would be quite impossible to hold the Salient, which had been bought at the cost of thousands of lives, and it was abandoned in favour of a tight defensive position close to Ypres. The evacuation began on 11 April, when Sir Douglas Haig issued the following special order.

SPECIAL ORDER OF THE DAY
By FIELD-MARSHAL SIR DOUGLAS HAIG
K.T., G.C.B., G.C.V.O., K.C.I.E.
Commander-in-Chief, British Armies in France
To ALL RANKS OF THE BRITISH ARMY IN FRANCE AND FLANDERS

Three weeks ago to-day the enemy began his terrific attacks against us on a fifty-mile front. His objects are to separate us from the French, to take the Channel Ports and destroy the British Army. In spite of throwing already 106 Divisions into the battle and enduring the most reckless sacrifice of human life, he has as yet made little progress towards his goals. We owe this to the determined fighting and self-sacrifice of our troops. Words fail me to express the admiration which I feel for the splendid resistance offered by all ranks of our Army under the most trying circumstances. Many amongst us now are tired. To those I would say that Victory will belong to the side which holds out the longest. The French Army is moving rapidly and in great force to our support. There is no other course open to us but to fight it out. Every position must be held to the last man: there must be no retirement. With our backs to the wall and believing in the justice of our cause each one of us must fight on to the end. The safety of our homes and the Freedom of mankind alike depend upon the conduct of each one of us at this critical moment.
    D. Haig, F.M.[5]

Plumer was authorised to withdraw his left flank to Pilckem Ridge, leaving outposts only at Passchendaele. This manoeuvre went unnoticed by German

---

4   Edmonds, J.E., *History of the Great War Based on Official Documents by Direction of the Historical Section of the Committee of Imperial Defence Military Operations. France and Belgium 1918* Volume 2 (London: Macmillan, 1937), p.118.
5   Duff Cooper, *Haig* (London: Faber and Faber Limited, 1935), p.275.

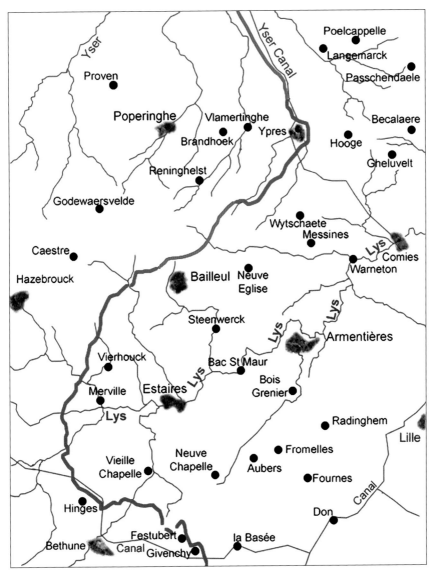

Figure 17.27 Map of the front line on 26 April 1918 following the Battle of The Lys.

forces at first when it was ascertained on 14 April that the British still occupied their original positions. By then, the Belgian Army had taken over the northern part of the line. Over the next few days, the British and adjacent Belgian forces withdrew until the line curved tightly around Ypres and was to the west of the Yser Canal north of Ypres (Figure 17.27).

All the effort and loss of life in 1917 had gone for nothing, as surviving British soldiers retired to the canal at Boesinghe, leaving their dead comrades buried in scattered graves throughout the Ypres Salient or lost forever beneath the mud.

EVENTS OF 28 SEPTEMBER 1918

The German offensives failed, and they were exhausted by their efforts. The tide turned and during the last 100 days of the war, the Allies were on the offensive. On 28 September, an attack was launched by the Flanders Group of Armies, nominally under command of King Albert of Belgium. The British Second Army at Ypres, which had borne the brunt of the fighting, took part in the attack, as did six French divisions. One by one, and very quickly, the places which had cost the British so many lives in 1917 were retaken.

Chapter 18

HILL 62 AND HILL 60

The preceding chapters focus on the three Battles of Ypres and deal with most of the important events which took place on the Ypres Salient between 1914 and 1918. We now consider events at two locations which were not always directly related to these battles, but were nevertheless of such importance that no description of the Ypres Salient would be complete without them.

Hill 60 was the scene of some of the fiercest fighting which took place on the Ypres Salient, while Hill 62, the adjacent Hill 61 (together known as Tor Top), Observatory Ridge and Mount Sorrel were fiercely contested between 2–13 June 1916 in an encounter between Canadian and German forces which became known as the Battle of Mount Sorrel.

HILL 62 AND THE BATTLE OF MOUNT SORREL

In June 1916, the British line adjacent to Bellewaarde Ridge passed just north of Hooge, before crossing the Menin Road and through Sanctuary Wood, Hill 62 and Hill 61. It then passed to the east of Observatory Ridge and Mount Sorrel before curving round Hill 60, which was in German hands (Figure 18.1). The Canadian Corps of three divisions (there would later be four) held the line from St Eloi in the south to Hooge in the north. On 2 June 1916, the Canadian line between Hooge and Hill 60 was subjected to an overwhelming German attack. Men of the Canadian 3rd Division were forced to retreat from Hooge to Zouave Wood and were ejected from Sanctuary Wood. They lost Hill 62, Observatory Ridge and Mount Sorrel (Figure 18.1). You will now go to Hill 62 and Observatory Ridge, where the Battle of Mount Sorrel will be explained.

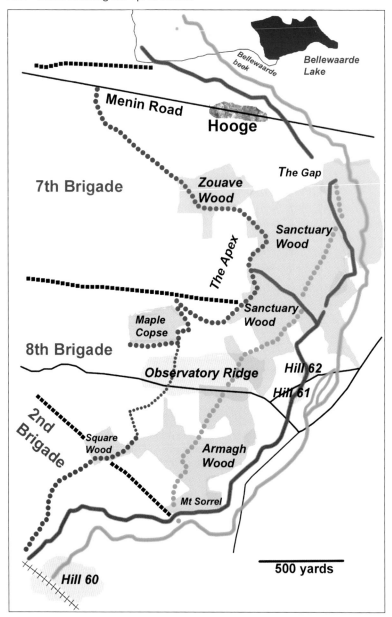

Figure 18.1 The solid red line is the British front line between Hooge and Hill 60 before the German attack on 2 June 1916. The dotted red line is the British front line after the attack. The German front line is in green. The line at Hill 60 was held by the Canadian 2nd Division and that between Mount Sorrel and Hooge by the Canadian 3rd Division.

Location 1: Canadalaan

Figure 18.2 Hooge is visible beyond Hooge Crater Cemetery. Sanctuary Wood is to the right.

There are two ways to reach Hill 62. The first is along Canadalaan. Stop and look to your left. You can see Hooge Crater Cemetery and the village of Hooge beyond. Sanctuary Wood is to the right (Figure 18.2). Keep going past Sanctuary Wood Museum. The Canadian Memorial is on top of Hill 62 straight ahead. Climb the steps to the memorial.

The second way to reach Hill 62, and suitable for a bicycle, is to go up the Menin Road to Clapham Junction, and turn right onto the Pappotstraat at the 18th Division Memorial, proceeding for three-quarters of a mile. Look to your right where you will see the Canadian Memorial on Hill 62 (Figure 18.3).

Location 2: Looking up to Canadian Memorial on Hill 62

The road marks the approximate position of the German front line on 2 June 1916, while the Canadians held the more advantageous ground on Hill 62 overlooking German trenches. At 0800 on 2 June, German guns of all calibres fired on the Canadian front line. The barrage continued until 1300, when mines exploded under Canadian positions. German infantry rose from trenches where you stand and advanced to occupy Hills 61 and 62. Go along

Figure 18.3 The Canadian Memorial marking Hill 62. Hill 61 is to its immediate left as you look; the combined 'peak' was known as Tor Top. This photograph was taken from the Pappotstraat and was the approximate position of the German front line before the attack on 2 June 1916.

the Pappotstraat a short distance and take the first turning to the right to the Canadian Memorial.

Location 3: Canadian Memorial on Hill 62

Stand close to the memorial and look in the direction of Ypres. You can appreciate the advantage the Germans had when they captured British trenches here (Figure 18.4).

Turn to your left. You can see Observatory Ridge with Armagh Wood and Mount Sorrel beyond. The German attack on 2 June forced the Canadians to retreat from all the ground seen in Figure 18.5 to new positions out of sight to the right.

Go back down the track and when you reach the bottom, turn right. Continue along the road until you reach a Y-junction. The road to your right leads over Observatory Ridge. The Canadian line before the attack on 2 June was roughly in the position of Figure 18.6.

Figure 18.4 A good view of Ypres is to be had from Hill 62.

Figure 18.5 The brown field marks the position of Observatory Ridge. The high ground in the distance partly covered by trees is Mount Sorrel. All the territory in this photograph was taken by the Germans on 2 June 1916.

Figure 18.6 Approximate position of the Canadian front line before the attack on 2 June 1916. The road to the right goes over Observatory Ridge, which is the elevated ground on both sides of the road. The Canadians were forced back from their front line, close to where the cyclist is standing, across the ridge to the far side.

Location 4: Summit of Observatory Ridge

Take the right fork. When you reach the top, turn round to face the way you have just come. Figure 18.7 was taken from the 'summit' of Observatory Ridge, looking back towards the Canadian front line. The Canadians were pushed back to Maple Copse, a wooded area approximately 250 yards behind your position. The wood straight ahead was called Shrewsbury Forest.

From your position on Observatory Ridge, turn to your right and you can see Mount Sorrel (Figure 18.8).

The commanding officer of the Canadian 3rd Division, Major General Malcolm Mercer, was killed near here. He was visiting the front line to assess defences when the Germans attacked. Mercer had the dubious distinction of being the most senior Canadian officer to be killed during the war. He is buried in Lijssenthoek Military Cemetery near Poperinghe.

As you stand on Observatory Ridge, you may consider events which occurred after 2 June. The Canadians launched an attack on 3 June in an attempt to retake lost positions, but failed because the attack was too hurried and lacked artillery support. A further attempt was made on 13 August, predominantly by the Canadian 1st Division supported by more than 200

Figure 18.7 The 'summit' of Observatory Ridge looking towards the Canadian front line (at the bottom of the hill ahead) before the German attack on 2 June 1916. The Canadians were forced to the far side of the ridge behind the camera.

Figure 18.8 Looking from the 'summit' of Observatory Ridge. Mount Sorrel can be seen, partly covered by the trees of Armagh Wood. The Canadians were pushed off Observatory Ridge and Mount Sorrel as German infantry advanced from left to right.

artillery pieces. The 3rd Battalion (Toronto) recaptured Mount Sorrel. The 16th Battalion (Western Canadian Scottish) and 13th Battalion (Black Watch of Montreal) recaptured Observatory Ridge, Hill 62 and Hill 61. The 58th Battalion (Central Ontario) attacked Sanctuary Wood and regained some positions. No attempt was made to recapture Hooge. Figure 18.9 shows the position of the new Canadian front line. Canadian losses between 2–13 June 1916 were 8,000 killed and wounded, and 536 were taken prisoner.[1]

HILL 60

You can reach Hill 60 from either of the forks in Figure 18.6. If you take the left fork, you pass Mount Sorrel on your right. At the end of the road turn right. After 600 yards, a signpost directs you to Hill 60 on your left. If you follow the right fork it takes you over Observatory Ridge to Zillebeke, where you should turn left up a steep hill out of the village. Turn right to Hill 60 at the top.

Hill 60 refers to the fact that it is 60 metres above sea level. It is the spoil on the east side of a railway cutting on the line between Ypres and Comines which was constructed more than 60 years before the war. You can see the railway line and cutting if you walk along the road to the bridge (Figure 18.10). There is another area of elevated ground created by spoil on the west side of the railway called the 'Caterpillar' because of its shape. Hill 60 (Figure 18.11) was regarded as a strategically important piece of ground and was of particular importance to the Germans, since it gave them a view of British positions around Zillebeke and of Ypres beyond. In recent years, houses have been built which obscure this view.

Initially held by French forces, Hill 60 was captured by the Germans on 10 December 1914 and changed hands several times, with the loss of hundreds of lives from both sides, many of whose bodies were never found. The British came here in February 1915.

Location I: Café Facing Hill 60

Orientate yourself to the location of British and German front lines. If you stand at the café facing Hill 60, then you are approximately at the position shown on Figure 18.12. To your right is the bridge over the railway and its cutting. The British line ran behind the road where you stand, and just before and after the bridge was in front of, and parallel to, the road.

---

1   Christie, N.M., *For King and Empire: The Canadians at Mount Sorrel* (Ottawa: CEF Books, 2000).

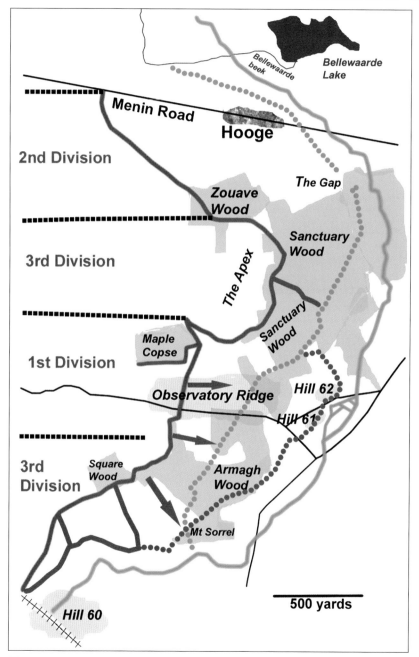

Figure 18.9 Map showing the position of the Canadian front line following the counter-attack on 13 June 1916.

Figure 18.10 This photograph shows the location of Hill 60 to the right, looking from across the bridge over the railway line. The Caterpillar is on the right side of the railway line. The British line was to the left of the road.

Figure 18.11 Wartime destruction on Hill 60. (Wikimedia)

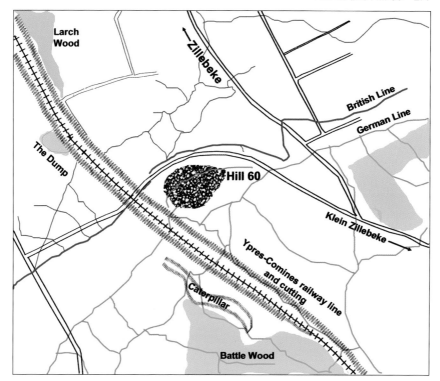

Figure 18.12 A drawn map showing the approximate positions of the British and German front lines at Hill 60.

As you look at Hill 60 from the vicinity of the British front line, imagine the scene of repeated attacks and counter-attacks; the British attacking from where you stand, and the Germans coming towards you from the other side of the hill, all to have control of this elevated ground with its tactical advantage. Fighting here was some of the fiercest in the Ypres Salient, and several Victoria Crosses were awarded for bravery. Look at Table 18.1 which lists key attacks which took place here.

Location 2: On Hill 60

Hill 60 was held initially by the French, but the Germans captured it during the Battle of Nonne Bosschen (Chapter 5). Go through a gate onto the hill. Look around and you will see small craters, some caused by exploding shells and others by French mines dating from the early months of the war, reflecting attempts made by the French to recapture the hill (Figure 18.13). In February 1915, the British took over the front line here, and plans were made to retake Hill 60.

272   Understanding the Ypres Salient

Table 18.1 The key battles for Hill 60 during the Great War.

Date	Event
4 August 1914	French army holds Hill 60
11 November 1914	German 30th Division captured Hill 60 during the First Battle of Ypres (Battle of Nonne Bosschen)
17 April 1915	British capture Hill 60
Night of 17/18 April 1915	Germans recapture part of Hill 60
18 April 1915	British retake all of Hill 60
18–22 April 1915	Concerted effort by Germans to retake Hill 60
1 May 1915	Germans use a gas attack but fail to capture Hill 60
5 May 1915	Germans capture Hill 60 using gas
7 May 1915	Small-scale British attempt to retake Hill 60 failed
7 June 1917	British retake Hill 60 as part of their major offensive with 19 mines including one under Hill 60 and one under the Caterpillar
15 April 1918	British withdraw from the Ypres Salient during the Second German Spring Offensive and evacuate Hill 60
28 September 1918	British recapture Hill 60 for the final time

Figure 18.13 The entrance to Hill 60, where the remnants of shell holes and mine craters can be seen as you follow the walkway onto the hill.

BRITISH ATTACK ON 17 APRIL 1915

These plans involved the construction of mines beneath German positions and were implemented almost as soon as the 28th Division, later replaced by the 5th Division, had taken up position in the front line. If you look back from your location, the tunnels began a few hundred yards behind the houses across the road. There were two major tunnels, each of which had two mines, and two smaller tunnels, constructed by 171st Tunnelling Company. All chambers were filled with explosives and ready to be used by early April 1915.

Make your way to the crest of Hill 60. As you go, you will see further craters, including one very large one which you skirt around to reach the crest and to which you will return later (Figure 18.14).

Location 3: Crest of Hill 60

The mines were detonated on 17 April 1915 at 1905. Tons of earth and German soldiers were blown more than 300ft into the air and scattered over a wide area. A British, French and Belgian artillery bombardment was followed by an infantry attack by the 1st Royal West Kents, 2nd King's Own Scottish Borderers and the 9th Queen Victoria Rifles. These men would have been making their way towards you on the crest of Hill 60, stumbling through and round shell

Figure 18.14 Towards the crest of the hill, further shell holes and mine craters can be seen all around you.

holes on the way. Surviving Germans were "dazed" and unsure what had happened. Many were bayoneted. The British attack threw the Germans off the hill. British casualties were light compared with German losses.

Unfortunately for the British, Hill 60 proved very hard to defend. A strong German counter- attack on the night of 17/18 April pushed the British back to the crest of the hill where you stand. Although German attacks continued next day, the British defended resolutely. At 1800, a British counter-attack (2nd Duke of Wellingtons and 2nd King's Own Yorkshire Light Infantry) drove the Germans from the ground they had taken the evening before. The British were subjected to fire from the front and sides, since they had created a vulnerable salient by capturing the hill without support on either side. The Germans made a further determined attack on 20 April, but the British held on. Lieutenant George Roupell of the East Surreys won the VC. His citation reads:

> For most conspicuous gallantry and devotion to duty on 20 April 1915, when he was commanding a company of his battalion in a front trench on 'Hill 60', which was subjected to a most severe bombardment throughout the day. Though wounded in several places, he remained at his post and led his company in repelling a strong German assault … Towards evening, his company being dangerously weakened, he went back to his battalion headquarters, represented the situation to his Commanding Officer, and brought up reinforcements, passing backwards and forwards over ground swept by heavy fire. With these reinforcements he held his position throughout the night and until his battalion was relieved next morning.
>
> *London Gazette* (Supplement) No. 29, 202, p.6, 115, 22 June 1915

Another East Surrey who won the VC that day was Private Edward Dwyer. In the afternoon of 20 April, his trench came under a grenade attack. Undeterred, he described his actions and what was happening:

> Fear's a funny thing. It gets at you in all kinds of funny ways. When we've been skirmishing in open order under heavy fire all the while I've felt myself go dumb, my tongue a bit of cotton. Then the blood has rushed into my face head and ears hot as fire, and the tip of my tongue swollen into a blob of blood. It's not nice, I can tell you, but the feeling passes. I've never expected to get out of any fight I've ever been in. And so I always just try to do my bit, and leave it at that.
>
> Well, they were shelling our trench pretty badly, and after a time all our chaps were either killed or wounded. Some of the papers have said that the other chaps retired. They didn't retire although the wounded may have crawled.

At last I was the only unwounded man left in the trench. There were three steps leading up to the parapet of the trench, and I sat crouched on the middle step. Shells and hand bombs were bursting all over and around, but nothing touched me at all. We had a lot of hand grenades in our trench, and I added to my stock by gathering up all I could find. I suppose I had about three hundred in all.

Then I went back to crouch on the middle step of the trench. The fear of being taken prisoner was very strong upon me. A straight shot, a round hole in the forehead, is all right. A soldier can't complain at that. But to be taken prisoner by those Huns ugh!

But funking drives a man to do mad things I found myself on the trench parapet hurling hand grenades. I won't say it wasn't fine fun, but there was the dread at the back of my mind that the devils might miss me, and take me alive before the trench was relieved. So I gave it to them good and hot. I did a few of them in. If they had only known that I was the last man left they would have rushed me, and by now I should have been a dead prisoner.[2]

Figure 18.15 Remnants of bunkers can be found at several locations on the hill as you walk around; this is just one example.

---

2   http://www.westernfrontassociation.com/great-war-people/victoria-crosses/
678-dwyer-vc.html.

The Germans made a counter-attack on the night of 20 April, and fighting continued into the early hours of the next morning. Lieutenant Harold Wooley and his company from the Queen Victoria Rifles (9th Battalion London Regiment) defended Hill 60 against repeated attacks and held the Germans off. This cost them dearly and only 14 men out of 150 survived. For his actions, Wooley (who a Church of England clergyman and a Territorial officer), was awarded the VC. His citation reads:

> For most conspicuous bravery on 'Hill 60' during the night of 20th–21st April, 1915. Although the only Officer on the hill at the time, and with very few men, he successfully resisted all attacks on his trench, and continued throwing bombs and encouraging his men till relieved. His trench during all this time was being heavily shelled and bombed and was subjected to heavy machine gun fire by the enemy.
>
> *London Gazette* (Supplement) No. 29, 170, p.4, 990, 22 May 1915

On 22 April, the Second Battle of Ypres began in the northern part of the Salient when the Germans used chlorine gas (Chapter 6). British plans for further attacks on Hill 60 were put on hold as resources were diverted to prevent a German breakthrough in the north.

On your way to your position on the crest, you will have noticed concrete remnants of several German blockhouses (Figure 18.15). There is one pillbox in the upper part of the hill on the forward slope (Figure 18.16) which has survived mostly intact. Initially a German bunker, this was modified subsequently and built on top of by Australians in 1918. You will see where it has been damaged by shellfire, and can also see inside through its slits and see how well constructed it was (Figure 18.17).

GERMAN ATTACKS COMMENCING ON 1 MAY 1915

From your position on the crest of Hill 60, facing in the direction of the entrance to the hill, turn left towards the railway line. A German attack was launched on 1 May 1915 at approximately 1900. It began with a heavy artillery bombardment against the 1st Dorsets in the front line. The Germans released chlorine gas from across the railway cutting, which drifted towards Hill 60. British communication trenches were bombarded to prevent reinforcements reaching the hill. The Germans attacked from both sides and inflicted heavy casualties. Despite this, the British held on and were reinforced by men of the 1st Bedfords and 1st Devons who managed to reach them. Edward Warner of the Bedfords won a VC. His citation reads:

Figure 18.16 From the crest of the hill, looking down over the ground that had been so fiercely contested during the fighting between 17–22 April 1915. This ground was taken and was held by the British, while the German trenches were close to where you stand.

Figure 18.17 This British bunker remains in good condition and can be found in the upper part of Hill 60.

278 Understanding the Ypres Salient

For most conspicuous bravery near 'Hill 60' on 1st May, 1915. After Trench 46 had been vacated by our troops, consequent on a gas attack, Private Warner entered it single-handed in order to prevent the enemy taking possession. Reinforcements were sent to Private Warner, but could not reach him owing to the gas. He then came back and brought up more men, by which time he was completely exhausted, but the trench was held until the enemy's attack ceased. This very gallant soldier died shortly afterwards from the effects of gas poisoning.

London Gazette (Supplement), p.6, 270, 19 June 1915

The Germans used gas again on 5 May at 0845. On this occasion the British, who were only equipped with the primitive respirators available at that time, were overcome by the gas. Many were forced to retire, while those who stayed were overwhelmed by Germans of the 30th Division. A third gas attack followed at 1100, and heavy fighting continued throughout the day. The Germans reached the crest and released more gas in the evening to complete the capture of the hill. The situation for the British was desperate. The 13th Division arrived late in the evening and launched a counter-attack at 2200. Men struggled to advance because of strong German opposition. Some reached the crest just after midnight, but were forced back by the Germans. A further relatively weak attempt was made to retake the hill on 7 May, but this was unsuccessful and Hill 60 remained in German hands until 7 June 1917. The fighting on Hill 60 had resulted in the loss of more than 3,000 British soldiers.

BRITISH ATTACK 7 JUNE 1917: BATTLE OF MESSINES RIDGE

Location 4: Mine Crater, 7 June 1917

From your position on the crest of Hill 60, make your way back to the large crater you walked around to reach the top of the hill.[3] Within the crater are smaller craters caused subsequently by high explosive shellfire. As you stand next to this crater, you may consider what happened here (Figure 18.18).

On 7 June 1917, in one of the most successful battles of the war thus far, the British Second Army removed the Germans from Messines Ridge. This was a necessary preliminary step for the Third battle of Ypres (Chapter 1). Nineteen mines were detonated under German positions; the two northern-most mines were at the Caterpillar and Hill 60. You are standing next to the Hill 60 mine crater. Extensive mining operations were started here in late summer 1915 by the Royal Engineers (175th Tunnelling Company). Mining was continued

---

3   The crest of Hill 60 used to be reached by walking through the June 1917 mine crater. A new walkway skirts around it.

Figure 18.18 Photograph showing the massive crater produced as a result of the mine explosion on 7 June 1917.

by the 3rd Canadian Tunnelling Company in April 1916, followed by the 1st Australian Tunnelling Company in November 1916. A memorial to the latter may be seen at the foot of Hill 60 (Figure 18.19). There was a tunnel called the Berlin Tunnel which started approximately 220 yards behind the British front line and ran at a depth of 90ft. Working conditions in the tunnel were almost intolerable, with the constant fear of discovery. The main tunnel split into two branches, which led to chambers. To the left, 'Hill 60 A' was beneath Hill 60, and to the right, 'Hill 60 B' was under the Caterpillar. The chambers were filled with explosives by late 1916. The Hill 60 mine had 45,700lb of ammonal, while the Caterpillar mine had 70,000lb, as detailed in the Australians' War Diary.

The Germans also tunnelled and counter-mined, and there was frequently underground fighting, either by design or accident. German mining activity carried the risk that the Hill 60 A and Hill 60 B mines would be discovered. The Germans could often be heard digging as they reached ever-closer to Australian mining operations.[4] The Germans were aware that the British were planning something, and made a trench raid in April 1917 in an attempt to find out more about British mining operations, but failed to do so.

---

4   https://www.awm.gov.au/images/collection/bundled/RCDIGI006639.pdf.

On 25 May, the Germans blew one of their own mines, which exploded in no man's land close to the railway cutting. Fortunately, although this did cause some damage to the British tunnelling system, it was successfully repaired.[5] At 0310 on 7 June, the 19 mines were detonated under the German front line. The blast at Hill 60 made a crater 33ft deep and 191ft wide. The Hill 60 and Caterpillar mines killed more than 650 soldiers from the German 204th Division. It is difficult to imagine what the scene must have been like, but the words of eyewitnesses perhaps give the best insight. The first account is by journalist Phillip Gibbs:

> The most diabolical splendour I have ever seen. Out of the dark ridges of Messines and Wytschaete and the ill-famed Hill 60, there gushed out and up enormous volumes of scarlet flame from the exploding mines and of earth and smoke all lighted by the flame spilling over into mountains of fierce colour, so that all the countryside was illuminated with red light. While some of us stood watching, aghast and spell bound by this burning horror, the ground trembled and surged violently to and fro. Truly the earth quaked.[6]

Lieutenant J. Todd described the scene:

> It was an appalling moment. We all had the feeling 'it's not going up'. Then a remarkable thing happened. The ground on which I was lying started to go up and down just like an earthquake. It lasted for seconds and then, suddenly in front of us, the Hill 60 mine went up.[7]

THE CATERPILLAR

It is a short walk to the Caterpillar. After coming out of Hill 60, turn left and walk across the bridge over the railway cutting. Immediately to your left is a small grass pathway alongside a small fence. Follow this, climb over a small stile and the pathway leads you through some trees and up a slight incline, which is the rim of the Caterpillar crater (Figure 18.20). The crater is now a tranquil place filled with water, which hides the reality of death and destruction when the explosion here made a crater 51ft deep and 260ft across.[8] The explosions at Hill 60 and the Caterpillar left German survivors too stunned to offer any resistance. Men of the British 23rd Division advanced almost unopposed.

---

5   https://www.awm.gov.au/images/collection/bundled/RCDIGI006639.pdf.
6   Phillip Gibbs of the *Daily Chronicle*.
7   Lieutenant J. Todd, Prince of Wales' Own Regiment of Yorkshire.
8   https://www.awm.gov.au/images/collection/bundled/RCDIGI006640.pdf.

Figure 18.19 The memorial to men of the 1st Australian Tunnelling Company that worked in this area and under Hill 60.

Figure 18.20 Caterpillar crater today.

EVENTS AFTER 7 JUNE 1917

After the capture of Hill 60 on 7 June, the British advanced approximately 1,500 yards and Hill 60 was left some distance behind the front line. When the Germans launched their Second Spring Offensive in April 1918, the British withdrew from the Ypres Salient and evacuated Hill 60 as part of this process on 15 April. Hill 60 remained in German hands until the final Allied offensive on 28 September 1918 pushed the Germans out of the Ypres Salient. On that day, the British 35th Division moved forward and retook Hill 60, which had changed hands for the final time.

Appendix

Nomenclature used in *The Official History of the Great War* and modern usage.

Becelaere	Beselare	Pilckem	Pilkem
Bellewaarde	Bellewaerde	Ploegsteert	Ploegsteert
Bixschoote	Bikschote	Poelcappelle	Poelkapelle
Boesinghe	Boezinge	Poperinghe	Popeninge
Broodseinde	Broodseinde	Roulers	Roeselare
Dickebusch	Dikkebus	St Eloi	St Elooi
Elverdinghe	Elverdinge	St Jean	Sint Jan
Frezenberg	Frezenberg	St Julien	Sint Juliaan
Gheluvelt	Geluveld	Vlamertinghe	Vlamertinge
Gravenstafel	s-Graventafel	Voormezele	Voormezele
Hollebeke	Hollebeke	Westhoek	Westhoek
Hooge	Hooge	Westroosebeke	Westrozebeke
Keerselare	Keerselar	Wieltje	Wieltje
Kortekeer	Kortekeer	Wytschaete	Wijtschate
Kruiseecke	Kruiseke	Ypres	Ieper
Langemarck	Langemark	Zandvoorde	Zandvoorde
Menin	Menen	Zillebeke	Zillebeke
Messines	Mesen	Zonnebeke	Zonnebeke
Passchendaele	Passendale		

Bibliography

UNPUBLISHED SOURCES

Gordon Highlanders Museum:
GHPB145.15: Copy of typed letter (2 pages) from Brig.- Gen. A.R. Hoskins to Sir Alexander Lyon, concerning action of 25.9.1915.
GHPB63.59: Copy of description of events from 10.10.1914–29.10.1914 at the 1st Battle of Ypres; from a typed account of the archives of the 2nd Battalion Gordon Highlanders from part of a donation of documents relating to Lieutenant Colonel James Dawson.
PB375: 'With the Highlanders by a Sassenach', the First World War diary of Major D.W. Pailthorpe.

PUBLISHED SOURCES

Bean, C.E.W., *Anzac to Amiens* (Canberra: Australian War Memorial, 1946).
Blake, R., *The Private Papers of Douglas Haig 1914–1919* (London: Eyre and Spottiswoode, 1952).
Brice, B., *The Battle Book of Ypres: A Reference to the Military Operations in the Ypres Salient 1914–1918* (Stevenage: Spa Books, 1987).
Butler, A.G., *Official History of the Australian Army Medical Services, 1914– 1918 Volume II – The Western Front* (Canberra: Australian War Memorial, 1940).
Carberry, A.D., *The New Zealand Medical Services in the Great War* (Auckland: Whitcombe and Tombs, 1924).
Cave, N., *Passchendaele: The Fight for the Village* (London: Leo Cooper, 1997).
Christie, N.M., *For King and Empire: The Canadians at Mount Sorrel* (Ottawa, Ontario: CEF Books, 2000).
Christie, N.M., *For King and Empire: The Canadians in the Second Battle of Ypres* (Ottawa, Ontario: CEF Books, 1999).
Christie, N.M., *For King and Empire: The Canadians at Passchendaele* (Ottawa, Ontario: CEF Books, 1999).
Cooper, Duff, *Haig* (London: Faber and Faber, 1935).
Edmonds, J.E., *History of the Great War Based on Official Documents by Direction of the Historical Section of the Committee of Imperial Defence. Military Operations. France and Belgium 1914* Volume 2 (London: Macmillan, 1925).

Edmonds, J.E., *History of the Great War Based on Official Documents by Direction of the Historical Section of the Committee of Imperial Defence. Military Operations. France and Belgium 1915* Volume 1 (London: Macmillan, 1927).

Edmonds, J.E., *History of the Great War Based on Official Documents by Direction of the Historical Section of the Committee of Imperial Defence. Military Operations. France and Belgium 1917* Volume 2 (London: HMSO, 1948).

Edmonds, J.E., *History of the Great War Based on Official Documents by Direction of the Historical Section of the Committee of Imperial Defence Military Operations. France and Belgium 1918* Volume 2 (London: Macmillan, 1937).

Falls, C., *Gordon Highlanders in the First World War* (Uckfield, East Sussex: Naval and Military Press, 2014, reprinted).

Hammerton, J.A., *A Popular History of the Great War Volume 2* (London: The Amalgamated Press, 1933).

MacDonald, L., *1915: The Death of Innocence* (London: Penguin Books, 1997).

MacDonald, L., *They Called it Passchendaele* (London: Macmillan Publishers, 1983).

McConachie, J., *The Student Soldiers* (Elgin: Moravian Press, 1995).

Neillands, R., *The Death of Glory: The Western Front 1915* (London: John Murray, 2006).

Neillands, R., *The Great War Generals on the Western Front* (London: Robinson Publishing, 1999).

Palmer, A., *The Salient: Ypres 1914–18* (London: Constable, 2007).

Prior, R., and Wilson, T., *Passchendaele, The Untold Story* (New Haven: Yale University Press, 2002).

Thomson, P.D., *The Gordon Highlanders* (Devonport; Swiss and Co, Military Printers, 1921).

Index

INDEX OF MILITARY FORMATIONS

INDEX OF PLACES

INDEX OF PEOPLE

INDEX OF GENERAL & MISCELLANEOUS TERMS